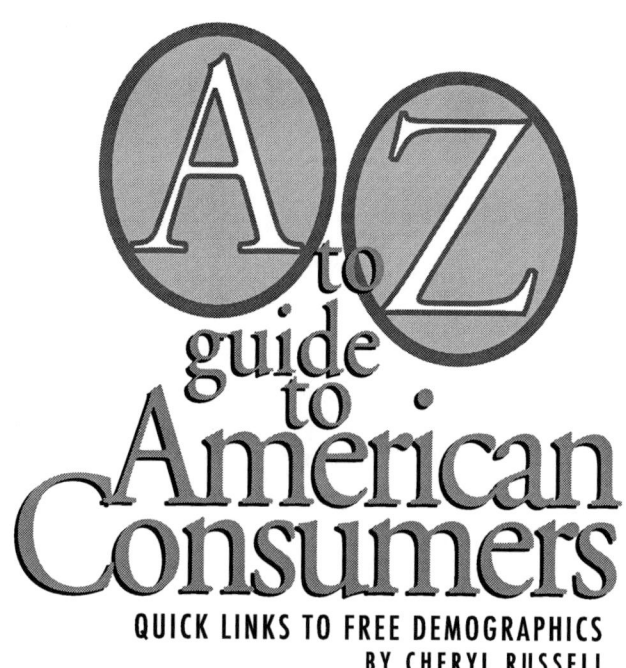

A to Z guide to American Consumers

QUICK LINKS TO FREE DEMOGRAPHICS
BY CHERYL RUSSELL

South University Library
Richmond Campus
2151 Old Brick Road
Glen Allen, Va 23060

New Strategist Publications, Inc.
Ithaca, New York

New Strategist Publications, Inc.
P.O. Box 242, Ithaca, New York 14851
800/848-0842; 607/273-0913
www.newstrategist.com

Copyright 2008. NEW STRATEGIST PUBLICATIONS, INC.

All rights reserved.

No part of this book may be reproduced, stored in a retrieval system, or transmitted in any form or by any means, electronic, mechanical, photocopying, microfilming, recording, or otherwise without written permission from the Publisher.

ISBN 978-1-933588-97-1
ISBN 1-933588-97-7

Printed in the United States of America

Table of Contents

Introduction 1

A
Abortion 3
Adoption 3
Adult Education 3
African Americans 4
After-School Programs 5
Age 5
Aging 6
Ask a Demographer: How Are the Generations Defined and Who Decides? 7
AIDS 8
Alabama 8
Alaska 8
Alcohol Consumption 8
Alternative Medicine 9
Alternative Workers 9
American Indians 9
Ancestry 10
Arizona 10
Arkansas 11
Arts Participation 11
Asians 11
Ask a Demographer: What's in Store for Books? 12
Assets 13
Attitudes 13

B
Baby Boom 15
Behavior 15
Benefits (Employee) 16
Birth Control 16
Births 17
Blacks 18
Ask a Demographer: Just How Fat Are Americans? 19
Body Mass Index 20
Business Owners 20

C
California 21
Careers 21
Caregivers 21
Cell Phone Demographics 21
Census of Population and Housing 22
Census Tract Demographics 22
Charitable Giving 22
Child Care Arrangements 22
Child Support 23
Children, Adopted and Step 23
Children, After-School Activities 23
Children, Family Life 23

Children, Health 24
Children in Poverty 24
Children, Living Arrangements 24
Children, Socioeconomics 24
Ask a Demographer: How Diverse Are American Children? 25
Chronic Conditions 26
Cigarette Smoking 26
Citizenship 27
City Demographics 27
College Costs 28
College Degrees Awarded 28
College Enrollment 28
Ask a Demographer: Is There a College Market Bubble? 29
College Student Attitudes 30
College Student Employment 30
Colorado 30
Commuting 30
Compensation 31
Computer Use 31
Congressional Demographics 31
Connecticut 31
Construction Statistics 32
Consumer Expenditures 32
Consumer Finances 32
Ask a Demographer: Is There an Easy Way to Adjust a Dollar Figure for Inflation? 33
Consumer Price Index 34
Contingent Workers 34
Contraceptive Use 34
Counties, Coastal 34
Ask a Demographer: How Fast Is the Coastal Population Growing? 35
County Demographics 36
Crime 36

D

Day Care 39
Daytime Population 39
Deaths 39
Debt 40
Degrees Awarded 40
Delaware 40
Demographic Data, General 40
Ask a Demographer: How Deep in Debt Are American Households? 41
Demographic Data, Historical 42
Demography 42
Dental Care 42
Diet and Nutrition 42
Disability 43
Discouraged Workers 43
Diseases 43
District of Columbia 44
Divorce 44
Doctor Visits 44
Drinking 44
Ask a Demographer: Do Half of Marriages End in Divorce? 45
Drug Use (Illegal) 46

Drug Use, Prescription 47
Dual Earners 47

E

Earnings 49
Economic Indicators 50
Economic Mobility 50
Economic Trends 50
Education, Adult 50
Education, Attitudes Toward 51
Education, General Statistics 51
Education, Homeschooling 51
Education, Private Schools 52
Education Projections 52
Education, Public Schools 52
Ask a Demographer: What's Wrong with Public Schools? 53
Education, School Enrollment 54
Educational Attainment 54
Elderly 54
Emergency Department Visits 55
Employee Benefits 56
Employee Compensation 56
Employee Tenure 56
Employment 56
Employment Projections 57
Energy Consumption 58
English, Ability to Speak 58
Enrollment, School 58
Estimates, Population 59
Exercise 59
Expenditures 59

F

Families, Employment Of 61
Family Formation 61
Family Planning 61
Family Statistics 62
Fathers 62
Fertility 62
Ask a Demographer: How High Is Fertility? 63
Fishing 64
Flextime 65
Florida 65
Food Consumption 65
Foreign-Born Population 65

G

Gays and Lesbians 67
Genealogy 67
Geographic Products 67
Ask a Demographer: How Many Americans Are Gay? 68
Geographical Mobility 69
Georgia 69
Graduation Rates 69
Grandparents 69
Group Quarters Population 70

H

Hawaii	71
Health and Aging	71
Health and Nutrition	72
Health Behavior	72
Health Care Costs	73
Health Care System, Attitudes Toward	73
Health Conditions	74
Health Insurance	74
Health-Related Quality of Life	75
Health Statistics	75
Ask a Demographer: Are Americans Feeling Better?	76
Health Status, Self-Reported	77
High-Income Households	77
High School Graduates	78
Higher Education	78
Hispanics	78
Ask a Demographer: What Is the Biggest Demographic Trend?	79
Historical Demographic Statistics	81
HIV	81
Home and Hospice Care	81
Homeownership	81
Homeschooling	82
Homosexuality	82
Hospital, Emergency Department Visits	82
Hospital, Outpatient Visits	83
Hospital, Overnight Stays	83
Households	83
Ask a Demographer: Why Are Houses Getting Bigger?	84
Housing	85
Housing Units, Estimates	86
Hunting	86

I

Idaho	87
Illegal Immigrants	87
Illinois	87
Immigration	87
Immunization	88
Income	88
Income Inequality	88
Independent Contractors	89
Indiana	89
Industry Employment	89
Infertility	90
Inflation Calculator	90
Insurance, Health	90
International Demographics	91
Internet	92
Interracial Marriage	92
Iowa	92

J
Job Benefits 93
Job Tenure 93
Job Training 93
Jobs 94
Journey to Work 95

K
Kansas 97
Kentucky 97

L
Labor Force 99
Language Spoken at Home 100
Latinos 100
Learning Disabilities 101
Leisure 102
Life Expectancy 102
Living Alone 102
Ask a Demographer: How Long Do We Live? 103
Living Arrangements 104
Living Standards 104
Long-Term Care 104
Louisiana 105

M
Maine 107
Mapping 107
Marital Status 107
Marriage 108
Maryland 109
Massachusetts 109
Media Demographics 109
Medicaid 109
Medical Expenditures 110
Medicare 110
Ask a Demographer: Who's Happy with Health Care? 111
Men 112
Mental Health 113
Metropolitan Area Statistics 114
Michigan 114
Migration 114
Military Demographics 115
Minimum Wage Workers 115
Minnesota 116
Mississippi 116
Missouri 116
Mobility, Economic 116
Mobility, Geographic 116
Montana 117
Mortality Data 117
Mothers 117
Multiple Job Holders 118
Mutual Fund Shareholders 118

N

Natality	121
National Parks	122
Nativity	122
Nebraska	122
Neighborhoods	122
Net Worth	122
Nevada	123
New Hampshire	123
New Jersey	123
New Mexico	123
New York	124
Non-Hispanic Whites	124
North Carolina	125
North Dakota	125
Nursing Homes	125
Nutrition and Diet	125

O

Obesity	127
Occupations	127
Ohio	128
Oklahoma	128
Older Population	128
Online Activities	129
Oregon	129
Overweight	129

P

Parents	131
Parks, National	132
Pennsylvania	133
Pensions	133
People Living Alone	133
Physical Activity	134
Physician Visits	134
Places of Birth	135
Play	135
Population Estimates	135
Ask a Demographer: How Much Elbow Room Do We Have?	136
Population Projections	137
Population, United States	137
Poverty	137
Pregnancy	138
Prescription Drugs	139
Price Index	139
Prison Population	139
Private Schools	139
Projections, Education	139
Projections, Employment	140
Projections, Population	140
Public Assistance	140
Public Schools	141

Q
Quality of Life. 143

R
Race. 145
Ask a Demographer: How Are the Races Defined?. 146
Recreational Activities 147
Regions 148
Religion. 148
Ask a Demographer: How Religious Are Americans? 149
Renters 150
Retirement. 150
Ask a Demographer: When Will the Baby-Boom Generation Retire?. 151
Rhode Island 152
Rural Population 153

S
Savings 154
School Enrollment 154
School, Private 155
School, Public. 155
Schools, General Statistics 156
Schools, Satisfaction With 156
Self-Employment 157
Sexual Behavior 157
Shift Work 157
Shopping. 157
Ask a Demographer: Does Religion Influence Sexual Behavior? 158
Sick Leave. 159
Single-Person Households 159
Sleep 159
Ask a Demographer: How Much Time Do We Spend Shopping? 160
Smoking 161
Social Security 161
South Carolina 162
South Dakota. 162
Spanish, Spoken at Home 162
Spending 163
Sports 163
Standard of Living 163
Ask a Demographer: How Much Does Gasoline Matter? 164
State Demographics 165
Statistics, Demographic 166
Stocks 166
Students, Attitudes of 167
Substance Abuse 167

T
Taxes 168
Technology 168
Teenagers 169
Telephones 169
Television Audience 170
Temporary Workers. 170
Tennessee 170

Tenure, Job	170
Texas	171
Time Use	171
Tobacco Use	171
Ask a Demographer: Who Does the Laundry?	172
Tract Data (Census)	173
Training, Job	173
Transportation	173
Travel	174
Travel to Work	174
Tribes, American Indian	174
Ask a Demographer: How Many Own a Vacation Home?	175
Tuition, College	176
Turnover (Labor)	176

U

Unemployment	177
Union Members	177
Unmarried Partners	178
Urban	178
Utah	178

V

Vacation Days	179
Vehicles	179
Vermont	179
Veterans	179
Ask a Demographer: Who Is the Average Voter?	180
Virginia	181
Vital Statistics	181
Volunteering	181
Voting	181

W

Wages	183
Washington	184
Wealth	184
Weekends	184
Weight	184
Ask a Demographer: Who Has Put on the Most Pounds?	185
Welfare	186
Well-Being	186
West Virginia	187
Whites	187
Widows	188
Wildlife-Associated Recreation	188
Wisconsin	188
Women	188
Work	190
Work Arrangements	191
Work-at-Home Population	191
Work Experience	192
Work Schedules	192
Work Time	192
Working Mothers	192

Working Poor 193
Working, Reasons for Not. 193
World Population 193
Wyoming. 194

Y
Youth. 195

Z
Zip Code Demographics 197

Appendix A: Major Demographic Surveys 199

Appendix B: Mailing Addresses, Telephone Numbers, Web Sites. 211

Appendix C: Glossary of Demographic Terms 215

Index 215

The best way to use the *A to Z Guide* is to download it as a pdf file. In that format, you will be able to literally click through to the sources listed in these pages. For those of you who have a printed copy of the directory, type the URL for the source into the address box of your browser and go.

Most of the links in the *A to Z Guide* are your conduit to the original source of demographic data available from the producing agency. For the most part, this directory does not include businesses and nonprofits that publish demographic statistics produced by others because they are not the original source of the data. This directory also does not include businesses that provide numbers for a fee. Most of the sources shown here are entirely free, although a few charge a nominal fee (such as the $5 charge to download a working paper from the National Bureau of Economic Research). The *A to Z Guide* is your link to original sources, the latest data, and the rich universe of free demographics. The *Guide* will be updated regularly, since Internet addresses and offerings change frequently.

Sprinkled throughout the directory are brief commentaries I have written for *American Consumers*, a free email newsletter about demographic trends available from New Strategist (to subscribe, go to http://www.newstrategist.com and click on "Get free American Consumers Newsletter"). These commentaries discuss how to think about demographics, what is revealed by demographic data, and how you can use demographics to talk about trends.

At the end of the *A to Z Guide* are three appendices for those who want to know more. Appendix A describes the many surveys that produce the demographic data on which government and industry depend. Appendix B lists physical addresses and telephone numbers for the major agencies that produce demographic data. While the Internet is the way most people retrieve data today, we believe the directory would be incomplete without these additional listings. Appendix C is a glossary of demographic terms for easy reference. Also at the back of the book is an index to help speed researchers on their way to finding the information they need.

Consider the *A to Z Guide* your research assistant. With its help, you are more likely to find the right number and make the best decision.

Cheryl Russell
Editorial Director
New Strategist Publications

(*Cheryl Russell is the editorial director of New Strategist Publications. She is a demographer and author who previously served as editor-in-chief of American Demographics magazine from 1984 to 1990, executive editor of The Boomer Report, and contributing editor to Money magazine. She holds an M.A. in Sociology/Demography from Cornell University.*)

A

ABORTION

- **Federal government data**

http://www.cdc.gov/reproductivehealth/Data_Stats/Abortion.htm

At this Centers for Disease Control site, you can find government figures on legal abortions by state, marital status, age, race, ethnicity, and many other characteristics.

- **Guttmacher Institute data**

http://www.guttmacher.org/sections/abortion.php

The Guttmacher Institute compiles statistics on abortion from a variety of sources, providing a comprehensive look at abortion in the United States.

ADOPTION

- **2000 census report**

http://www.census.gov/population/www/cen2000/phc-t21.html

Here you can access a report and tables on adopted and stepchildren in the United States, with data from the 2000 census.

- **The Children's Bureau**

http://www.childwelfare.gov/systemwide/statistics/adoption.cfm

The Children's Bureau provides state and national data on adoption and foster care, child abuse and neglect, and child welfare. Here you can access reports and statistics on adoption, those who seek to adopt, and those who have relinquished their child for adoption.

ADULT EDUCATION

- **National Household Education Survey**

http://nces.ed.gov/nhes/

From this page you can access data on adult education from the National Household Education Survey. This survey is fielded every few years by the National Center for Health Statistics to measure participation in educational activities ranging from early childhood programs to work-related adult education courses.

AFRICAN AMERICANS

• 2000 census data

http://www.census.gov/population/www/cen2000/briefs.html

On this page, scroll down to Census 2000 Special Report 25, *We The People: Blacks in the United States*. This will give you an overview of the black population as of 2000.

• Business owners

http://www.census.gov/csd/sbo/black2002.htm

The Survey of Business Owners, taken every five years as part of the Economic Census, provides details on black-owned businesses in the United States.

• Demographics from the American Community Survey

http://factfinder.census.gov/home/saff/main.html?_lang=en

The American Community Survey provides annual statistics on the population by race and Hispanic origin. To retrieve the information, go to this site—the Census Bureau's Fact Finder page. Click on "get data" under "American Community Survey." On the next page, click on the "Selected Population Profiles" link. On the next page, specify the desired geography (for national totals, just click "add" and "next"). On the following page, select the desired racial group. One more click and you have the latest demographic profile of the African American population. You can also create custom tables of American Community Survey data with the "Custom Table" link.

• Estimates by age

http://www.census.gov/popest/national/asrh/

To get the latest numbers on the black population—including estimates of the population by age—visit the Census Bureau's population estimates site.

• Gateway at the Census Bureau

http://www.census.gov/population/www/socdemo/race/black.html

Here you can access the Census Bureau's reports on African Americans, including 2000 census data.

• Health data from the Centers for Disease Control

http://www.cdc.gov/omhd/Populations/BAA/BAA.htm

For information on the health of the black population, this is the place to start. This page has links to a variety of statistics revealing the health of the black population, including information on health disparities.

• Income data

http://www.census.gov/hhes/www/income/dinctabs.html

Every March the Current Population Survey collects income data by race and Hispanic origin through the Annual Social and Economic Supplement. The gateway to the data for households, families, and persons is available here.

- **Poverty data**

http://www.census.gov/hhes/www/poverty/detailedpovtabs.html

Every year, the Census Bureau measures the poverty population by race and Hispanic origin. The poverty estimates are based on income data collected by the Annual Social and Economic Supplement of the March Current Population Survey. The poverty tables are available here.

AFTER-SCHOOL PROGRAMS

- **A Child's Day reports**

http://www.census.gov/population/www/socdemo/2004_detailedtables.html

This site allows you to access the many tables of data on the family life of children contained in the latest *A Child's Day* report—including children's participation in after-school activities. The data are from the Census Bureau's Survey of Income and Program Participation.

- **National Household Education Survey**

http://nces.ed.gov/pubsearch/pubsinfo.asp?pubid=2006076

This page is your gateway to information about children's participation in after-school programs. The National Household Education Survey is fielded every few years by the National Center for Health Statistics to measure participation in educational activities ranging from early childhood programs to work-related adult education courses.

AGE

- **Age at first marriage**

http://www.census.gov/population/www/socdemo/hh-fam.html

For current as well as historical data on the age of men and women when they marry for the first time, go to this page, scroll down to the Marital Status section of the Historical Time Series tables, and click on table MS-2.

- **Age data from the American Community Survey**

http://factfinder.census.gov/home/saff/main.html?_lang=en

The American Community Survey publishes annual data on the age of the population. To see the latest information, go to this site—the Census Bureau's Fact Finder Page. Click "get data" under "American Community Survey," then click "Subject Tables." Select your geography, then click "next." On the subject table list, select "Age and Sex."

- **Estimates by age from the Census Bureau**

http://www.census.gov/popest/national/asrh/

The latest official estimates of the age of the population by sex, race, and Hispanic origin can be downloaded from this site.

AGING

- **Gateway at the Census Bureau**

http://www.census.gov/population/www/socdemo/age.html

This is the Census Bureau's access point to its voluminous data on the age of the American population, including links to censuses, surveys, estimates, and projections.

- **Projections by age from the Census Bureau**

http://www.census.gov/ipc/www/usinterimproj/

The latest Census Bureau projections of the age of the population by sex, race, and Hispanic origin can be downloaded from this site.

AGING

- **AARP research**

http://www.aarp.org/research/

To lobby for the older population, the AARP must research its needs. At the AARP site you can benefit from its work. This page is your gateway to the AARP's studies and statistics.

- **Gateway at the Census Bureau**

http://www.census.gov/population/www/socdemo/age.html

This is the Census Bureau's access point to its voluminous data on the age of the American population. Scroll down to the sections on the older (55+) and elderly (65+) populations.

- **Health and Retirement Study data book**

http://hrsonline.isr.umich.edu/docs/sho_refs.php?hfyle=index&xtyp=7

Here you can access *Growing Older in America: The Health and Retirement Study*, a free pdf download that places some of the University of Michigan's Health and Retirement Study into the hands of the public. The Health and Retirement Study is a longitudinal survey, launched in 1992 and funded by the National Institute on Aging, which tracks a nationally representative sample of Americans aged 50 or older as they age. HRS data are available primarily as datasets, limiting their use to academic researchers. *Growing Older in America* allows the public to review the survey's most important findings.

- **Older Americans: Key Indicators of Well-Being report**

http://www.agingstats.gov/agingstatsdotnet/main_site/default.aspx

Here you can download the summary report, *Older Americans 2008*, which provides data on 37 indicators of the socioeconomic status of older Americans.

- **The State of 50+ America report**

http://www.aarp.org/research/reference/statistics/fifty_plus_2006.html

Every two years the AARP analyzes the socioeconomic well-being of Americans aged 50 or older in its report *The State of 50+ America*. The report can be downloaded here.

How Are the Generations Defined and Who Decides?

Dividing a population into generations is one way to explore its characteristics. Many researchers segment populations by age. Generational segmentation goes beyond age by tracking a cohort—a group of people born in certain years—as the cohort moves through the age structure. People's wants and needs change with age, but attitudes and values tend to form in early adulthood and remain with a cohort throughout its life. Consequently, understanding generational differences is important to businesses and policy makers.

Because there are no official definitions, experts often disagree on generational boundaries. The Baby Boom is the only generation whose definition is widely agreed upon because it is clearly defined by its size. Births spiked in 1946, climbed to a peak in 1957, and fell in 1965. The Baby-Boom generation includes all those born from 1946 through 1964. Because this 19-year span is so broad, marketers often separate Boomers into older and younger halves.

Two living generations precede Boomers: The Swing (or Silent) generation (born from 1933 through 1945), and the World War II generation (born before 1933). The Swing generation is a relatively small group because of the declining number of births during the Depression and World War II. The youngest members of the Swing generation are now in their sixties. Many of the nation's most powerful corporate and political leaders are members of the Swing generation. The oldest Americans are members of the World War II generation—people in their late 70s and older. This group accounts for a small share of the population, but because it votes at an above-average rate it continues to wield political power.

Two generations follow the Baby Boom: Generation X (born from 1965 through 1976) and the Millennials (born from 1977 through 1994). Like the Swing generation, Gen Xers are a small cohort born during an era of fewer births. When Boomers finally began to have children, however, births surged once again. The result was the Millennial generation, the oldest of whom are now entering their thirties.

The generation that follows Millennials remains unnamed. Because the oldest members of the "post-Millennial" generation are only in their midteens, it is too soon to say what will distinguish them from the rest of us—but no doubt something will.

AIDS

• Centers for Disease Control

http://www.cdc.gov/hiv/topics/surveillance/index.htm

For statistics on AIDS and HIV, this is the place to go. Many reports and statistics on AIDS at the national and state level are available by age, sex, race, and Hispanic origin.

ALABAMA

• State Data Center

http://cber.cba.ua.edu/

At this web site you can access demographic and economic statistics for Alabama, including current population estimates, population projections, employment statistics, and 2000 census data. Local area data are also available here.

ALASKA

• State Data Center

http://almis.labor.state.ak.us/

At this web site you can access the range of demographic and economic statistics for Alaska, including current population estimates, population projections, employment statistics, 2000 census data, and American Community Survey numbers. Local area data are also available here.

ALCOHOL CONSUMPTION

• Behavioral Risk Factor Surveillance System

http://www.cdc.gov/brfss/

This annual survey collects data nationally and by state on the health behaviors of adults, including alcohol consumption.

• Gateway at the Centers for Disease Control

http://www.cdc.gov/alcohol/surveillance.htm

To find out how much people drink, start at this site and explore the links to many government and other surveys that collect data on alcohol consumption, including the National Health Interview Survey and the Monitoring the Future survey.

• High school students

http://www.monitoringthefuture.org/

The annual Monitoring the Future survey fielded by the Institute for Social Research at the University of Michigan tracks the behavior and attitudes of American 8th, 10th, and 12th graders toward alcohol, drugs, and tobacco.

- **National Health Interview Survey**

http://www.cdc.gov/nchs/nhis.htm

In the National Center for Health Statistics' annual report, *Summary Health Statistics for U.S. Adults*, available on this page, you can access tables on alcohol consumption by a variety of demographic characteristics. Tables 26 and 27 have the numbers.

- **Youth Risk Behavioral Surveillance System**

http://www.cdc.gov/HealthyYouth/yrbs/

Every two years the Youth Risk Behavioral Surveillance System examines the behavior of 9th through 12th graders nationally and by state. Alcohol, drug, and tobacco use are examined.

ALTERNATIVE MEDICINE

- **National Center for Complementary and Alternative Medicine**

http://www.nccam.nih.gov/news/camstats.htm

More than two-thirds of Americans have used some form of complementary or alternative medicine, according to a 2002 study by the National Center for Health Statistics. The report, *Complementary and Alternative Medicine Use Among Adults: United States, 2002*, is available for download at this site.

ALTERNATIVE WORKERS

- **Bureau of Labor Statistics**

http://www.bls.gov/news.release/conemp.toc.htm

Every few years the Bureau of Labor Statistics collects data on the nontraditional workforce, which includes independent contractors, temporary workers, on-call workers, and contract workers. The data can be accessed at this site.

AMERICAN INDIANS

- **2000 Census**

http://www.census.gov/population/www/cen2000/briefs.html

On this page, scroll down to Census 2000 Special Report 28, *We The People: American Indians and Alaskan Natives in the United States*. This will give you an overview of the American Indian population by tribe as of 2000.

- **Business owners**

http://www.census.gov/csd/sbo/aian2002.htm

The Survey of Business Owners, taken every five years as part of the Economic Census, provides details on American Indian-owned businesses in the United States.

- **Demographics from the American Community Survey**

http://factfinder.census.gov/home/saff/main.html?_lang=en

The American Community Survey provides annual statistics on the population by race and Hispanic origin. To retrieve the information, go to this site—the Census Bureau's Fact Finder page. Click on "get data" under "American Community Survey." On the next page, click on the "Selected Population Profiles" link. On the next page, specify the desired geography (for national totals, just click "add" and "next"). On the following page, select the desired racial group. One more click and you have the latest demographic profile of American Indians. You can also create custom tables of American Community Survey data with the "Custom Table" link.

- **Estimates by age**

http://www.census.gov/popest/national/asrh/

To get the latest numbers on the American Indian population—including estimates of the size of the population by age—visit the Census Bureau's population estimates site.

- **Gateway at the Census Bureau**

http://www.census.gov/population/www/socdemo/race/indian.html

This is the federal government's official site for data about American Indians and Native Americans from the 2000 Census, supplemented by more recent population estimates and projections.

- **Health data from the Centers for Disease Control**

http://www.cdc.gov/omhd/Populations/AIAN/AIAN.htm

For information on the health of the American Indian population, this is the place to start. This page has links to a variety of statistics revealing the health of American Indians, including information on health disparities.

ANCESTRY

- **Census Bureau**

http://www.census.gov/population/www/ancestry.html

Ancestry data from the Census Bureau are available from this site via links to annual data from the American Community Survey and 2000 census data.

ARIZONA

- **State Data Center**

http://www.workforce.az.gov/

At this web site you can access demographic and economic statistics for Arizona, including current population estimates, population projections, employment statistics, and 2000 census data. Local area data are also available here.

ARKANSAS

• **State Data Center**

http://www.aiea.ualr.edu/census/default.html

At this web site you can access demographic and economic statistics for Arkansas, including current population estimates, population projections, employment statistics, and 2000 census data. Local area data are also available here.

ARTS PARTICIPATION

• **National Endowment for the Arts**

http://www.nea.gov/research/ResearchReports_chrono.html

The National Endowment for the Arts has a number of reports on the demographics of arts participation that can be downloaded from this site, including the 2007 report *To Read or Not to Read: A Question of National Consequence*.

ASIANS

• **2000 Census**

http://www.census.gov/population/www/cen2000/briefs.html

On this page, scroll down to Census 2000 Special Report 17, *We The People: Asians in the United States*. This will give you an overview of the Asian population as of 2000.

• **Business owners**

http://www.census.gov/csd/sbo/asian2002.htm

The Survey of Business Owners, taken every five years as part of the Economic Census, provides details on Asian-owned businesses in the United States.

• **Demographics from the American Community Survey**

http://factfinder.census.gov/home/saff/main.html?_lang=en

The American Community Survey provides annual statistics on the population by race and Hispanic origin. To retrieve the information, go to this site—the Census Bureau's Fact Finder page. Click on "get data" under "American Community Survey." On the next page, click on the "Selected Population Profiles" link. On the next page, specify the desired geography (for national totals, just click "add" and "next"). On the following page, select the desired racial group. One more click and you have the latest demographic profile of Asians. You can also create custom tables of American Community Survey data with the "Custom Table" link.

• **Estimates by age**

http://www.census.gov/popest/national/asrh/

To get the latest numbers on the Asian population—including estimates of the size of the population by age—visit the Census Bureau's population estimates site.

What's in Store for Books?

The National Endowment for the Arts reports that there has been a decline in book reading over the past decade. How big is the decline? The percentage of adults who have read a book for pleasure (that is, it was not required for work or school) in the past year fell from 61 to 57 percent between 1992 and 2002—down 4 percentage points. Is this a cause for concern or, rather, a sign of the book's staying power? To get a better perspective, let's look at trends in two other traditional media outlets—the daily newspaper and the network evening news.

Between 1991 and 2002, the percentage of people who read a newspaper every day fell from 52 to 41 percent—a much larger decline than the one experienced by books, according to the General Social Survey. Even more telling, unit sales of trade books have been increasing, while weekday newspaper circulation is decreasing. Yes, average household spending on books is down, according to the Consumer Expenditure Survey, falling by a painful 28 percent between 1991 and 2006 after adjusting for inflation. But much of the decline in spending can be explained by the growing sales of used books and the deep discounts offered by Amazon.com and other Internet retailers. No such benign factors can explain why household spending on newspapers and magazines fell by a heartrending 60 percent during the same years.

Network evening news is also experiencing a precipitous decline. The average number of people who watch the network evening news plummeted from 42 million to 30 million between 1992 and 2002, according to an analysis by the Project for Excellence in Journalism. Not only is the audience shrinking, it is also aging. The median age of the viewers of network evening news has now surpassed 60.

The fact is, the percentage of people reading for pleasure has remained remarkably stable over the past decade considering the enormous expansion of television channels and the adoption of computers and the Internet. Even more important, the demographics of book readers are healthy. Young adults are almost as likely as older Americans to be regular book readers. Forty-three percent of busy 18-to-24-year-olds have read a work of fiction in the past year, not too far below the peak of 52 percent among 45-to-54-year-olds. Contrast that 9 percentage point gap with this one: only 18 percent of 18-to-29-year-olds regularly watch network evening news compared with the peak of 56 percent among people aged 65 or older—a gap of 38 percentage points. Or this one: only 16 percent of 18-to-29-year-olds read a newspaper every day compared with 66 percent of people aged 65 or older, a gap of 50 percentage points.

Newspapers and network evening news are being supplanted by more efficient ways of getting up-to-the-minute information. Some claim electronic devices such as Kindle will replace books. But handheld electronic devices are no more likely to replace books read for pleasure than video screens have replaced original art, virtual tours have replaced travel, or pills have replaced food.

- **Gateway at the Census Bureau**

http://www.census.gov/population/www/socdemo/race/api.html

Here you can access the Census Bureau's reports on Asians, including 2000 census data.

- **Health data from the Centers for Disease Control**

http://www.cdc.gov/omhd/Populations/AsianAm/AsianAm.htm

For information on the health of the Asian population, this is the place to start. This page has links to a variety of statistics revealing the health of Asians, including information on health disparities.

- **Income data**

http://www.census.gov/hhes/www/income/dinctabs.html

Every March the Current Population Survey collects income data by race and Hispanic origin through the Annual Social and Economic Supplement. The gateway to the data for households, families, and persons is available here.

- **Poverty data**

http://www.census.gov/hhes/www/poverty/detailedpovtabs.html

Every year, the Census Bureau measures the poverty population by race and Hispanic origin. The poverty estimates are based on income data collected by the Annual Social and Economic Supplement of the March Current Population Survey. The poverty tables are available here.

ASSETS

- **Survey of Consumer Finances**

http://www.federalreserve.gov/pubs/oss/oss2/scfindex.html

The Federal Reserve Board's Survey of Consumer Finances, taken every three years, can be accessed at this site. The SCF is the only comprehensive source of data on the wealth of Americans at the household level. Here you can download the latest numbers detailing household net worth, financial and nonfinancial assets, and debts. Historical data back to 1989 are also available.

ATTITUDES

- **Gallup Poll**

http://www.gallup.com/poll/101905/Gallup-Poll.aspx

Gallup polls are a mainstay of public opinion research and have been for 70 years. This site is your gateway to the many topics examined by Gallup. Use the A to Z index to access public opinion on topics ranging from abortion to work.

ATTITUDES

- **General Social Survey**

http://sda.berkeley.edu/cgi-bin32/hsda?harcsda+gss06

Until now, tapping into General Social Survey results has been difficult, limited to academic researchers with the expertise to run statistical programs. To the rescue comes the Computer Assisted Survey Methods Program at the University of California, Berkeley, which has created a web-based program for retrieving and analyzing the data. This online application allows you to choose a GSS question and get an answer in table and chart format by demographic segment.

- **Harris Poll**

http://www.harrisinteractive.com/harris_poll/

The Harris Poll has been examining public opinion since 1963. At this address you can access Harris Poll data.

- **Pew Research Center**

http://pewresearch.org/

The Pew Research Center is a nonpartisan "fact tank" that provides information on the issues, attitudes, and trends shaping America and the world. Its work is carried out by eight projects: The Pew Research Center for the People & the Press (*http://people-press.org/*), the Project for Excellence in Journalism (*http://journalism.org/*), Stateline.org (*http://www.stateline.org/live/*), Pew Internet & American Life Project (*http://www.pewinternet.org/*), Pew Forum on Religion & Public Life (*http://pewforum.org/*), Pew Hispanic Center (*http://pewhispanic.org/*), Pew Global Attitudes Project (*http://pewhispanic.org/*), and Social & Demographic Trends (*http://pewsocialtrends.org/*).

- **Roper Center for Public Opinion Research**

http://www.ropercenter.uconn.edu/

The Roper Center for Public Opinion Research, one of the world's leading archives of social science data, specializes in surveys of public opinion. While access to much of the data is restricted to paying members, limited searches are available for free.

- **World Public Opinion**

http://www.worldpublicopinion.org/

The Program on International Policy Attitudes was established in 1992 with the purpose of giving public opinion a greater voice in international relations. PIPA launched WorldPublicOpinion.org in January 2006 to provide a source of in-depth information and analysis on public opinion from around the world on international issues.

B

BABY BOOM

• Special studies from AARP

http://www.aarp.org/research/reference/boomers

Research reports, fact sheets, speeches—just about anything the AARP has ever published about baby boomers is accessible here. A quick look reveals topics covering socially conscious shopping behavior, characteristics of uninsured 50-to-64-year-olds, and a snapshot of boomers' travel and adventure experiences.

BEHAVIOR

• Behavioral Risk Factor Surveillance System

http://apps.nccd.cdc.gov/brfss/index.asp

If you want to know the health status and behavior of Americans nationally or by state, the Centers for Disease Control's Behavioral Risk Factor Surveillance System, accessible at this site, can tell you. The BRFSS bills itself as the largest telephone survey in the world. It has to be large to provide annual state-level details by age, race, sex, income, and education.

• High school students

http://www.monitoringthefuture.org/

Monitoring the Future is an ongoing study of the behaviors and attitudes of American secondary school students. Each year the survey queries 50,000 students in 8th, 10th, and 12th grade about their use of drugs, alcohol, and tobacco.

• National Survey on Drug Use and Health

http://www.oas.samhsa.gov/nsduh.htm

At this site you can access tables from the annual National Survey on Drug Use and Health, which examines the drug, alcohol, and tobacco use of Americans aged 12 or older in detail by a variety of characteristics.

• Sexual and family formation behavior

http://www.cdc.gov/nchs/about/major/nsfg/nsfgcycle6reports.htm

The National Survey of Family Growth provides a wealth of data about the sexual and family formation behavior of American men and women aged 15 to 44. Reports from the survey are available here.

- **Youth Risk Behavior Surveillance System**

http://www.cdc.gov/HealthyYouth/yrbs/index.htm

The Youth Risk Behavior Surveillance System monitors the health risk behavior of 9th through 12th graders nationally and by state. These behaviors include tobacco, alcohol and drug use, diet, physical activity, sexual behavior, and risk behavior that contributes to injury and violence.

BENEFITS (EMPLOYEE)

- **Employee Benefit Research Institute**

http://www.ebri.org/

The Employee Benefit Research Institute is one of the premier sources of information on employment benefits, including analysis of pension coverage, 401(k) account balances, health insurance coverage, and Social Security. EBRI also sponsors the annual Retirement Confidence and Health Confidence surveys, which can be accessed here.

- **National Compensation Survey**

http://www.bls.gov/ncs/ebs/home.htm

Get the facts about employee benefits from the Bureau of Labor Statistics' National Compensation Survey here. This annual survey examines the entire range of employee benefits provided by the nation's private companies—from vacation days to employee bonuses. Retirement and health care benefits are examined in detail.

BIRTH CONTROL

- **Gateway at the Centers for Disease Control**

http://www.cdc.gov/reproductivehealth/UnintendedPregnancy/Contraception.htm

This is the gateway to the Centers for Disease Control data on contraceptive use in the United States, which is awkwardly titled "unintended pregnancy prevention." At this site you can find links to a variety of reports and organizations that track contraceptive use.

- **National Survey of Family Growth**

http://www.cdc.gov/nchs/about/major/nsfg/nsfgcycle6reports.htm

From this page you can access a series of reports on sexual behavior, fertility, and use of family planning services by men and women aged 15 to 44. The data come from the 2002 National Survey of Family Growth, which is fielded every few years by the National Center for Health Statistics. Note in particular the report *Use of Contraception and Use of Family Planning Services in the United States: 1982–2002*.

BIRTHS

• Birth statistics from the National Center for Health Statistics

http://www.cdc.gov/nchs/fastats/births.htm

The National Center for Health Statistics, the official source of data on births in the United States, collects and analyzes records from every state. This site is the access point for the information. The annual series, *Births: Final Data* provides statistics on childbearing by age, race and Hispanic origin, marital status, and other characteristics.

• Data from the American Community Survey

http://factfinder.census.gov/home/saff/main.html?_lang=en

The American Community Survey collects data on fertility. To see the latest information, go to this site—the Census Bureau's Fact Finder Page. Click "get data" under "American Community Survey," then click "Subject Tables." Select your geography, then click "next." Scroll down to the table "Fertility."

• Data from the Current Population Survey

http://www.census.gov/population/www/socdemo/fertility.html

Every two years the Current Population Survey asks American women about their childbearing experiences, which results in a report on the fertility of American women. The information includes a profile of the characteristics of women who have had a child in the past year.

• Maternity leave

http://www.census.gov/Press-Release/www/releases/archives/employment_occupations/011536.html

The Census Bureau report *Maternity Leave and Employment Patterns, 1961–2003* provides the most comprehensive data available on women's labor force participation before and after giving birth.

• National Survey of Family Growth

http://www.cdc.gov/nchs/products/pubs/pubd/series/sr23/pre-1/sr23_25.htm

This address will take you to the comprehensive report on women's sexual and reproductive behavior, *Fertility, Family Planning, and Reproductive Health of U.S. Women*. The report is based on the 2002 National Survey of Family Growth, which asked women aged 15 to 44 about their sexual behavior, contraceptive use, fertility, and motherhood status. The NSFG, fielded every few years by the National Center for Health Statistics, also examines whether births were wanted or unwanted, parameters of maternity leave, and use of family planning services.

BLACKS

• 2000 Census

http://www.census.gov/population/www/cen2000/briefs.html

On this page, scroll down to Census 2000 Special Report 25, *We The People: Blacks in the United States*. This will give you an overview of the black population as of 2000.

• Business owners

http://www.census.gov/csd/sbo/black2002.htm

The Survey of Business Owners, taken every five years as part of the Economic Census, provides details on black-owned businesses in the United States.

• Demographics from the American Community Survey

http://factfinder.census.gov/home/saff/main.html?_lang=en

The American Community Survey provides annual statistics on the population by race and Hispanic origin. To retrieve the information, go to this site—the Census Bureau's Fact Finder page. Click on "get data" under "American Community Survey." On the next page, click on the "Selected Population Profiles" link. On the next page, specify the desired geography (for national totals, just click "add" and "next"). On the following page, select the desired racial group. One more click and you have the latest demographic profile of the African American population. You can also create custom tables of American Community Survey data with the "Custom Table" link.

• Estimates by age

http://www.census.gov/popest/national/asrh/

To get the latest numbers on the black population—including estimates of the population by age—visit the Census Bureau's population estimates site.

• Gateway at the Census Bureau

http://www.census.gov/population/www/socdemo/race/black.html

Here you can access the Census Bureau's reports on blacks, including 2000 census data.

• Health data from the Centers for Disease Control

http://www.cdc.gov/omhd/Populations/BAA/BAA.htm

For information on the health of the black population, this is the place to start. This page has links to a variety of statistics revealing the health of the black population, including information on health disparities.

• Income data

http://www.census.gov/hhes/www/income/dinctabs.html

Every March the Current Population Survey collects income data by race and Hispanic origin through the Annual Social and Economic Supplement. The gateway to the data for households, families, and persons is available here.

Just How Fat Are Americans?

Too fat, according to the latest statistics. Obesity has become the health concern *du jour* for good reason. Data from the National Health and Nutrition Examination Survey reveal the growing size of Americans: 66 percent of adults are overweight.

The National Health and Nutrition Examination Survey produces "official" statistics on the weight of Americans. They are considered "official" because, to derive the numbers, survey researchers actually measure the height and weight of a representative sample of the population. Measuring provides more accurate data than simply asking people to report their height and weight, since many women understate their weight and many men overstate their height. This tendency to fib about weight and height lowers body mass index calculations based on self-reports, making us more complacent than we should be about our weight.

The percentage of people who are overweight (defined as having a body mass index of 25.0 or more) has grown from 47 percent in 1976–80 to 66 percent in 2003–04, the most recent data available. The percentage of people who are obese (defined as having a body mass index of 30.0 or more) climbed from 15 to 33 percent during those years. In every age group, most are overweight.

- **Poverty data**

http://www.census.gov/hhes/www/poverty/detailedpovtabs.html

Every year, the Census Bureau measures the poverty population by race and Hispanic origin. The poverty estimates are based on income data collected by the Annual Social and Economic Supplement of the March Current Population Survey. The poverty tables are available here.

BODY MASS INDEX

- **Measured weight, historical data**

http://www.cdc.gov/nchs/pressroom/04news/americans.htm

Here you can download the eye-opening report *Mean Body Weight, Height, and Body Mass Index*, which tells you just how much weight Americans have gained over the decades. From the early 1960s to 2002, the average weight of both men and women increased by 24 pounds. The data come from the National Health and Nutrition Examination Survey.

- **Measured weight, latest data**

http://www.cdc.gov/nchs/about/major/nhanes/nhanesmmwrs_obesity.htm

When asked to self-report their weight, most Americans say they weigh less than they really do. At this site you can access the latest data on how much men and women weigh, based on the National Health and Nutrition Examination Survey, which, rather than asking people how much they weigh, actually puts them on the scale and records the numbers.

- **Self-reported weight**

http://www.cdc.gov/nchs/nhis.htm

In the annual report *Summary Health Statistics for U.S. Adults*, available on this page, you can access tables on body mass index based on self-reported weight and height by a variety of demographic characteristics. Tables 30 and 31 have the numbers, based on the National Health Interview Survey.

BUSINESS OWNERS

- **Survey of Business Owners**

http://www.census.gov/csd/sbo/

Results from the Census Bureau's 2002 Survey of Business Owners, part of the economic censuses fielded by the bureau every five years, can be found at this site. Reports on American Indian, black, Hispanic, Asian, Native Hawaiian, and women-owned businesses are available. Hundreds of pages in length, the reports include the number of businesses, types of businesses, sizes of firms, and their revenues in 2002. The data are shown for the nation as a whole and for states, metropolitan areas, counties, and cities. For those wanting a comprehensive picture of minority and women-owned businesses, this is it.

C

CALIFORNIA

- **State Data Center**

http://www.dof.ca.gov/Research/Research.php

At this web site you can access demographic and economic statistics for California, including current population estimates, population projections, employment statistics, and 2000 census data. Local area data are also available here.

CAREERS

- **Bureau of Labor Statistics**

http://www.bls.gov/bls/occupation.htm

This is the access point for the Bureau of Labor Statistics voluminous data on occupations, including links to compensation data.

CAREGIVERS

- **AARP**

http://www.aarp.org/research/housing-mobility/caregiving/

Available here is a list of reports on caregiving in the United States.

CELL PHONE DEMOGRAPHICS

- **Cell-phone-only households**

http://www.cdc.gov/nchs/nhis.htm

Sometimes the most interesting bits of information come from unlikely places. The National Health Interview Survey is a source of information on cell-phone-only households. Scroll down this page, which lists reports from the NHIS, to *Wireless Substitution: Estimates from the National Health Interview Survey*, for the latest numbers. The survey tracks cell-phone-only use because of the growing difficulty of surveying Americans by landline phone.

- **Occasional surveys from Pew**

http://www.pewinternet.org/index.asp

The Pew Internet & American Life Project, one of the eight Pew Research Center groups, surveys the public about its computer and Internet use. Occasionally, it produces reports on cell phone use, which you can find here.

CENSUS OF POPULATION AND HOUSING

- **Census Bureau**

http://www.census.gov/main/www/cen2000.html

This is the gateway to the 2000 census and its voluminous and geographically detailed data. Here you can find ranking tables, special reports, and geographic products and create custom tables.

CENSUS TRACT DEMOGRAPHICS

- **Census Bureau**

http://www.census.gov/geo/www/tractez.html

If you need demographic data by census tract, this is the place to start. This site explains how to determine a census tract number from a street address and guides you in retrieving the demographic information.

CHARITABLE GIVING

- **Boston College Center of Wealth and Philanthropy**

http://www.bc.edu/research/cwp/

New York, Utah, California, Connecticut, Maryland, New Jersey, Georgia, Massachusetts, Hawaii, and South Carolina are the ten leaders in charitable giving among the 50 states. This is one of the findings in *Charitable Giving Indices: Social Indicators of Philanthropy by State*, a report from the Boston College Center on Wealth and Philanthropy.

CHILD CARE ARRANGEMENTS

- **National Center for Education Statistics**

http://nces.ed.gov/pubs2006/earlychild/04.asp

Here you can access results from the Childhood Program Participation Survey, which is part of the government's National Household Education Survey. Data are available on participation in early child care programs, length of time in child care, cost of child care, and reasons for selecting the child care arrangement.

- **Who's Minding the Kids reports**

http://www.census.gov/population/www/socdemo/childcare.html

This page is the gateway to *Who's Minding the Kids* reports on child care arrangements. The data come from the Census Bureau's Survey of Income and Program Participation.

CHILD SUPPORT

• Census Bureau

http://www.census.gov/hhes/www/childsupport/childsupport.html

This page is your gateway to the Census Bureau's data on child custody and support in its report series entitled *Custodial Mothers and Fathers and Their Child Support*. The data come from the Census Bureau's Survey of Income and Program Participation.

CHILDREN, ADOPTED AND STEP

• 2000 Census

http://www.census.gov/population/www/cen2000/phc-t21.html

Here you can access the 2000 census report on adopted and stepchildren in the United States.

• The Children's Bureau

http://www.childwelfare.gov/systemwide/statistics/adoption.cfm

The Children's Bureau provides state and national data on adoption and foster care, child abuse and neglect, and child welfare. Here you can access reports and statistics on adoption, those who seek to adopt, and those who have relinquished their child for adoption.

CHILDREN, AFTER-SCHOOL ACTIVITIES

• A Child's Day reports

http://www.census.gov/population/www/socdemo/2004_detailedtables.html

This site allows you to access the many tables of data on the family life of children from the Census Bureau's series entitled *A Child's Day*. Some of the unique findings available in these reports include whether children participate in sports and after-school activities. The data are from the Census Bureau's Survey of Income and Program Participation.

• National Household Education Survey

http://nces.ed.gov/pubsearch/pubsinfo.asp?pubid=2006076

This page is your gateway to information about children's participation in after-school programs collected by the National Center for Education Statistics in its National Household Education Survey.

CHILDREN, FAMILY LIFE

• A Child's Day reports

http://www.census.gov/population/www/socdemo/2004_detailedtables.html

This site allows you to access the many tables of data on the family life of children from the Census Bureau's series entitled *A Child's Day*. Some of the unique findings available in these reports include whether parents feel angry with their children, whether children participate in sports and after-school activities, and whether a family has rules about television viewing. The data are from the Census Bureau's Survey of Income and Program Participation.

CHILDREN, HEALTH

• Medical Expenditure Panel Survey

http://www.meps.ahrq.gov/mepsweb/data_stats/MEPS_topics.jsp?topicid=2Z-1

The full range of data and reports on children's use of health care services can be accessed at this site. The data are from the federal government's Medical Expenditure Panel Survey.

• Summary Health Statistics for Children report

http://www.cdc.gov/nchs/nhis.htm

Here you can download the report *Summary Health Statistics for U.S. Children*, updated annually, with detailed data on the health status of the population under age 18.

CHILDREN IN POVERTY

• Poverty data

http://www.census.gov/hhes/www/poverty/detailedpovtabs.html

Every year, the Census Bureau measures the poverty population by age. The poverty estimates are based on income data collected by the Annual Social and Economic Supplement of the March Current Population Survey. The poverty tables are available here.

CHILDREN, LIVING ARRANGEMENTS

• 2000 Census

http://www.census.gov/population/www/cen2000/phc-t30.html

The comprehensive 2000 census report on children's living arrangements can be accessed at this site.

• Latest data from the Current Population Survey

http://www.census.gov/population/www/socdemo/hh-fam.html

The latest tables revealing the living arrangements of children, available annually from the Current Population Survey, are here.

CHILDREN, SOCIOECONOMICS

• American Community Survey

http://factfinder.census.gov/home/saff/main.html?_lang=en

The American Community Survey collects annual data on the characteristics of children. To see the latest information, go to this site—the Census Bureau's Fact Finder Page. Click

How Diverse Are American Children?

The population under age 18 is the leading edge of demographic change in the United States. According to Census Bureau population estimates for 2007, only 57 percent of the nation's children under age 18 are non-Hispanic white. Among people aged 65 or older, a much larger 81 percent are non-Hispanic white. Children are more diverse than older people because most immigrants are young adults in their childbearing years and because the fertility of immigrants is greater than that of the native-born population.

By 2050, only 43 percent of the nation's children will be non-Hispanic white, according to projections by the Census Bureau. Nearly 30 percent of children will be Hispanic, 16 percent black, and 7 percent Asian. Although older Americans will become more diverse as younger generations age, the disparity between young and old will continue for decades to come. Among people aged 65 or older in 2050, the 61 percent majority will be non-Hispanic white.

"get data" under "American Community Survey," then click "Subject Tables." Select your geography, then click "next." Scroll down to the table "Children Characteristics."

- **America's Children: Key National Indicators of Well-Being reports**

http://www.childstats.gov/

For those who want to know the status of America's children, the web site of the Federal Interagency Forum on Child and Family Statistics is a good place to start. From here you can download the latest *America's Children: Key National Indicators of Well-Being*. This annual report compiles statistics on children in one convenient volume. The site also provides a long list of other government contacts for more information about children.

CHRONIC CONDITIONS

- **Gateway at the Centers for Disease Control**

http://www.cdc.gov/DiseasesConditions/

The A to Z index on this page is a useful gateway to the Centers for Disease Conrol's voluminous statistics and reports on just about any chronic condition.

- **Medical Expenditure Panel Survey data**

http://www.meps.ahrq.gov/mepsweb/survey_comp/household.jsp

Go to this page and click on the link to the right, called "Expenditures by Medical Condition," to see a list of tables showing health care service utilization (doctor visits, hospital stays, prescription drug use, and emergency department services) by medical condition such as asthma, diabetes, and high blood pressure.

- **Medical Expenditure Panel Survey reports**

http://www.meps.ahrq.gov/mepsweb/data_stats/MEPS_topics.jsp?topicid=4Z-1

This site provides access to a broad range of reports on health care visits and spending for a variety of chronic conditions. The data come from the Medical Expenditure Panel Survey.

- **Summary Health Statistics reports**

http://www.cdc.gov/nchs/nhis.htm

On this page you gain access to the National Center for Health Statistics' *Summary Health Statistics* reports for the population as a whole, for children, and for adults. Each report examines a variety of diseases such as asthma, cardiovascular disease, arthritis, and learning disabilities.

CIGARETTE SMOKING

- **Behavioral Risk Factor Surveillance System**

http://www.cdc.gov/brfss/

This annual survey collects data nationally and by state on the health behaviors of adults, including tobacco use.

- **Gateway at the Centers for Disease Control**

http://www.cdc.gov/tobacco/data_statistics/index.htm

This is the Center for Disease Control's gateway to government information on tobacco use, with links to many surveys and statistics.

- **High school students**

http://www.monitoringthefuture.org/

The annual Monitoring the Future survey fielded by the Institute for Social Research at the University of Michigan tracks the behavior and attitudes of American 8th, 10th, and 12th graders toward alcohol, drugs, and tobacco.

- **Summary Health Statistics reports**

http://www.cdc.gov/nchs/nhis.htm

In the annual report, *Summary Health Statistics for U.S. Adults,* available on this page, you can access tables on cigarette smoking by a variety of demographic characteristics. Tables 24 and 25 have the numbers, based on the National Health Interview Survey.

- **Youth Risk Behavioral Surveillance System**

http://www.cdc.gov/HealthyYouth/yrbs/

Every two years the Youth Risk Behavioral Surveillance System examines the behavior of 9th through 12th graders nationally and by state. Drug, tobacco, and alcohol use are examined.

CITIZENSHIP

- **American Community Survey**

http://factfinder.census.gov/home/saff/main.html?_lang=en

The American Community Survey collects annual data on citizenship. To see the latest information, go to this site—the Census Bureau's Fact Finder Page. Click "get data" under "American Community Survey," then click "Subject Tables." Select your geography, then click "next." Scroll down to the section on "Origins and Language," and click on the table, "Selected Characteristics of the Native and Foreign-Born Populations."

CITY DEMOGRAPHICS

- **American Community Survey**

http://factfinder.census.gov/home/saff/main.html?_lang=en

The American Community Survey collects annual data on city demographics. To see the latest information, go to this site—the Census Bureau's Fact Finder Page. Click "get data" under "American Community Survey," then click "Data Profiles." Select your geography, and you can retrieve the latest demographic and socioeconomic data on the city of your choice.

- **County and City Data Book**

http://www.census.gov/prod/www/abs/ccdb07.html

Which city has the fastest growing labor force? Which one gets the most rainfall? You can find out at this site, where you can access the *County and City Data Book: 2007* for population, housing and business data for counties, cities with 25,000 or more population, and places of 2,500 or more residents. The book incorporates information from government agencies and private nonprofit organizations.

COLLEGE COSTS

- **College Board**

http://www.collegeboard.com/student/pay/add-it-up/4494.html

On this page you can access the College Board's annual publication *Trends in College Pricing*, with the latest available data on college costs by type of institution. Historical data are also included in the publication.

- **National Center for Education Statistics**

http://nces.ed.gov/pubsearch/pubsinfo.asp?pubid=2006186

Everyone knows college costs are in the stratosphere and rising. But few pay full freight to go to school. This report from the National Center for Education Statistics, *Student Financing of Undergraduate Education: 2003–04*, reveals how much families actually pay, out of pocket, to send their kids to school—or what the NCES calls the net price of attendance.

COLLEGE DEGREES AWARDED

- **National Center for Education Statistics**

http://nces.ed.gov/programs/digest/d07/tables_3.asp#Ch3aSub4

This address takes you to the many tables on postsecondary degrees in the latest *Digest of Education Statistics*.

COLLEGE ENROLLMENT

- **Census Bureau**

http://www.census.gov/population/www/socdemo/school.html

The annual Current Population Survey collects data on school enrollment, including enrollment at the college level. This is where you can access links to those tables.

- **National Center for Education Statistics**

http://nces.ed.gov/programs/digest/d07/tables_3.asp#Ch3aSub1

This address takes you to the many tables on college enrollment in the latest *Digest of Education Statistics*.

Is There a College Market Bubble?

Prices are high and rapidly rising. Millions are clamoring to buy. Many are taking on debt to cover the cost. A stock market bubble? A housing market bubble? No, the college market bubble.

A speculative bubble occurs when the price of a product or service exceeds its fundamentals, yet excessive numbers of buyers keep driving up the price. This is happening in the college market today. The fundamentals of a bachelor's degree—greater lifetime earnings, ticket to the middle class—have long been worth the price. But that era may be ending. Is a college education still worth the cost? Yes, but the returns are diminishing, and they are no longer guaranteed.

Over the past few years, college graduates have not fared well. Between 2000 and 2006, the median earnings of men with a bachelor's degree who work full-time fell 5 percent, after adjusting for inflation. Growth in the median earnings of their female counterparts came to a halt in 2003. Everyone from the former chairman of the Federal Reserve Board, Alan Greenspan, to the local high school guidance counselor is encouraging teenagers to go to college. Teenagers—and their parents—are listening. Today, more than 80 percent of parents expect their children to get a college degree, according to the Census Bureau's Survey of Income and Program Participation. Two out of three high school graduates enroll in college within a few months of getting a high school diploma.

Buyers are in a frenzy, and prices are going through the roof. The average charge for tuition at the nation's colleges is growing by an unsustainable 5.6 percent a year, much faster than family incomes. Here is the consequence: In 1976–77, one year of college tuition at a four-year public university cost the equivalent of $2,225 (in today's dollars), according to the College Board. In 2007–08, one year of tuition at a public university cost $6,185—nearly three times as much. The cost of one year of tuition at a private school grew from $9,172 to $23,712 during those years, after adjusting for inflation.

As further proof of a speculative market, these bloated prices have not reduced demand. Instead they have fueled an aggressive and questionable student loan business. With parents unable to pay the bills but still urging their children to get a college degree, and children afraid they will be left behind in an increasingly competitive economy, college is a seller's market no matter the cost. Sixty-five percent of college students graduate in debt, according to the National Center for Education Statistics.

By now, we should know better. We have weathered two economic bubbles in the past decade, and we should be able to finesse this one. The key, as always, is to buy low and sell high. To buy low, students should find a school they can afford without taking on debt. To sell high, students should focus on preparing themselves for a financially rewarding career. A gentleman's diploma is no longer enough. But a carefully chosen career path, free of debt, should allow newly minted college graduates to be bystanders, rather than victims, when the college market bubble bursts.

COLLEGE STUDENT ATTITUDES

• The American Freshman Survey

http://www.gseis.ucla.edu/heri/heri.html

At this site you can order results from the latest American Freshman Survey. Sponsored by the Higher Education Research Institute at UCLA's Graduate School of Education and Information Studies, the well-known survey of college freshmen has been taken annually for more than 40 years. The site itself does not offer much data, but you can download the press release and a few charts from the most recent survey. For $25 you can order the annual publication *The American Freshman: National Norms*.

COLLEGE STUDENT EMPLOYMENT

• Bureau of Labor Statistics

http://www.bls.gov/news.release/hsgec.toc.htm

The web site provides the latest data on the employment status of college and high school students.

COLORADO

• State Data Center

http://dola.colorado.gov/dlg/demog/index.html

At this web site you can access demographic and economic statistics for Colorado, including current population estimates, employment statistics, and 2000 census data. Local area data are also available here.

COMMUTING

• 2000 Census

http://www.census.gov/population/www/socdemo/journey.html

At this site you can access detailed census data on the journey to work.

• American Community Survey

http://factfinder.census.gov/home/saff/main.html?_lang=en

The American Community Survey collects annual data on commuting. To see the latest information, go to this site—the Census Bureau's Fact Finder Page. Click "get data" under "American Community Survey," then click "Subject Tables." Scroll down to the table "Commuting Characteristics by Sex."

COMPENSATION

• **Bureau of Labor Statistics**

http://www.bls.gov/bls/wages.htm

Want to know how much people make in any occupation, even at the state or metropolitan level? You can find it here.

COMPUTER USE

• **Current statistics from Pew Internet & American Life Project**

http://www.pewinternet.org/

The Pew Internet & American Life Project produces reports that explore the impact of computers and the Internet. At this site you can access historical and current survey data revealing what Americans do online. You can also take The Internet Typology Test to find out what kind of information technology user you are.

• **Historical statistics from the Census Bureau**

http://www.census.gov/population/www/socdemo/computer.html

For historical data on household computer ownership and use, the Census Bureau has data that can be accessed here.

CONGRESSIONAL DEMOGRAPHICS

• **Congressional Research Service**

http://www.senate.gov/reference/resources/pdf/RS22007.pdf

How do the demographics of Congress compare with those of the average American? This report, prepared by the Congressional Research Service, will tell you. It examines the age, occupation, education, religion, sex, race, Hispanic origin, nativity status, and military service of House and Senate members. The Senate has never been older, according to the report, with an average age of 60. House members are slightly younger, with an average age of 55. The 109th Congress has a record number of women (85), blacks (43), and Hispanics (30).

CONNECTICUT

• **State Data Center**

http://ctsdc.uconn.edu/

At this web site you can access demographic and economic statistics for Connecticut, including current population estimates, population projections, employment statistics, and 2000 census data. Local area data are also available here.

CONSTRUCTION STATISTICS

• Census Bureau

http://www.census.gov/const/www/

On a monthly basis, the Census Bureau tracks the number of housing units authorized by permits, started, sold, and completed. It measures the dollar value of all construction put in place each month. It tracks residential construction in 30 metropolitan areas across the country each quarter, and it reports the sales of new one-family houses in those areas each year. These numbers and historical data on housing characteristics and home prices are available here.

CONSUMER EXPENDITURES

• 100 Years of Consumer Spending

http://www.bls.gov/opub/uscs/home.htm

This is where you can access the Bureau of Labor Statistics report, *100 Years of U.S. Consumer Spending: Data for the Nation, New York City, and Boston*. The report draws on a wide range of consumer expenditure data to present a 100-year history of significant changes in consumer spending in the country as a whole, New York City, and Boston.

• Consumer Expenditure Survey

http://www.bls.gov/cex/

This is the site of the Bureau of Labor Statistics Consumer Expenditure Survey (CEX), which releases annual data on household spending. Summary statistics back to 1984 are available here. The data are shown by a variety of demographic characteristics such as age of householder, household type, and household income. Detailed spending data from the CEX are available only by special request.

CONSUMER FINANCES

• Survey of Consumer Finances

http://www.federalreserve.gov/pubs/oss/oss2/scfindex.html

The Federal Reserve Board's Survey of Consumer Finances, taken every three years, can be accessed at this site. The SCF is the only comprehensive source of data on the wealth of Americans at the household level. Here you can download the latest statistics showing household assets (financial and nonfinancial) and debts. Historical data back to 1989 are available.

Is There an Easy Way to Adjust a Dollar Figure for Inflation?

The easiest way to adjust a figure for inflation is to use the inflation calculator on the Bureau of Labor Statistics home page at *http://www.bls.gov*.

Click on the Inflation Calculator link on the left side of the page, under the heading Inflation and Consumer Spending. A pop-up window will appear, allowing you to adjust a figure for inflation.

For example, let's say you want to know whether households are spending more money on pets. You know the average household spent $209 on their pets in 2000 and $316 on pets in 2006. To determine whether the average household is spending more or whether the increase is simply due to inflation, you need to adjust the 2000 figure for inflation, turning it into 2006 dollars. Plug the number $209 into the upper box of the Inflation Calculator and select the year 2000—indicating that it is the amount spent in 2000. Then select the year 2006 in the lower scroll bar and click "calculate." A box pops up showing the number $244.68. This means an expenditure of $209 in 2000 was the equivalent of an expenditure of $245 in 2006. Since the average household spent $316 on pets in 2006, the difference between $245 and $316 is how much more the average household spent on pets—a substantial 29 percent more in 2006 than in 2000, after adjusting for inflation.

CONSUMER PRICE INDEX

• Bureau of Labor Statistics

http://www.bls.gov/cpi/home.htm

On this web page you gain access to the government's Consumer Price Indexes over time, item by item. Examine the government's tabulated data or create custom tables.

CONTINGENT WORKERS

• Bureau of Labor Statistics

http://www.bls.gov/news.release/conemp.toc.htm

An annual profile of the number and demographics of the nation's alternative workers (including independent contractors, on-call, temporary, and contract workers) is here.

CONTRACEPTIVE USE

• Gateway at the Centers for Disease Control

http://www.cdc.gov/reproductivehealth/UnintendedPregnancy/Contraception.htm

This is the gateway to the Centers for Disease Control data on contraceptive use in the United States, which is awkwardly titled "unintended pregnancy prevention." At this site you can find links to a variety of reports and organizations that track contraceptive use.

• National Survey of Family Growth

http://www.cdc.gov/nchs/about/major/nsfg/nsfgcycle6reports.htm

From this page you can access a series of reports on sexual behavior, fertility, and use of family planning services by men and women aged 15 to 44. The data come from the 2002 National Survey of Family Growth, which is fielded every few years by the National Center for Health Statistics. Note in particular the report *Use of Contraception and Use of Family Planning Services in the United States: 1982–2002*.

COUNTIES, COASTAL

• National Oceanic and Atmospheric Administration

http://www.noaa.gov/coasts.html

For information about the nation's coasts and trends in the coastal population, the web site of the National Oceanic and Atmospheric Administration is the place to go. Here you can download the NOAA-Census study, *Population Trends Along the Coastal United States: 1980 to 2008*, part of the Coastal Trends Report Series.

How Fast Is the Coastal Population Growing?

With all the talk about Americans moving to warmer climates and the expansion of retirement and resort areas, you would think the number of people living along the nation's coast would be growing much faster than the number of people living inland. But you would be wrong.

The government actually measures these things. Specifically, the U.S. National Oceanic and Atmospheric Agency defines "coastal" counties or equivalents and tracks their population growth. According to NOAA, there are 673 coastal counties, which are areas with at least 15 percent of their land in or between coastal watersheds. NOAA divides coastal counties into six regions: Atlantic, Gulf of Mexico, Pacific, Alaskan, Hawaiian, and Great Lakes. The most populous coastal region is the Atlantic, which consists of 285 counties and more than 60 million people.

Between 2000 and 2006, coastal counties grew more slowly than noncoastal counties, up 5 percent compared with an 8 percent gain for inland areas. Overall, the 52 percent majority of Americans (156 million people) lived in a coastal county in 2006. But this share had been 53 percent in 2000. One reason for the slower growth of coastal counties is that many of the nation's largest metropolitan areas are on the coast. As those areas grow, they have only one way to go and that's inland.

COUNTY DEMOGRAPHICS

• American Community Survey

http://factfinder.census.gov/home/saff/main.html?_lang=en

The American Community Survey collects annual data on county demographics. To see the latest information, go to this site—the Census Bureau's Fact Finder Page. Click "get data" under "American Community Survey," then "Data Profiles." Select your geography, and you get the latest demographic and socioeconomic data on the county of your choosing.

• County and City Data Book

http://www.census.gov/prod/www/abs/ccdb07.html

Which county is growing the fastest? Which one has the most crime? You can find out at this site, where you can access the *County and City Data Book: 2007* for population, housing and business data for counties, cities with 25,000 or more population, and places of 2,500 or more residents. The book incorporates information from government agencies and private nonprofit organizations.

• State and County QuickFacts

http://quickfacts.census.gov/qfd

This link takes you to an interactive map of the United States where you click on a state and pull up a demographic snapshot of the state based on the range of Census Bureau data. Comparisons with national totals are shown alongside the state data. Once on a state page, you can select a county or city within the state. Comparisons with state totals are shown alongside the local data.

CRIME

• Bureau of Justice Statistics

http://www.ojp.usdoj.gov/bjs/

The United States has more prisoners than any other country in the world. At this site you can access the Bureau of Justice Statistics' reports on crime, law enforcement, the courts, prisons, and prisoners.

• FBI, Uniform Crime Reports

http://www.fbi.gov/ucr/ucr.htm

The FBI's Uniform Crime Reports are based on data provided to the agency by nearly 17,000 law enforcement agencies across the country. Here you can access those reports as well as the annual publication *Crime in the United States*.

- **Safety of the nation's schools**

http://nces.ed.gov/surveys/ssocs/

How safe are the nation's schools? Find out at this site, where you gain access to the National Center for Education Statistics' School Survey on Crime and Safety, the primary source of school-level data on crime and safety in the nation's public schools.

- **Sourcebook of Criminal Justice Statistics**

http://www.albany.edu/sourcebook/

This site is the source for comprehensive and up-to-date criminal justice statistics, which are published each year in the *Sourcebook of Criminal Justice Statistics*. The data are compiled for the Bureau of Justice Statistics by the Utilization of Criminal Justice Statistics Project at the State University of New York, Albany. The Sourcebook has been produced annually since 1973.

D

DAY CARE

- **National Center for Education Statistics**

http://nces.ed.gov/pubs2006/earlychild/04.asp

Here you can access results from the Childhood Program Participation Survey, which is part of the government's National Household Education Survey. Data are available on participation in early child care programs, length of time in child care, cost of child care, and reasons for selecting the child care arrangement.

- **Who's Minding the Kids reports**

http://www.census.gov/population/www/socdemo/childcare.html

This page is the gateway to *Who's Minding the Kids* reports on child care arrangements. The data come from the Census Bureau's Survey of Income and Program Participation.

DAYTIME POPULATION

- **Census Bureau**

http://www.census.gov/population/www/socdemo/daytime/daytimepop.html

The term "daytime population" refers to the number of people who are present in an area during normal business hours, including workers. This is in contrast to the "resident" population present during the evening and nighttime hours. Information on the expansion or contraction experienced by different communities between nighttime and daytime populations is important for many purposes. At this site you can access the Census Bureau's data on daytime populations by geographic area.

DEATHS

- **Death statistics from the National Center for Health Statistics**

http://www.cdc.gov/nchs/deaths.htm

Everything you need to know about mortality statistics can be accessed via this site, which has links to annual reports on deaths by cause as well as life expectancy.

DEBT

• Survey of Consumer Finances

http://www.federalreserve.gov/pubs/oss/oss2/scfindex.html

The Federal Reserve Board's Survey of Consumer Finances, taken every three years, can be accessed at this site. The SCF is the only comprehensive source of data on the wealth of Americans at the household level. Here you can download the latest analysis detailing household assets and debts. Historical data back to 1989 are also available.

DEGREES AWARDED

• National Center for Education Statistics

http://nces.ed.gov/programs/digest/d07/tables_3.asp#Ch3aSub4

This address takes you to the many tables on postsecondary degrees in the latest *Digest of Education Statistics*.

DELAWARE

• State Data Center

http://stateplanning.delaware.gov/census_data_center/

At this web site you can access the range of demographic and economic statistics for Delaware, including current population estimates, population projections, employment statistics, 2000 census data, and American Community Survey numbers. Local area data are also available here.

DEMOGRAPHIC DATA, GENERAL

• Census Bureau

http://www.census.gov/

Do you love demographics but don't know quite what you're looking for? Then stop by the Census Bureau's home page where the entire range of demographic data is at your fingertips.

• Statistical Abstract

http://www.census.gov/compendia/statab/

The premier book of numbers, the *Statistical Abstract of the United States*, is available at this site, which provides direct access to the latest and earlier editions of the *Abstract* (all the way back to 1878). The *Abstract* is the authoritative and comprehensive summary of statistics on the social, political, and economic organization of the United States. Use the *Abstract* as a convenient volume for statistical reference and as a guide to sources of more information both in print and on the web.

How Deep in Debt Are American Households?

While the U.S. government cannot balance its budget, American households are more disciplined. The median amount of debt carried by the average household is a surprisingly modest $55,300, according to the most authoritative source of information on household wealth, the Survey of Consumer Finances. And this figure includes mortgage debt. While most households are in debt, most are not in over their heads.

Every three years the Federal Reserve Board's Survey of Consumer Finances examines the assets and liabilities of American households, providing the most comprehensive picture available of household wealth. The latest data are from the 2004 survey. While the numbers are somewhat dated and personal debt is certainly larger today than it was in 2004, the median debt calculation is based on the behavior of more than 100 million households. In other words, it is unlikely to change radically in just a few years. The modest amount owed by the average household brings us to one conclusion: Americans are careful with their money.

Three out of four households were in debt in 2004, a figure that has not changed much over the years. The amount of money owed by the average household has been climbing. Between 2001 and 2004, median debt rose by 34 percent, after adjusting for inflation. This is a considerable increase, but most of it was due to greater mortgage debt as the large baby-boom generation bought homes. In fact, 75 percent of household debt is accounted for by mortgages and home equity loans.

Three types of debt are about equally common: mortgage and home equity (owed by 48 percent of households), installment loans (such as car loans, owed by 46 percent), and credit card balances (46 percent). The largest debts by far are mortgage and home equity. Despite horror stories about credit card debt, households that carry a credit card balance from one month to the next owed a median of only $2,200 on their cards.

Bottom line: Few families are in financial trouble. American households manage their money wisely—more wisely than many of the so-called professionals in the field of finance.

DEMOGRAPHIC DATA, HISTORICAL

• Statistical Abstract

http://www.census.gov/compendia/statab/2007/hist_stats.html
http://www.census.gov/prod/www/abs/statab.html

Historical demographic data organized by topic is available from a selection of the Census Bureau's *Statistical Abstracts* at the first listed site. The second site is the gateway to individual *Statistical Abstracts* dating back to 1878.

DEMOGRAPHY

• Population Association of America

http://www.popassoc.org/

If you need insight into population trends, you can find a demographer—or hundreds of them—at this official site of the Population Association of America. Here you can browse the PAA membership directory by area of specialization, such as business demography or aging. The site also contains the latest news on government funding for population-related matters.

DENTAL CARE

• Medical Expenditure Panel Survey

http://www.meps.ahrq.gov/mepsweb/data_stats/MEPS_topics.jsp?topicid=10Z-1

This site provides access to tables and reports on dental care based on data from the Medical Expenditure Panel Survey.

DIET AND NUTRITION

• Food availability spreadsheets

http://www.ers.usda.gov/Data/FoodConsumption/FoodAvailIndex.htm

At this site you can access the federal government's food availability spreadsheets, which reveal how much food—item by item—is available for human consumption in the United States. You discover, for example, that 23 pounds of candy per capita disappear from store shelves every year, as do 25 gallons of alcoholic beverages—far more than Americans claim to drink on surveys.

• Gateway at the Centers for Disease Control

http://www.cdc.gov/nccdphp/dnpa/nutrition/health_professionals/data/index.htm

From here you can access a variety of reports and statistics on the eating habits of Americans, including the Behavioral Risk Factor Surveillance System, the Pediatric Nutrition Surveillance System, and obesity reports.

DISABILITY

• Census Bureau

http://www.census.gov/hhes/www/disability/disability.html

Perhaps no population characteristic is more difficult to nail down than disability. Everyone, and every government survey, defines disability differently. Here you can access several different surveys revealing the demographics of the disabled and decide which one best fits your needs.

DISCOURAGED WORKERS

• Bureau of Labor Statistics

http://www.bls.gov/news.release/empsit.t12.htm

Here you find the continually updated table Alternative Measures of Labor Underutilization, which tracks unemployed and discouraged workers.

DISEASES

• Gateway at the Centers for Disease Control

http://www.cdc.gov/DiseasesConditions/

The A to Z index on this page is a useful gateway to the Center for Disease Control's voluminous statistics and reports on just about any chronic condition.

• Medical Expenditure Panel Survey data

http://www.meps.ahrq.gov/mepsweb/survey_comp/household.jsp

Go to this page and click on the link to the right, called "Expenditures by Medical Condition," to see a list of tables showing health care service utilization (doctor visits, hospital stays, prescription drug use, and emergency department services) by medical condition such as asthma, diabetes, and high blood pressure.

• Medical Expenditure Panel Survey reports

http://www.meps.ahrq.gov/mepsweb/data_stats/MEPS_topics.jsp?topicid=4Z-1

This site provides access to a broad range of reports on health care visits and spending for a variety of chronic conditions. The data come from the Medical Expenditure Panel Survey.

• Summary Health Statistics reports

http://www.cdc.gov/nchs/nhis.htm

On this page you gain access to the National Center for Health Statistics' *Summary Health Statistics* reports for the population as a whole, for children, and for adults. Each report examines a variety of diseases such as asthma, cardiovascular disease, arthritis, and learning disabilities.

DISTRICT OF COLUMBIA

• State Data Center

http://www.planning.dc.gov/planning/site/default.asp

At this web site you can access 2000 census data for the District of Columbia.

DIVORCE

• Gateway at the National Center for Health Statistics

http://www.cdc.gov/nchs/fastats/divorce.htm

In 2005, the nation had a divorce rate of 3.6 per 1,000 population. At this site you can find the latest divorce rates, along with links to divorce data available from the National Survey of Family Growth and the Census Bureau.

• Divorce history

http://www.census.gov/population/www/socdemo/marr-div.html

This address will take you to the Census Bureau's web page devoted to its data on marriage and divorce. Here you can access the report *Number, Timing and Duration of Marriages and Divorces: 2004*, with data on the marital history of Americans including the percentage who have ever divorced.

DOCTOR VISITS

• Doctor visit reports

http://www.cdc.gov/nchs/about/major/ahcd/adata.htm

Every year the federal government collects data on the characteristics of people visiting the doctor through the National Ambulatory Medical Care Survey. At this site you can access the many reports about those visits.

• Medical Expenditure Panel Survey

http://www.meps.ahrq.gov/mepsweb/survey_comp/household.jsp

On this page, click on the link to the right, "Expenditures by Health Care Service," to see a list of tables showing the demographics of those using a variety of health care services including physician visits.

DRINKING

• Behavioral Risk Factor Surveillance System

http://www.cdc.gov/brfss/

This annual survey collects data nationally and by state on the health behaviors of adults, including alcohol consumption.

Do Half of Marriages End in Divorce?

Once upon a time, the National Center for Health Statistics collected and published statistics on marriage and divorce. Its researchers calculated marriage and divorce rates, determined the percentage of marriages ending in divorce, and contributed greatly to our understanding of this important milestone in the lives of most Americans. But that worthy effort came to an unfortunate halt more than a decade ago due to limitations in the data collected by states and tighter federal budgets.

The NCHS marriage and divorce reports are greatly missed. Pundits and politicians have filled the statistical vacuum, pontificating on the topic with little factual information. For those who want the facts, the only place to turn to is occasional surveys—such as the National Survey of Family Growth. The NSFG, taken every five years or so, is a survey of the sexual and family formation behavior of the nation's 15-to-44 year olds. The latest NSFG survey, taken in 2002, can answer the question of how many marriages end in divorce.

The likelihood of divorce depends on when you were born, your age at marriage, your educational level, and even the type of family in which you were raised. Among ever-married women aged 15 to 44 in 2002, a substantial 35 percent had seen their first marriage end in divorce. But this figure ranged from a high of 63 percent among those who married before age 18 to just 22 percent among those who married at age 23 or older. The percentage of women divorced from their first husband was as high as 45 percent for those with only a high school education and a much smaller 20 percent among college graduates. Among ever-married women raised in a two-parent family, only 32 percent had divorced from their first husband. Among those raised by single parents, a larger 44 percent had divorced.

So how many marriages end in divorce? The answer is, it depends.

Drug Use (Illegal)

- **Gateway at the Centers for Disease Control**

http://www.cdc.gov/alcohol/surveillance.htm

To find out how much people drink, start at this site and explore the links to many government and other surveys that collect data on alcohol consumption, including the National Health Interview Survey and Monitoring the Future survey.

- **High school students**

http://www.monitoringthefuture.org/

The annual Monitoring the Future survey fielded by the Institute for Social Research at the University of Michigan tracks the behavior and attitudes of American 8th, 10th, and 12th graders toward alcohol, drugs, and tobacco.

- **National Health Interview Survey**

http://www.cdc.gov/nchs/nhis.htm

In the annual National Center for Health Statistics' report *Summary Health Statistics for U.S. Adults*, available on this page, you can access tables on alcohol consumption by a variety of demographic characteristics. Tables 26 and 27 have the numbers.

- **Youth Risk Behavioral Surveillance System**

http://www.cdc.gov/HealthyYouth/yrbs/

Every two years the Youth Risk Behavioral Surveillance System examines the behavior of 9th through 12th graders nationally and by state. Alcohol, drug, and tobacco use are examined.

DRUG USE (ILLEGAL)

- **Gateway at the National Center for Health Statistics**

http://www.cdc.gov/nchs/fastats/druguse.htm

This page is a gateway to the federal government's many statistics on illegal drug use by Americans.

- **High school students**

http://www.monitoringthefuture.org/

The annual Monitoring the Future survey fielded by the Institute for Social Research at the University of Michigan tracks the behavior and attitudes of American 8th, 10th, and 12th graders toward alcohol, drugs, and tobacco.

- **National Survey on Drug Use and Health**

http://oas.samhsa.gov/nsduh.htm

This annual survey of illegal drug use by Americans aged 12 or older provides detailed data by drug and by demographic characteristic.

- **Youth Risk Behavioral Surveillance System**

http://www.cdc.gov/HealthyYouth/yrbs/

Every two years the Youth Risk Behavioral Surveillance System examines the behavior of 9th through 12th graders nationally and by state. Alcohol, drug, and tobacco use are examined.

DRUG USE, PRESCRIPTON

- **Medical Expenditure Panel Survey**

http://www.meps.ahrq.gov/mepsweb/data_stats/MEPS_topics.jsp?topicid=14Z-1

This site provides access to tables and reports on prescription drug use based on data from the Medical Expenditure Panel Survey.

DUAL EARNERS

- **Incomes from the Current Population Survey**

http://pubdb3.census.gov/macro/032007/faminc/toc.htm

For the latest data on the incomes of dual-earner married couples, see table FINC-05, which can be accessed on this page.

- **Wives who earn more**

http://www.census.gov/hhes/www/income/histinc/incfamdet.html

For the latest statistics on wives who earn more than their husbands, go to this page and scroll down to table F22.

E

EARNINGS

• Annual earnings

http://pubdb3.census.gov/macro/032007/perinc/toc.htm

The latest annual earnings data from the Current Population Survey can be accessed at this site by downloading tables PINC-03 to PINC-07. The data are available by sex, race, and other demographic characteristics.

Earnings from the Current Employment Statistics Program

http://www.bls.gov/ces/home.htm

Each month the Current Employment Statistics program surveys about 150,000 businesses and government agencies, representing approximately 390,000 individual worksites, in order to provide detailed industry data on employment, hours, and earnings of workers on nonfarm payrolls nationally.

• Earnings from the Occupational Employment Statistics Survey

http://www.bls.gov/bls/blswage.htm

From this site you can retrieve wage data from the Bureau of Labor Statistics' Occupational Employment Statistics Survey. The OES is a survey of the nation's business establishments, producing detailed estimates of earnings by occupation for the nation, regions, states, and metropolitan areas.

• Weekly earnings

http://www.bls.gov/cps/home.htm

This page is the gateway to accessing the latest labor force characteristics compiled by the Bureau of Labor Statistics, including median weekly earnings. Scroll down to "Annual Averages—Household Data" and click on tables 37, 38, and 39 for median weekly earnings data, including earnings by detailed occupation.

• Wives who earn more

http://www.census.gov/hhes/www/income/histinc/f22.html

This table has data from the Current Population Survey on the number of wives who earn more than their husbands.

ECONOMIC INDICATORS

• Bureau of Labor Statistics

http://www.bls.gov/bls/newsrels.htm

If you want to track unemployment, consumer prices, or other economic indicators produced by the Bureau of Labor Statistics, then visit this site to get the latest numbers.

• Census Bureau

http://www.census.gov/cgi-bin/briefroom/BriefRm/

This site links you to the latest government statistics on homeownership and housing sales.

ECONOMIC MOBILITY

• Economic Mobility Project

http://economicmobility.org/

The Economic Mobility Project is a nonpartisan collaboration of The Pew Charitable Trusts and four leading policy institutes—the American Enterprise Institute, the Brookings Institution, the Heritage Foundation, and the Urban Institute. Together, these groups analyze economic mobility in the United States and produce reports on the status of the American Dream. At this site you can download reports and access studies of economic mobility.

ECONOMIC TRENDS

• National Bureau of Economic Research

http://www.nber.org/

The National Bureau of Economic Research is the organization that officially decides when recessions begin and end. It also investigates socioeconomic trends, making the findings available through its Working Paper series. These studies examine everything from why Americans weigh so much to why college costs so much. You can download individual working papers for just $5.

EDUCATION, ADULT

• National Center for Education Statistics

http://nces.ed.gov/nhes/

From this page you can access reports with data from the adult education portion of the National Household Education Survey. This survey is fielded every few years to measure participation in educational activities ranging from early childhood programs to work-related adult education courses.

EDUCATION, ATTITUDES TOWARD

• The American Freshman Survey

http://www.gseis.ucla.edu/heri/heri.html

At this site you can order results from the latest American Freshman Survey. Sponsored by the Higher Education Research Institute at UCLA's Graduate School of Education and Information Studies, the well-known survey of college freshmen has been taken annually for more than 40 years. The site itself does not offer much data, but you can download the press release and a few charts from the most recent survey. For $25 you can order the annual publication *The American Freshman: National Norms*.

• Attitudes toward public schools

http://www.pdkintl.org/kappan/kpollpdf.htm

If you want to know what Americans think about public education, visit the Phi Delta Kappa International web site. Phi Delta Kappa International is an association of professional educators committed to public education. Of particular interest is the Phi Delta Kappa/Gallup Poll of the Public's Attitudes Toward the Public Schools, an annual survey the organization has conducted for more than three decades. The polls provide a wealth of current and historical data on attitudes toward public education.

EDUCATION, GENERAL STATISTICS

• Digest of Education Statistics

http://nces.ed.gov/programs/digest/

The *Digest of Education Statistics* is the comprehensive source of statistics on education in the United States, from prekindergarten through graduate school and adult education. Updated annually, the *Digest* covers a variety of topics, including school enrollment, SAT scores, high school graduates, college degrees awarded, as well as data on schools, teachers, and school finances.

EDUCATION, HOMESCHOOLING

• National Household Education Survey

http://nces.ed.gov/pubsearch/pubsinfo.asp?pubid=2006042

Here you can access the government's statistics on the homeschool population, based on the National Household Education Survey. The findings reveal that more than 1 million American children are being schooled at home.

EDUCATION, PRIVATE SCHOOLS

• Digest of Education Statistics

http://nces.ed.gov/programs/digest/d07/tables_2.asp#Ch2Sub2

The National Center for Education Statistics' annual *Digest of Education Statistics* contains many tables on the nation's private elementary and high schools. Those tables can be accessed here.

• Private School Survey

http://nces.ed.gov/surveys/pss/

On this page you can access statistics and reports from the federal government's biennial Private School Survey. You can retrieve data on private schools by size, level, religious orientation, geographic region, community type, and program emphasis. If you want data for a particular private school, use the search function to find out more.

EDUCATION PROJECTIONS

• National Center for Education Statistics

http://nces.ed.gov/programs/projections/projections2016/

If you want to know how many bachelor's degrees will be awarded in 2016, or the number and share of female college students in that year, then take a look at the National Center for Education Statistics' education projections available at this site.

EDUCATION, PUBLIC SCHOOLS

• Attitudes toward public schools

http://www.pdkintl.org/kappan/kpollpdf.htm

If you want to know what Americans think about public education, visit the Phi Delta Kappa International web site. Phi Delta Kappa International is an association of professional educators committed to public education. Of particular interest is the Phi Delta Kappa/Gallup Poll of the Public's Attitudes Toward the Public Schools, an annual survey the organization has conducted for more than three decades. The polls provide a wealth of current and historical data on attitudes toward public education.

• Digest of Education Statistics

http://nces.ed.gov/programs/digest/d07/tables_2.asp

The National Center for Education Statistics' annual *Digest of Education Statistics* contains hundreds of tables of data on the nation's public elementary and high schools. Those tables can be accessed from this site.

What's Wrong with Public Schools?

Americans are concerned about the nation's public schools—so what else is new? Education always ranks as a top concern. Educating children, after all, is one of the most important tasks of governments and parents. When asked for their opinion of the public school system, Americans always give it low marks. The latest data show no change in this trend. Fully 80 percent of the public give the nation's public schools a grade of C or lower, according to the 2007 Phi Delta Kappa/Gallup Poll of the Public's Attitudes toward Public Schools. Only 16 percent give public schools an A or B.

Phi Delta Kappa/Gallup researchers have polled the public each year for more than three decades, and in all of those years they have found many more people willing to give low rather than high marks to public schools. But does the general public know enough about schools to make an informed decision? After all, few households include school-aged children, and aren't the parents of school children much more likely to know how well schools perform? The PDK/Gallup poll looks into this issue by examining the opinions of parents of public school children. Alas, it finds little difference between the opinions of parents and the general public. Among parents, 84 percent give the nation's public schools a C or lower grade; only 14 percent give them an A or B.

But zoom in for a close-up and the picture improves. Ask the general public to rate their local schools, and a larger 45 percent give them an A or B. Among parents of schoolchildren, an even larger 53 percent give the local schools a high grade. The more specific the question, the more positive the results. When researchers ask parents of public school children to grade the school their oldest child attends, an impressive 67 percent give the school an A or B.

So are the public schools in trouble or not? Clearly, some schools are troubled. Eight percent of parents give the school attended by their oldest child a D or F. This number is not insignificant, but since a much larger percentage give their child's school a high grade, the nation's public schools may not be as bad as we think.

EDUCATION, SCHOOL ENROLLMENT

- **Local schools**

http://nces.ed.gov/ccd/schoolsearch/

If you need data on a specific public school, then visit this National Center for Education Statistics' site and retrieve information on the total number of students in a school as well as the number of students by grade, sex, race, and Hispanic origin. The data come from the federal government's Common Core of Data Program, an annual survey of the nation's public schools.

- **School districts**

http://nces.ed.gov/surveys/sdds/index.asp

Want to know the demographics of a particular school district? The National Center for Education Statistics' School District Demographics System allows users to retrieve population profiles of school districts for analysis or comparison, based on data from the American Community Survey.

EDUCATION, SCHOOL ENROLLMENT

- **Gateway at the Census Bureau**

http://www.census.gov/population/www/socdemo/school.html

This site is the gateway to the Census Bureau's data on school enrollment from the Current Population Survey.

- **Digest of Education Statistics**

http://nces.ed.gov/programs/digest/d07/tables_2.asp#Ch2Sub1

The *Digest of Education Statistics* provides enrollment data for public and private schools from prekindergarten through graduate school and adult education programs. The *Digest*'s enrollment data can be accessed here.

EDUCATIONAL ATTAINMENT

- **Census Bureau**

http://www.census.gov/population/www/socdemo/educ-attn.html

Each year the Current Population Survey collects data on the educational attainment of Americans, and you can access the data at this site.

ELDERLY

- **AARP research**

http://www.aarp.org/research/

To lobby for the older population, the AARP must research its needs. At the AARP site you can benefit from its work. This page is your gateway to the AARP's studies and statistics.

- **Gateway at the Census Bureau**

http://www.census.gov/population/www/socdemo/age.html

This is the Census Bureau's access point to its voluminous data on the age of the American population. Scroll down to the sections on the older (55+) and elderly (65+) populations.

- **Health and Retirement Study data book**

http://hrsonline.isr.umich.edu/docs/sho_refs.php?hfyle=index&xtyp=7

Here you can access *Growing Older in America: The Health and Retirement Study*, a free pdf download that places some of the University of Michigan's Health and Retirement Study into the hands of the public. The Health and Retirement Study is a longitudinal survey, launched in 1992 and funded by the National Institute on Aging, which tracks a nationally representative sample of Americans aged 50 or older as they age. HRS data are available primarily as datasets, limiting their use to academic researchers. *Growing Older in America* allows the public to review the survey's most important findings.

- **Older Americans: Key Indicators of Well-Being report**

http://www.agingstats.gov/agingstatsdotnet/main_site/default.aspx

Here you can download the summary report, *Older Americans 2008*, which provides data on 37 indicators of the socioeconomic status of older Americans.

- **The State of 50+ America report**

http://www.aarp.org/research/reference/statistics/fifty_plus_2006.html

Every two years the AARP analyzes the socioeconomic well being of Americans aged 50 or older in its report *The State of 50+ America*. The report can be downloaded here.

EMERGENCY DEPARTMENT VISITS

- **Emergency department visit reports**

http://www.cdc.gov/nchs/about/major/ahcd/adata.htm#Emergency

Every year the federal government collects data on the characteristics of people visiting hospital emergency departments through the National Ambulatory Medical Care Survey. At this site you can access reports about those visits.

- **Medical Expenditure Panel Survey**

http://www.meps.ahrq.gov/mepsweb/survey_comp/household.jsp

On this page, click on the link to the right, "Expenditures by Health Care Service," to see a list of tables showing the demographics of those using a variety of health care services including hospital emergency departments.

EMPLOYEE BENEFITS

• Employee Benefit Research Institute

http://www.ebri.org

The Employee Benefit Research Institute is one of the premier sources of information on employment benefits, including analysis of pension coverage, 401(k) account balances, health insurance coverage, and Social Security. EBRI also sponsors the annual Retirement Confidence and Health Confidence surveys, which can be accessed here.

• National Compensation Survey

http://www.bls.gov/ncs/ebs/home.htm

Get the facts about employee benefits from the Bureau of Labor Statistics' National Compensation Survey here. This annual survey examines the entire range of employee benefits provided by the nation's private companies—from vacation days to employee bonuses. Retirement and health care benefits are examined in detail.

EMPLOYEE COMPENSATION

• Bureau of Labor Statistics

http://www.bls.gov/opub/cwc/home.htm

To keep tabs on employee compensation and working conditions, visit the Bureau of Labor Statistics' Compensation and Working Conditions Online. Here you will find a variety of reports on such topics as employer costs, employee benefits, occupational injuries, and collective bargaining.

EMPLOYEE TENURE

• Bureau of Labor Statistics

http://www.bls.gov/news.release/tenure.toc.htm

Want to know how long workers have been at their current job? The Bureau of Labor Statistics tracks employee tenure by age, sex, race and Hispanic origin, occupation, and education. Get the numbers here.

EMPLOYMENT

• American Community Survey

http://factfinder.census.gov/home/saff/main.html?_lang=en

The American Community Survey collects annual data on the labor force. To see the latest information, go to this site—the Census Bureau's Fact Finder Page. Click "get data" under "American Community Survey," then click "Subject Tables." Select your geography, then click "next." Scroll down to the section on employment to retrieve labor force data.

- **Demographics of the labor force**

http://www.bls.gov/cps/home.htm

This site is the federal government's central repository of data on the demographics of the labor force. Here you can access just about everything you would want to know about labor force topics, such as working mothers, the decline in long-term employment, and the characteristics of minimum wage workers. The site also provides access to the Bureau of Labor Statistics' annual average employment tables.

- **Employment statistics from the Current Employment Statistics Program**

http://www.bls.gov/ces/home.htm
http://www.bls.gov/sae/home.htm

Each month the Current Employment Statistics Program surveys about 150,000 businesses and government agencies, representing approximately 390,000 individual worksites, in order to provide detailed industry data on employment, hours, and earnings of workers on nonfarm payrolls nationally (available at the first URL), and for all 50 states and over 300 metropolitan areas (available at the second URL).

- **Gateway at the Bureau of Labor Statistics**

http://www.bls.gov/bls/employment.htm

This is the Bureau of Labor Statistics' gateway to the entire range of statistics on employment. Everything you want to know about employment and unemployment can be accessed through this web page.

- **Projections**

http://www.bls.gov/emp/home.htm

Every two years the Bureau of Labor Statistics issues updated employment projections. The latest are available at this site. The projections show big changes on the horizon as the workforce ages.

- **State and local area employment statistics from the Current Population Survey**

http://www.bls.gov/lau/#data

Here you can access local area employment, unemployment, and labor force data from the Current Population Survey, a monthly survey of households. The data are available for regions and divisions, states, counties, metropolitan areas, and many cities.

EMPLOYMENT PROJECTIONS

- **Bureau of Labor Statistics**

http://www.bls.gov/emp/home.htm

Every two years the Bureau of Labor Statistics issues updated employment projections. The latest are available at this site. The projections show big changes on the horizon as the workforce ages.

ENERGY CONSUMPTION

• Energy Information Administration

http://www.eia.doe.gov/emeu/recs/contents.html

This site, home of the Residential Energy Consumption Survey, will answer your questions about household energy consumption.

ENGLISH, ABILITY TO SPEAK

• American Community Survey

http://factfinder.census.gov/home/saff/main.html?_lang=en

The American Community Survey collects annual data on how well Americans speak English. To see the latest information, go to this site—the Census Bureau's Fact Finder Page. Click "get data" under "American Community Survey," then click "Subject Tables." Select your geography, then click "next." On the Subject Table page, scroll down to the tables on Origins and Language: "Characteristics of People by Language Spoken at Home" and "Language Spoken at Home."

• Gateway at the Census Bureau

http://www.census.gov/population/www/socdemo/lang_use.html

This site is the Census Bureau's gateway to 1990 and 2000 census information on language spoken at home.

ENROLLMENT, SCHOOL

• All levels

http://www.census.gov/population/www/socdemo/school.html

Here you will find Current Population Survey data on all levels of school enrollment by a variety of demographic characteristics.

• Elementary and secondary school

http://nces.ed.gov/programs/digest/d07/tables_2.asp#Ch2Sub1

This address will take you to tables on elementary and secondary school enrollment from the *Digest of Education Statistics*.

• Higher education

http://nces.ed.gov/programs/digest/d07/tables_3.asp

This address will take you to tables on enrollment in higher education from the *Digest of Education Statistics*.

ESTIMATES, POPULATION

• Census Bureau

http://www.census.gov/popest/estimates.php

This site is the gateway to the Census Bureau's official population estimates. Here you can access monthly estimates of the total population, as well as annual estimates of the population by age, sex, race, and Hispanic origin. Estimates by state, county, and metropolitan area are also available.

EXERCISE

• Behavioral Risk Factor Surveillance System

http://www.cdc.gov/nccdphp/dnpa/physical/stats/index.htm

Here you can access physical activity statistics and reports from the Behavioral Risk Factor Surveillance System, a state-by-state telephone survey of a nationally representative sample of Americans.

• Demographics of exercisers

http://www.cdc.gov/nchs/nhis.htm

In the annual report *Summary Health Statistics for U.S. Adults*, available on this page, you can access tables on leisure-time physical activity by a variety of demographic characteristics. Tables 28 and 29 have the numbers, based on the National Health Interview Survey.

• Gateway at the National Center for Health Statistics

http://www.cdc.gov/nchs/fastats/exercise.htm

This is the National Center for Health Statistics gateway to its data on the physical activity of Americans.

• Public school programs

http://nces.ed.gov/pubsearch/pubsinfo.asp?pubid=2006057

This address is the link to *Calories In, Calories Out: Food and Exercise in Public Elementary Schools, 2005*, a report examining the food and physical activity programs available at the nation's public elementary schools.

EXPENDITURES

• 100 Years of Consumer Spending

http://www.bls.gov/opub/uscs/home.htm

This is where you can access the Bureau of Labor Statistics report *100 Years of U.S. Consumer Spending: Data for the Nation, New York City, and Boston*. The report draws on a wide range of consumer expenditure data to present a 100-year history of significant changes in consumer spending in the country as a whole, New York City, and Boston.

EXPENDITURES

• Consumer Expenditure Survey

http://www.bls.gov/cex/

This is the site of the Bureau of Labor Statistics Consumer Expenditure Survey (CEX), which releases annual data on household spending. Summary statistics back to 1984 are available here. The data are shown by a variety of demographic characteristics such as age of householder, household type, and household income. Detailed spending data from the CEX are available only by special request.

F

FAMILIES, EMPLOYMENT OF

- **Bureau of Labor Statistics**

http://www.bls.gov/news.release/famee.toc.htm

Both mother and father are employed in 62 percent of the nation's nuclear families (married couples with children). This is just one of the findings in the Bureau of Labor Statistics' annual Employment Characteristics of Families tabulation, available at this site.

FAMILY FORMATION

- **National Survey of Family Growth**

http://www.cdc.gov/nchs/about/major/nsfg/nsfgcycle6reports.htm

Every few years the National Center for Health Statistics collects information on the sexual and family formation behavior of men and women aged 15 to 44 through the National Survey of Family Growth. Links to those studies are on this web page.

FAMILY PLANNING

- **Gateway at the Centers for Disease Control**

http://www.cdc.gov/reproductivehealth/UnintendedPregnancy/Contraception.htm

This is the gateway to the Center for Disease Control's data on contraceptive use in the United States, which is awkwardly titled "unintended pregnancy prevention." At this site you can find links to a variety of reports and organizations that track contraceptive use.

- **National Survey of Family Growth**

http://www.cdc.gov/nchs/about/major/nsfg/nsfgcycle6reports.htm

From this page you can access a series of reports on sexual behavior, fertility, and use of family planning services by men and women aged 15 to 44. The data come from the 2002 National Survey of Family Growth, which is fielded every few years by the National Center for Health Statistics. Note in particular the report *Use of Contraception and Use of Family Planning Services in the United States: 1982–2002*.

FAMILY STATISTICS

• A Child's Day reports

http://www.census.gov/population/www/socdemo/2004_detailedtables.html

This site allows you to access the many tables of data on the family life of children from the Census Bureau's series entitled *A Child's Day*. The unique findings available in these reports include whether parents feel angry with their children, whether children participate in sports and after-school activities, and whether a family has rules about television viewing. The data are from the Census Bureau's Survey of Income and Program Participation.

• Gateway at the Census Bureau

http://www.census.gov/population/www/socdemo/hh-fam.html

This site is your gateway to the Census Bureau's voluminous data on families and households, with current and historical data from the Current Population Survey, links to the American Community Survey, the census, and other relevant sites.

FATHERS

• Fathers of U.S. Children Born in 2001

http://nces.ed.gov/pubsearch/pubsinfo.asp?pubid=2006002

The report *Fathers of U.S. Children Born in 2001* is based on data collected by the Early Childhood Longitudinal Program, which is tracking a cohort of children born in 2001. The report profiles the demographic characteristics of resident and nonresident biological fathers, the extent of their involvement in pregnancy and birth, their attitudes toward fathering, and their participation in child care.

• Fertility, Contraception, and Fatherhood report

http://www.cdc.gov/nchs/pressroom/06facts/fatherhood.htm

This page will take you to the groundbreaking report *Fertility, Contraception, and Fatherhood*, which details men's sexual and reproductive behavior. The report is based on the 2002 National Survey of Family Growth, which asked men, for the first time, about their fertility, contraceptive use, and fatherhood status. The NSFG, fielded every few years by the National Center for Health Statistics, typically examines the sexual behavior and fertility status of American women aged 15 to 44. Now men are included too.

FERTILITY

• Birth statistics from the National Center for Health Statistics

http://www.cdc.gov/nchs/fastats/births.htm

The National Center for Health Statistics is the official source of data on births in the United States, collecting and analyzing records from every state. This site is the access point for the information. The annual series *Births: Final Data* provides statistics on childbearing by age, race and Hispanic origin, marital status, and other characteristics.

How High Is American Fertility?

The U.S. population has surpassed 300 million. Every 12 seconds, our population grows by one additional person. There are only two ways this can happen—through births or immigration. Births contribute the most to our population growth by far, with one birth occurring in the United States every 7 seconds. International migration adds one person to the population every 29 seconds. Death subtracts one person every 12 seconds.

For a developed country, the U.S. birth rate is high. In the world as a whole, the average woman has 2.59 children during her lifetime, according to data published by the CIA in its publication *The World Factbook*. The CIA ranks countries by their total fertility rate—a measure of the number of children a woman will have in her lifetime based on current age-specific fertility rates. From the highest fertility rate to the lowest, the United States ranks 126 out of 222 countries. Mali was number 1, with 7.38 children born per woman. In the United States, the average woman has 2.09 children. Our fertility rate is higher than the rate in 43 percent of the world's countries, including Chile, Turkey, Vietnam, and Brazil. Hong Kong has the lowest fertility rate, the average woman having only 0.98 children in her lifetime.

In 2007, the United States recorded 4.1 million births, rivaling the numbers during the peak of the baby boom. Of course our population is much larger now than it was then, meaning the fertility rate has dropped sharply since the 1950s and 1960s. Nevertheless, our rate remains above those in most of the developed world. While the higher fertility rate of the nation's Hispanics (2.9 children) sometimes gets the credit (or blame) for this, in fact the fertility rate of non-Hispanic white women (1.8 children) is higher than the fertility rate of 31 percent of the world's countries including most of Western Europe and Canada. The fertility rate of non-Hispanic white women is higher than the fertility rate of women in Cuba, Puerto Rico, China, and Iran.

- **Data from the American Community Survey**

http://factfinder.census.gov/home/saff/main.html?_lang=en

The American Community Survey collects annual data on fertility. To see the latest information, go to this site—the Census Bureau's Fact Finder Page. Click "get data" under "American Community Survey," then click "Subject Tables." Select your geography, then click "next." Scroll down to the table "Fertility."

- **Data from the Current Population Survey**

http://www.census.gov/population/www/socdemo/fertility.html

Every two years the Current Population Survey asks American women about their childbearing experiences, resulting in a report on the fertility of American women. The information includes a profile of the characteristics of women who have had a child in the past year.

- **Maternity leave**

http://www.census.gov/Press-Release/www/releases/archives/employment_occupations/011536.html

This Census Bureau report, *Maternity Leave and Employment Patterns, 1961–2003*, provides the most comprehensive data available on women's labor force participation before and after giving birth.

- **National Survey of Family Growth**

http://www.cdc.gov/nchs/products/pubs/pubd/series/sr23/pre-1/sr23_25.htm

This address will take you to the comprehensive report on women's sexual and reproductive behavior, *Fertility, Family Planning, and Reproductive Health of U.S. Women*. The report is based on the 2002 National Survey of Family Growth, which asked women aged 15 to 44 about their sexual behavior, contraceptive use, fertility, and motherhood status. The NSFG, fielded every few years by the National Center for Health Statistics, also examines whether births were wanted or unwanted, maternity leave, and use of family planning services.

FISHING

- **U.S. Fish & Wildlife Service**

http://www.census.gov/prod/www/abs/fishing.html

According to the 2006 National Survey of Fishing, Hunting, and Wildlife-Associated Recreation, nearly 88 million Americans fished, hunted, or watched wildlife in 2006. The survey, which has been conducted about every five years since 1955, explores Americans' participation in and spending on fishing, hunting, bird watching, animal feeding, and wildlife photography.

FLEXTIME

- **Bureau of Labor Statistics**

http://www.bls.gov/news.release/flex.toc.htm

More than 27 million full-time wage and salary workers had flexible work schedules that allowed them to vary the time they begin or end their work. This is one of the findings in the Workers on Flexible and Shift Schedules tabulations from the Bureau of Labor Statistics available at this site.

FLORIDA

- **State Data Center**

http://www.labormarketinfo.com/library/census.htm

At this web site you can access demographic and economic statistics for Florida, including current population estimates, population projections, employment statistics, and 2000 census data. Local area data are also available here.

FOOD CONSUMPTION

- **Food availability spreadsheets**

http://www.ers.usda.gov/Data/FoodConsumption/FoodAvailIndex.htm

At this site you can access the federal government's food availability spreadsheets, which reveal how much food—item by item—is available for human consumption in the United States. You discover, for example, that 23 pounds of candy per capita disappear from store shelves every year, as do 25 gallons of alcoholic beverages, far more than Americans claim to drink on surveys.

- **Gateway at the Centers for Disease Control**

http://www.cdc.gov/nccdphp/dnpa/nutrition/health_professionals/data/index.htm

From here you can access a variety of reports and statistics on the eating habits of Americans, including the Behavioral Risk Factor Surveillance System, the Pediatric Nutrition Surveillance System, and obesity reports.

FOREIGN-BORN POPULATION

- **American Community Survey**

http://factfinder.census.gov/home/saff/main.html?_lang=en

The American Community Survey collects annual data on the foreign-born population. To see the latest information, go to this site—the Census Bureau's Fact Finder Page. Click "get data" under "American Community Survey," then click "Subject Tables." Select your geography, then click "next." Scroll down to the section on Origins and Language and download the tables on the foreign-born population.

• Historical data from the Census Bureau

http://www.census.gov/population/www/socdemo/foreign/datatbls.html

To access historical data on the foreign-born population, this is the site to visit.

G

GAYS AND LESBIANS

- **Sexual behavior report**

http://www.cdc.gov/nchs/products/pubs/pubd/ad/361-370/ad362.htm

If you want government estimates of the number of gays and lesbians in the United States, the report *Sexual Behavior and Selected Health Measures: Men and Women 15-44 Years of Age, United States, 2002*, which can be downloaded at this site, is the best information available. The data come from the 2002 National Survey of Family Growth, in which a representative sample of men and women aged 15 to 44 were asked to identify their sexual orientation and tell whether they were attracted to people of the same or the opposite sex.

GENEALOGY

- **1930 Census**

http://www.census.gov/pubinfo/www/1930census_media.html

The decennial censuses are an important source of information for historians and genealogists. By law, however, individual census records cannot be released to the public for 72 years following the census in which they were collected. On April 1, 2002, the National Archives and Records Administration released the individual records from the 1930 census. You can find out more about how to access those records at this site.

- **Surname File**

http://www.census.gov/genealogy/www/freqnames2k.html

At this site you can access the Census Bureau's surname file from the 2000 census, which reveals that Smith is the most common surname in the United States. Two Hispanic surnames make the top ten list: Garcia (number 8) and Rodriguez (9).

GEOGRAPHIC PRODUCTS

- **Census Bureau**

http://www.census.gov/geo/www/maps/
http://www.census.gov/population/www/cen2000/censusatlas/

At the first URL, you can access the Census Bureau's broad range of mapping products, including maps of the latest metropolitan statistical areas and congressional districts. At the second URL, you can access the *Census 2000 Atlas of the United States*, with nearly 800 maps based on census data.

How Many Americans Are Gay?

Believe it or not, the government asks and tells. According to results from the 2002 National Survey of Family Growth (NSFG), nine out of ten people aged 15 to 44 (the survey is limited to that age group) identify themselves as heterosexual. The proportions are almost identical for men (90.2 percent) and women (90.3 percent) and do not vary significantly by age within the 15-to-44 age group.

Does this mean the remaining 10 percent are homosexual? Maybe, but it's hard to say. The government allows respondents to identify themselves as homosexual, bisexual, or "something else." Among men aged 15 to 44, only 2.3 percent identify themselves as homosexual, 1.8 percent say they are bisexual, 3.9 percent say they are something else, and 1.8 percent did not answer the question. Among women the proportions are 1.3 percent homosexual, 2.8 percent bisexual, 3.8 percent something else, and 1.8 percent refused to answer. Just what is "something else"? According to the government report *Sexual Behavior and Selected Health Measures: Men and Women 15–44 Years of Age, United States, 2002*, some of those saying they are something else may not understand the terminology. So the 10 percent figure may be too large—or maybe not.

The NSFG explores sexual orientation in other ways as well. It asks respondents whether they are attracted more to people of the same sex or the opposite sex. It also asks about lifetime and past-year sexual contact with opposite-sex and same-sex partners. On the attraction question, 92 percent of men aged 15 to 44 say they are attracted only to females—more than the 90 percent of men who say they are heterosexual. Among women, 86 percent say they are attracted only to males—less than the 90 percent who say they are heterosexual. Six percent of men say they have had oral or anal sex with another man in their lifetime. A smaller 2.9 percent say they have done so in the past 12 months. Eleven percent of women say they have had a sexual experience with another woman in their lifetime, and 4.4 percent have done so in the past year (the survey asked men and women different questions regarding same-sex experiences, making it difficult to compare results by gender).

It is likely that many people do not want the government to know their sexual leanings—especially if they are gay. The NSFG interviews were conducted in a way to minimize this hesitancy. Respondents wore headphones and entered their responses into a computer, preventing the interviewer from knowing how they answered the questions. Nevertheless, there's little doubt homosexuality will be underreported, making the 10 percent figure as good a guess as any.

GEOGRAPHICAL MOBILITY

- **2000 census reports**

http://www.census.gov/population/www/cen2000/migration.html

Every ten years the census provides detailed data on the migration of Americans from one area to another. You can access the 2000 census reports here.

- **Data from the American Community Survey**

http://factfinder.census.gov/home/saff/main.html?_lang=en

The American Community Survey collects annual data on mobility. To see the latest information, go to this site—the Census Bureau's Fact Finder Page. Click "get data" under "American Community Survey," then click "Subject Tables." Select your geography, then click "next." Scroll down to the tables on Mobility and click on "Geographic Mobility" or "Movers between Regions."

- **Data from the Current Population Survey**

http://www.census.gov/population/www/socdemo/migrate.html

This is the access point for the Census Bureau's data on geographic mobility, including the annual Current Population Survey data and decennial census data.

GEORGIA

- **State Data Center**

http://www.gadata.org/

At this web site you can access demographic and economic statistics for Georgia, including employment statistics and 2000 census data. Local area data are also available here.

GRADUATION RATES

- **National Center for Education Statistics**

http://nces.ed.gov/programs/digest/d07/tables_2.asp#Ch2Sub5

Here you can access tables on high school graduates and dropouts in the *Digest of Education Statistics*.

GRANDPARENTS

- **Census Bureau**

http://www.census.gov/population/www/socdemo/grandparents.html

If you want to know how many children live with their grandparents, the data are available at this site. Most children who live with grandparents also live with one or both parents.

GROUP QUARTERS POPULATION

- **Census Bureau**

http://factfinder.census.gov/home/saff/main.html?_lang=en

The American Community Survey collects data on the group quarters population. To see the latest information, go to this site—the Census Bureau's Fact Finder Page. Click "get data" under "American Community Survey," then click "Subject Tables." Select your geography, then click "next." Scroll down to the Group Quarters section and download tables with the latest data on how many live in prisons or college dorms and their characteristics.

H

HAWAII

• State Data Center

http://hawaii.gov/dbedt/info/economic/census/

At this web site you can access the range of demographic and economic statistics for Hawaii, including current population estimates, population projections, visitor statistics, 2000 census data, and American Community Survey numbers. Local area data are also available here.

HEALTH AND AGING

• Gateway at the National Center for Health Statistics

http://209.217.72.34/aging/ReportFolders/ReportFolders.aspx

This is the site of the Trends in Health and Aging electronic data warehouse. The site provides access to many reports and tables revealing trends in older Americans' health-related behavior, health status, health care utilization, and cost of care. Reports include titles such as *The Oral Health of Older Americans*. Many tables include state-level data.

• Health and Retirement Study data book

http://hrsonline.isr.umich.edu/docs/sho_refs.php?hfyle=index&xtyp=7

Here you can access *Growing Older in America: The Health and Retirement Study*, a free pdf download that places some of the University of Michigan's Health and Retirement Study into the hands of the public. The Health and Retirement Study is a longitudinal survey, launched in 1992 and funded by the National Institute on Aging, which tracks a nationally representative sample of Americans aged 50 or older as they age. HRS data are available primarily as datasets, limiting their use to academic researchers. *Growing Older in America* allows the public to review the survey's most important findings.

• Medical Expenditure Panel Survey

http://www.meps.ahrq.gov/mepsweb/data_stats/MEPS_topics.jsp?topicid=8Z-1

The Medical Expenditure Panel Survey results for older Americans are accessible from this site. MEPS is a set of large-scale surveys of families and individuals, collecting data on the health services they use, how frequently they use them, the cost of these services, and how they pay for them.

HEALTH AND NUTRITION

• National Center for Health Statistics

http://www.cdc.gov/nchs/about/major/nhanes/survey_results_and_products.htm

Here you can explore findings from the National Health and Nutrition Examination Survey, a continuing survey that provides data on the health and nutritional status of children and adults in the United States. The survey is unique in that it includes physical examinations. Its findings are used to create the growth charts used by pediatricians.

HEALTH BEHAVIOR

• Behavioral Risk Factor Surveillance System

http://apps.nccd.cdc.gov/brfss/index.asp

If you want to know the health status and behavior of Americans nationally or by state, the Centers for Disease Control's Behavioral Risk Factor Surveillance System, accessible at this site, can tell you. The BRFSS bills itself as the largest telephone survey in the world. It has to be large to provide annual state-level details by age, race, sex, income, and education.

• High school students

http://www.monitoringthefuture.org/

Monitoring the Future Survey is an ongoing study of the behaviors and attitudes of American secondary school students. Each year the survey queries 50,000 students in 8th, 10th, and 12th grade about their drug, alcohol, and tobacco use.

• National Survey on Drug Use and Health

http://www.oas.samhsa.gov/nsduh.htm

At this site you can access the annual National Survey on Drug Use and Health, which examines the detailed drug, alcohol, and tobacco use of Americans aged 12 or older by a variety of characteristics.

• State rankings

http://www.unitedhealthfoundation.org/ahr2007/states.html

This United Health Foundation site tells you how states rank in health. Right now the winner is Vermont. This page allows you to click on a state and get details about its health status. State health trends as far back as 1990 are available here.

• Youth Risk Behavior Surveillance System

http://www.cdc.gov/HealthyYouth/yrbs/index.htm

The Youth Risk Behavior Surveillance System monitors the health risk behavior of 9th through 12th graders nationally and by state. These behaviors include tobacco, alcohol, and drug use; diet; physical activity; sexual behavior; and risk behavior that contributes to injury and violence.

HEALTH CARE COSTS

• Health Confidence Survey

http://www.ebri.org/surveys/hcs/

The Health Confidence Survey is an annual look at Americans' attitudes towards health care, including health insurance. The survey, accessible at the above address, has been fielded annually since 1998.

• Kaiser Family Foundation

http://www.kff.org/insurance/index.cfm

The Kaiser Family Foundation is a nonprofit foundation focusing on how Americans cope with health care issues. Health care costs are one of the issues investigated by Kaiser, and the findings can be accessed here.

• Medical Expenditure Panel Survey

http://www.meps.ahrq.gov/mepsweb/survey_comp/household.jsp

The Medical Expenditure Panel Survey collects household spending data for a variety of health care services and conditions. You can access the results from this page by clicking on the Summary Data Table links "Expenditures by Health Care Service" and "Expenditures by Medical Condition."

• Medicare and Medicaid

http://www.cms.hhs.gov/DataCompendium/

To get the latest numbers on the cost and benefits of the Medicare and Medicaid programs, download the *Data Compendium* from the Centers for Medicare & Medicaid Services from this site.

• National Health Expenditures Data

http://www.cms.hhs.gov/NationalHealthExpendData/

From this Centers for Medicare & Medicaid Services site, you can access historical and projected figures on health care spending in the United States.

HEALTH CARE SYSTEM, ATTITUDES TOWARD

• Kaiser Family Foundation

http://www.kff.org/kaiserpolls/

There is no better way to stay on top of the public's attitudes toward health care than through the Kaiser polls, accessible at this site. The Kaiser Family Foundation surveys public opinion on health care issues every other month. Some of the topics examined by the polls include the importance of health care among issues, the public's perception of health care quality, the Medicare prescription drug plan, employer health benefits, and much more. The Kaiser Health Poll Search allows users to sort through more than 60,000 health-related survey questions organized by topic.

HEALTH CONDITIONS

• Gateway at the Centers for Disease Control

http://www.cdc.gov/DiseasesConditions/

The A to Z index on this page is a useful gateway to the Centers for Disease Control's voluminous statistics and reports on just about any chronic condition.

• Medical Expenditure Panel Survey data

http://www.meps.ahrq.gov/mepsweb/survey_comp/household.jsp

Go to this page and click on the link to the right, called "Expenditures by Medical Condition," to see a list of tables showing health care service utilization (doctor visits, hospital stays, prescription drug use, and emergency department services) by medical condition such as asthma, diabetes, and high blood pressure.

• Medical Expenditure Panel Survey reports

http://www.meps.ahrq.gov/mepsweb/data_stats/MEPS_topics.jsp?topicid=4Z-1

This site provides access to a broad range of reports on health care visits and spending for a variety of chronic conditions. The data come from the Medical Expenditure Panel Survey.

• Summary Health Statistics reports

http://www.cdc.gov/nchs/nhis.htm

On this page you gain access to the National Center for Health Statistics' *Summary Health Statistics* reports for the population as a whole, for children, and for adults. Each report examines one of a variety of diseases such as asthma, cardiovascular disease, arthritis, and learning disabilities.

HEALTH INSURANCE

• Annual data from the Census Bureau

http://www.census.gov/hhes/www/hlthins/hlthins.html

The Current Population Survey collects data each year on health insurance coverage. This is the gateway to those numbers.

• Employee Benefit Research Institute

http://www.ebri.org/

The Employee Benefit Research Institute is one of the premier sources of information on employment benefits, including health insurance coverage. Here you can download reports with the latest findings on the health insurance coverage of the nation's workers.

• Gateway at the National Center for Health Statistics

http://www.cdc.gov/nchs/fastats/hinsure.htm

This is the National Center for Health Statistics gateway to statistics on the population's health insurance coverage, collected by several of its surveys.

- **Health Confidence Survey**

http://www.ebri.org/surveys/hcs/

The Health Confidence Survey is an annual look at Americans' attitudes towards health care, including health insurance. The survey, accessible at the above address, has been fielded annually since 1998.

- **Kaiser Family Foundation**

http://www.kff.org/insurance/index.cfm

The Kaiser Family Foundation is a nonprofit organization focusing on health care issues in the United States. Kaiser investigates various facets of health insurance, and the findings can be accessed here.

- **Medical Expenditure Panel Survey**

http://www.meps.ahrq.gov/mepsweb/data_stats/MEPS_topics.jsp?topicid=7Z-1

The Medical Expenditure Panel Survey findings on health insurance can be accessed here. MEPS is a set of large-scale surveys of families and individuals, collecting data on the health care services Americans use, how frequently they use them, the cost of these services, and how they pay for them.

- **Medicare and Medicaid coverage**

http://www.cms.hhs.gov/DataCompendium/

To get the latest numbers on the Medicare and Medicaid health insurance programs, download the *Data Compendium* from this site.

HEALTH-RELATED QUALITY OF LIFE

- **National Center for Chronic Disease Prevention and Health Promotion**

http://apps.nccd.cdc.gov/HRQOL/

If you want to know how good—or bad—Americans feel, then this web site is the place to start. Here you can find statistics on our health-related quality of life, with handy summary measures of unhealthy days, both physical and mental.

HEALTH STATISTICS

- **Health, United States**

http://www.cdc.gov/nchs/hus.htm

The annual edition of *Health, United States* is available here, on the National Center for Health Statistics web site. This invaluable reference is a compilation of a wide array of health statistics, ranging from the demographics of cigarette smokers to the percentage of the population that has taken a prescription drug in the past month.

Are Americans Feeling Better?

We are living longer, but are we feeling better? Apparently the answer is no. Although life expectancy in the United States is at a record high, self-reported health status is declining. These contradictory trends are an unexpected and unwelcome finding, and they call into question the basic paradigm of modern medicine—that improvements in the diagnosis and treatment of a variety of diseases will result not just in a longer life, but a better life as well.

According to the federal government's Behavioral Risk Factor Surveillance System, the percentage of adults aged 18 or older who report being in excellent or very good health fell from 58 to 55 percent between 1996 and 2006. The aging of the population explains some of the decline, since older Americans are less likely to report being in tip-top shape. But an examination of the trends by age reveals the decline occurring among people aged 25 to 54, not among older adults.

Who is most likely to report feeling worse? A closer look at the demographics shows the biggest decline in health status among Hispanics. The percentage of Hispanics who feel "excellent" or "very good" fell by an enormous 13 percentage points between 1996 and 2006. Why is the health of Hispanics getting so much worse? The lack of health insurance could be the explanation. Among all Americans, Hispanics are the ones least likely to have health insurance. More than one-third of Hispanics do not have coverage.

- **Medical Expenditure Panel Survey**

http://www.meps.ahrq.gov/mepsweb/data_stats/data_overview.jsp

The federal government's Medical Expenditure Panel Survey, which began in 1996, is a set of large-scale surveys of families and individuals, their medical providers (doctors, hospitals, pharmacies, etc.), and employers in the United States. MEPS collects data on the health services Americans use, how frequently they use them, the cost of services, and how they pay for them. The MEPS site allows users to customize tables to examine health care consumption and spending by specific demographic segment.

- **National Center for Health Statistics**

http://www.cdc.gov/nchs/

This is the go-to place for statistics on the health of Americans, with links to birth and death data as well as to surveys of Americans' health status, doctor visits, hospital use, sexual behavior, HIV, and more.

HEALTH STATUS, SELF-REPORTED

- **Behavioral Risk Factor Surveillance System**

http://apps.nccd.cdc.gov/brfss/index.asp

If you want to know whether people feel excellent, very good, good, fair, or poor, then visit the Behavioral Risk Factor Surveillance System. On this web page, choose the nation as a whole, all the states, or an individual state. Pick a year, and then select the category "Health Status." Choose the question "How is Your General Health?" You can retrieve the data for the population as a whole, and by age, race, sex, income, or education.

HIGH-INCOME HOUSEHOLDS

- **Census Bureau**

http://pubdb3.census.gov/macro/032007/hhinc/new06_000.htm
http://pubdb3.census.gov/macro/032007/faminc/new07_000.htm

For those who need information on the number of households with incomes of $100,000 or more, these tables are all the Current Population Survey provides. Each of the above addresses will take you to one of the 2007 Current Population Survey cross-tabulations of income by race and Hispanic origin. The first is for households and the second for families. The tables show the number of households with incomes up to $250,000 or more, in $50,000 increments.

HIGH SCHOOL GRADUATES

• Current and historical data from the Census Bureau

http://www.census.gov/population/www/socdemo/educ-attn.html

This page is the gateway to the Census Bureau's educational attainment statistics. Scroll down to "Historical Tables" to access data on the percentage of the population with a high school diploma or a college degree since 1940.

• National Center for Education Statistics

http://nces.ed.gov/programs/digest/d07/tables_2.asp#Ch2Sub5

This address will take you to tables of data on high school graduates and dropouts from the *Digest of Education Statistics*.

HIGHER EDUCATION

• College enrollment data from the Census Bureau

http://www.census.gov/population/www/socdemo/school.html

This site is the gateway to the Census Bureau's data on school enrollment, including enrollment at the college level, from the Current Population Survey.

• Digest of Education Statistics

http://nces.ed.gov/programs/digest/d07/tables_3.asp

Everything you need to know about college enrollment is available here, in the postsecondary education chapter of the *Digest of Education Statistics*.

• Educational attainment data from the Census Bureau

http://www.census.gov/population/www/socdemo/educ-attn.html

This page is the gateway to the Census Bureau's educational attainment statistics, many of which reveal the characteristics of Americans with a college degree.

• Field of training

http://www.census.gov/population/www/socdemo/fld-of-trn.html

To find out just how much a college degree is worth, the *What's It Worth: Field of Training and Economic Status* reports from the Census Bureau's Survey of Income and Program Participation provide the numbers.

HISPANICS

• 2000 Census

http://www.census.gov/population/www/cen2000/briefs.html

On this page, scroll down to Census 2000 Special Report 18, *We The People: Hispanics in the United States*. This will give you an overview of the Hispanic population as of 2000.

What Is the Biggest Demographic Trend?

Move over Academy Awards, Emmys, Grammies, Nobels, Pulitzers, and Tonys. Make room for the Demographic Trend of the Year Award, given in recognition of the demographic trend that has caused the most consternation. This year's award goes to the Hispanic Population. The 46 million Hispanics in the United States swept all five categories of demographic melodrama. Here is a review of the results:

1. Fastest Growing Demographic Segment
Between 2000 and 2007, The Hispanic Population grew by an enormous 28 percent. At the same time, the number of non-Hispanic whites increased by a miniscule 2 percent.

2. Demographic Segment Getting the Biggest Bang for the Buck
The Hispanic Population accounts for only 15 percent of the U.S. population. But because of its strategic location, its influence is far greater. In California and Texas, the two most populous states, Hispanics are fully 36 percent of the population, amplifying their influence.

3. Demographic Segment with the Greatest Reach
The age structure of The Hispanic Population makes it a powerhouse in the all-important youth market. The median age of Hispanics is just 28 compared with a median age of 41 for non-Hispanic whites. Because of their relative youth, Hispanics account for a disproportionate share of newborns, students, and entry-level workers.

4. Demographic Segment Confusing the Most Pundits
The Hispanic Population is large enough to influence the nation's demographic trends, fooling the pundits. Example: The small decline in the labor force participation rate of young women over the past few years does not herald a return of the stay-at-home mom—as some pundits have suggested—but is a consequence of the lower labor force participation rate of Hispanic women. Among women aged 20 to 24, only 63 percent of Hispanics work compared with 72 percent of non-Hispanic whites. As Hispanics represent an ever-growing share of young adults, the labor force participation rate of young women is slipping.

5. Demographic Segment Enraging the Most Politicians
With Hispanics accounting for most immigrants, both legal and illegal, they have become the political target du jour. The consequence is not just fence building along our border with Mexico, but efforts to make English the official language, and new laws that make life increasingly difficult for Hispanics in general and immigrants in particular.

After sweeping all five categories, The Hispanic Population is the hands-down winner of The Demographic Trend of the Year Award. The runners-up—Gays, Unmarried Mothers, Boomers Who Refuse to Save for Retirement, and Young Adults who Spend Too Much Time Texting—mark your calendar for next year's competition.

- **Business owners**

http://www.census.gov/csd/sbo/hispanic2002.htm

The Survey of Business Owners, taken every five years as part of the Economic Census, provides details on Hispanic-owned businesses in the United States.

- **Demographics from the American Community Survey**

http://factfinder.census.gov/home/saff/main.html?_lang=en

The American Community Survey provides annual statistics on the population by race and Hispanic origin. To retrieve the information, go to this site—the Census Bureau's Fact Finder page. Click on "get data" under "American Community Survey." On the next page, click on the "Selected Population Profiles" link. On the next page, specify the desired geography (for national totals, just click "add" and "next"). On the following page, select the desired race or Hispanic origin group.

- **Estimates by age**

http://www.census.gov/popest/national/asrh/

To get the latest numbers on the Hispanic population—including estimates of the size of the population by age—visit the Census Bureau's population estimates site.

- **Gateway at the Census Bureau**

http://www.census.gov/population/www/socdemo/hispanic/ho06.html

The Census Bureau has compiled a great deal of data on the Hispanic population that can be accessed here. The tables provide details on Hispanics by age, living arrangement, labor force status, education, income, and more.

- **Health data from the Centers for Disease Control**

http://www.cdc.gov/omhd/Populations/HL/HL.htm

For information on the health of the Hispanic population, this is the place to start. This page has links to a variety of statistics revealing the health of Hispanics, including information on health disparities.

- **Hispanic attitudes**

http://pewhispanic.org/

The Pew Hispanic Center tracks the attitudes of the Hispanic population in surveys exploring language, attitudes toward immigration, socioeconomic status, political orientation, and more.

- **Income data**

http://www.census.gov/hhes/www/income/dinctabs.html

Every March the Current Population Survey collects income data by race and Hispanic origin through the Annual Social and Economic Supplement. The gateway to the data for households, families, and individuals is available here.

- **Poverty data**

http://www.census.gov/hhes/www/poverty/detailedpovtabs.html

Every year, the Census Bureau measures the poverty population by race and Hispanic origin. The poverty estimates are based on income data collected by the Annual Social and Economic Supplement of the March Current Population Survey. The poverty tables are available here.

HISTORICAL DEMOGRAPHIC STATISTICS

- **Statistical Abstract**

http://www.census.gov/compendia/statab/2007/hist_stats.html
http://www.census.gov/prod/www/abs/statab.html

Historical demographic data, organized by topic, are available from a selection of the Census Bureau's *Statistical Abstracts* at the first listed site. The second site is the gateway to individual *Statistical Abstracts* dating back to 1878.

HIV

- **Centers for Disease Control**

http://www.cdc.gov/hiv/topics/surveillance/index.htm

The full range of statistics and reports on HIV and AIDS are available at this Centers for Disease Control site.

HOME AND HOSPICE CARE

- **National Center for Health Statistics**

http://www.cdc.gov/nchs/about/major/nhhcsd/nhhcslist.htm

The National Home and Hospice Care Survey is a continuing series of surveys of home and hospice care agencies in the United States. You can access those surveys at this site.

HOMEOWNERSHIP

- **American Community Survey**

http://factfinder.census.gov/home/saff/main.html?_lang=en

The American Community Survey collects annual data on homeownership. To see the latest information, go to this site—the Census Bureau's Fact Finder Page. Click "get data" under "American Community Survey," then click "Subject Tables." Select your geography, then click "next." Scroll down to the three sections of tables on housing.

- **Annual homeownership statistics**

http://www.census.gov/hhes/www/housing/hvs/hvs.html

At this Census Bureau address you can access the most up-to-date statistics on homeownership from the Housing Vacancy Survey.

- **Characteristics of owners and renters**

http://www.census.gov/hhes/www/housing/ahs/ahs.html

The American Housing Survey, taken every two years, provides voluminous data on homeownership including a detailed profile of mortgages and home equity loans by selected demographic characteristics.

HOMESCHOOLING

- **National Center for Education Statistics**

http://nces.ed.gov/pubsearch/pubsinfo.asp?pubid=2006042

Here you can access the government's statistics on the homeschool population, based on data from the National Household Education Survey. The findings reveal that more than 1 million American children are being schooled at home.

HOMOSEXUALITY

- **Sexual behavior report**

http://www.cdc.gov/nchs/products/pubs/pubd/ad/361-370/ad362.htm

If you want government estimates of the number of gays and lesbians in the United States, the report *Sexual Behavior and Selected Health Measures: Men and Women 15–44 Years of Age, United States, 2002*, which can be downloaded at this site, is the best information available. The data come from the 2002 National Survey of Family Growth, in which a representative sample of men and women aged 15 to 44 were asked to identify their sexual orientation and tell whether they were attracted to people of the same or the opposite sex.

HOSPITAL, EMERGENCY DEPARTMENT VISITS

- **Emergency department visit reports**

http://www.cdc.gov/nchs/about/major/ahcd/adata.htm#Emergency

Every year the federal government collects data on the characteristics of people visiting hospital emergency departments, based on the National Ambulatory Medical Care Survey. At this site you can access reports about those visits.

- **Medical Expenditure Panel Survey**

http://www.meps.ahrq.gov/mepsweb/survey_comp/household.jsp

On this page, click on the link to the right, "Expenditures by Health Care Service," to see a list of tables showing the demographics of those using a variety of health care services including hospital emergency departments.

HOSPITAL, OUTPATIENT VISITS

- **Medical Expenditure Panel Survey**

http://www.meps.ahrq.gov/mepsweb/survey_comp/household.jsp

On this page, click on the link to the right, "Expenditures by Health Care Service," to see a list of tables showing the demographics of those spending on a variety of health care services including hospital outpatient departments.

- **Outpatient department visit reports**

http://www.cdc.gov/nchs/about/major/ahcd/adata.htm

This is your access point to the government's reports on the demographics of hospital outpatients, based on the National Hospital Ambulatory Medical Care Survey.

HOSPITAL, OVERNIGHT STAYS

- **Medical Expenditure Panel Survey**

http://www.meps.ahrq.gov/mepsweb/survey_comp/household.jsp

On this page, click on the link to the right, "Expenditures by Health Care Service," to see a list of tables showing the demographics of those spending on a variety of health care services including overnight hospital stays.

- **National Hospital Discharge Survey**

http://www.cdc.gov/nchs/about/major/hdasd/listpubs.htm

This is your access point to the government's reports on the demographics of inpatients discharged from the hospital, based on the National Hospital Discharge Survey. The survey has been conducted annually since 1965.

HOUSEHOLDS

- **Census Bureau**

http://www.census.gov/population/www/socdemo/hh-fam.html

Everything the government knows about the living arrangements of Americans is here, including households by type, marital status of men and women, and living arrangements of children. The data are from the Current Population Survey Annual Social and Economic Supplement.

Why Are Houses Getting Bigger?

The average American home is getting larger. During the years between 1976 and 2006, the median size of a new single-family home grew 38 percent, from 1,620 to 2,237 square feet, according to the Census Bureau. During the first decade of that time period, new single-family homes increased in size by just 30 square feet, to 1,650. During the second decade, the typical new home expanded by a much larger 290 square feet. And during the third decade, the typical new home added another 297 square feet. What accounts for this expansion?

The common thread is the aging of the population. Between 1976 and 1986, the oldest boomers aged from 30 to 40. Most of the baby-boom generation was still in its teens and twenties and too young to own a home, placing little upward pressure on the size of new houses coming to market. Between 1986 and 1996, the oldest boomers aged from 40 to 50. Most boomers were marrying and having children, and most were buying homes—pressuring builders to offer more for the money. Builders responded by adding more bathrooms and bedrooms for expanding families.

Between 1996 and 2006, the oldest boomers aged from 50 to 60 and millions became empty-nesters. Demographically speaking, the pressure on new homes to expand should have eased, if not reversed, as boomers downsized. But the downsizing did not occur for one reason: the home office. For millions of Americans, the home office has become a necessity to house the space-hungry computers, monitors, and printers vital to today's workers—many of whom work some of the time at home. Between 1996 and 2006, computer ownership became the norm in America, crowding homes and driving demand for home office space. According to the American Housing Survey, a substantial 32 percent of new owner-occupied homes include a room used for business.

HOUSING

- **American Community Survey**

http://factfinder.census.gov/home/saff/main.html?_lang=en

The American Community Survey collects annual data on housing. To see the latest information, go to this site—the Census Bureau's Fact Finder Page. Click "get data" under "American Community Survey," then click "Subject Tables." Select your geography, then click "next." Scroll down to the three sections of tables on housing.

- **American Housing Survey**

http://www.census.gov/hhes/www/housing/ahs/ahs.html

The American Housing Survey, taken every two years, provides voluminous data on the characteristics of owner- and renter-occupied housing.

- **Construction statistics**

http://www.census.gov/const/www/

On a monthly basis, the Census Bureau tracks the number of housing units authorized by permits, started, sold, or completed. It measures the dollar value of all construction put in place each month. It tracks residential construction in 30 metropolitan areas across the country each quarter, and it reports the sales of new one-family houses in those areas each year. These numbers and historical data on housing characteristics and home prices are available here.

- **Housing Vacancy Survey**

http://www.census.gov/hhes/www/housing/hvs/hvs.html

At this Census Bureau address you can access the most up-to-date statistics on housing—owner-occupied, renter-occupied, and vacant—from the Census Bureau's Housing Vacancy Survey.

- **Joint Center for Housing Studies**

http://www.jchs.harvard.edu/

The Joint Center for Housing Studies generates new information on housing and mortgage markets by analyzing large-scale databases and designing housing market indicators. Its annual publication, *The State of the Nation's Housing*, is available as a free download.

- **National Association of Realtors**

http://www.realtor.org/research.nsf/pages/linkDB

This page will take you to a variety of sources of data on housing, the real estate market, and housing finances.

HOUSING UNITS, ESTIMATES

• Census Bureau

http://www.census.gov/popest/housing/

Just as the Census Bureau estimates the size of the U.S. population, it also estimates the number of housing units nationally, by state, and by county. This is where you can access those data.

HUNTING

• U.S. Fish & Wildlife Service

http://www.census.gov/prod/www/abs/fishing.html

According to the 2006 National Survey of Fishing, Hunting, and Wildlife-Associated Recreation, nearly 88 million Americans fished, hunted, or watched wildlife in 2006. The survey, which has been conducted about every five years since 1955, explores Americans' participation in and spending on fishing, hunting, bird watching, animal feeding, and wildlife photography.

I

IDAHO

- **State Data Center**

http://commerce.idaho.gov/

By clicking on the Statistics and Research link on the left side of the page, you can access demographic statistics for Idaho. Local area data are available in the City/County Profiles.

ILLEGAL IMMIGRANTS

- **Department of Homeland Security**

http://www.dhs.gov/ximgtn/statistics/

Go to this site and scroll down to the report *Estimates of the Unauthorized Immigrant Population: 2006*. Download the Department of Homeland Security's latest estimates of the number of "unauthorized immigrants" living in the United States.

ILLINOIS

- **State Data Center**

http://www.illinoisbiz.biz/dceo/Bureaus/Facts_Figures/Illinois_Census_Data

At this site you can access 2000 census data and population projections for Illinois. Local area data are also available here.

IMMIGRATION

- **Yearbook of Immigration Statistics**

http://www.dhs.gov/ximgtn/statistics/publications/yearbook.shtm

The *Yearbook of Immigration Statistics*, which can be downloaded from this Department of Homeland Security site, provides current and historical data on immigration to the United States. In addition to the *Yearbook*, the Office of Immigration Statistics in the Department of Homeland Security provides data on legal permanent residents, refugees and asylum seekers, nonimmigrant admissions, naturalizations, and enforcement actions.

IMMUNIZATION

• Centers for Disease Control

http://www.cdc.gov/vaccines/stats-surv/imz-coverage.htm#nis

The National Immunization Survey is a large, ongoing survey of immunization coverage among preschoolers aged 19 to 35 months. The tables and related articles available at this site describe vaccination coverage at the national and state levels.

INCOME

• American Community Survey

http://factfinder.census.gov/home/saff/main.html?_lang=en

The American Community Survey collects annual data on income. To see the latest information, go to this site—the Census Bureau's Fact Finder Page. Click "get data" under "American Community Survey," then click "Subject Tables." Select your geography, then click "next." Scroll down to the income tables to access the latest annual statistics on household incomes and the earnings of men and women. You can extract income data for the nation, states, counties, and metropolitan areas.

• Current Population Survey

http://www.census.gov/hhes/www/income/dinctabs.html

Taken in March every year, the Current Population Survey's Annual Social and Economic Supplement queries a large, nationally representative sample of Americans about their economic status in the previous year. From these data come the official income and poverty statistics produced by the federal government. The numbers can be accessed at this site.

• Gateway at the Census Bureau

http://www.census.gov/hhes/www/income/income.html

This is the Census Bureau's gateway to the government's income statistics including the Current Population Survey, the American Community Survey, the Survey of Income and Program Participation, and other sources. Historical income tables also can be accessed at this site. Click on "Historical Income Tables" to retrieve data on income trends.

INCOME INEQUALITY

• Census Bureau

http://www.census.gov/hhes/www/income/histinc/ineqtoc.html

The Census Bureau not only collects the nation's income statistics, but it has various ways of tracking income inequality. At this site you can access a variety of tables with historical and current data on income inequality.

- **Economic Mobility Project**

http://economicmobility.org/

The Economic Mobility Project is a nonpartisan collaboration of The Pew Charitable Trusts and four leading policy institutes—the American Enterprise Institute, the Brookings Institution, the Heritage Foundation, and the Urban Institute. Together, these groups analyze income inequality and economic mobility in the United States, producing reports on the status of the American Dream. At this site you can download reports and access studies on income inequality.

INDEPENDENT CONTRACTORS

- **Bureau of Labor Statistics**

http://www.bls.gov/news.release/conemp.toc.htm

Every few years the Bureau of Labor Statistics collects data on the nontraditional workforce, which includes independent contractors, temporary workers, on-call workers, and contract workers. More about their numbers and demographics can be accessed at this site.

INDIANA

- **State Data Center**

http://www.ibrc.indiana.edu/

Click on the "Stats Indiana" link at the top of the page to access demographic and economic statistics for Indiana, including population estimates, population projections, employment statistics, and 2000 census data. Local area data are also available here.

INDUSTRY EMPLOYMENT

- **Current Employment Statistics Survey**

http://www.bls.gov/ces/home.htm

Each month the Current Employment Statistics Program surveys about 150,000 businesses and government agencies, representing approximately 390,000 individual worksites, in order to provide detailed industry data on employment, hours, and earnings of workers on nonfarm payrolls.

- **Current Population Survey**

http://www.bls.gov/cps/home.htm

On this page, scroll down to the "Annual Average Household Tables—Characteristics of the Employed." Here you will find the latest data on the employed by industry based on the Current Population Survey.

- **Projections**

http://www.bls.gov/emp/home.htm

Every two years the Bureau of Labor Statistics issues updated employment projections. The latest are available at this site. The projections show continued employment growth in service-producing industries and a decline in manufacturing.

INFERTILITY

- **National Survey of Family Growth**

http://www.cdc.gov/nchs/about/major/nsfg/nsfgcycle6reports.htm

The National Survey of Family Growth is the source of information on fertility and infertility among American men and women aged 15 to 44. Reports from the latest (2002) survey can be accessed here.

INFLATION CALCULATOR

- **Bureau of Labor Statistics**

http://www.bls.gov/

Visit the Bureau of Labor Statistics' home page and click on the "inflation calculator" link in the Inflation and Consumer Spending block at the top left of the page. This will open a pop-up calculator allowing you to estimate the inflation-adjusted value—either backward or forward—of any sum as far back as 1913. In case you're wondering, a dollar in 1913 is equal to $20.94 today.

INSURANCE, HEALTH

- **Annual data from the Census Bureau**

http://www.census.gov/hhes/www/hlthins/hlthins.html

The Current Population Survey collects data each year on health insurance coverage. This is the gateway to those numbers.

- **Employee Benefit Research Institute**

http://www.ebri.org/

The Employee Benefit Research Institute is one of the premier sources of information on employment benefits, including health insurance coverage. Here you can download reports with the latest findings on the health insurance coverage of the nation's workers.

- **Gateway at the National Center for Health Statistics**

http://www.cdc.gov/nchs/fastats/hinsure.htm

This is the National Center for Health Statistics gateway to statistics on the population's health insurance coverage, collected by several of its surveys.

- **Health Confidence Survey**

http://www.ebri.org/surveys/hcs/

The Health Confidence Survey is an annual look at Americans' attitudes towards health care. The survey, accessible at the above address, has been fielded annually since 1998.

- **Kaiser Family Foundation**

http://www.kff.org/insurance/index.cfm

The Kaiser Family Foundation is a nonprofit organization focusing on health care issues in the United States. Kaiser investigates various facets of health insurance, and the findings can be accessed here.

- **Medical Expenditure Panel Survey**

http://www.meps.ahrq.gov/mepsweb/data_stats/MEPS_topics.jsp?topicid=7Z-1

The Medical Expenditure Panel Survey findings on health insurance can be accessed here. MEPS is a set of large-scale surveys of families and individuals, collecting data on the health care services Americans use, how frequently they use them, the cost of these services, and how they pay for them.

- **Medicare and Medicaid coverage**

http://www.cms.hhs.gov/DataCompendium/

To get the latest numbers on the Medicare and Medicaid health insurance programs, download the *Data Compendium* from this site.

INTERNATIONAL DEMOGRAPHICS

- **Central Intelligence Agency**

https://www.cia.gov/library/publications/the-world-factbook/index.html

If you want up-to-date demographic and political information on any nation in the world, check out the CIA's *The World Factbook*. The online edition of the factbook is updated periodically throughout the year, and provides national-level data for countries, territories, and dependencies.

- **International Database at the Census Bureau**

http://www.census.gov/ipc/www/idb/

To access population statistics for just about any country, this is the place to start—the Census Bureau's International Database. The database is a computerized data bank containing statistical tables of demographic and socioeconomic information for 227 countries and areas of the world. Just pick a country and get the data, including population projections.

- **Population Reference Bureau**

http://www.prb.org/Datafinder.aspx

Here you can access the Population Reference Bureau's database of international demographic statistics. Select a country and a topic, and retrieve the numbers you need.

INTERNET

• Pew Internet & American Life Project

http://www.pewinternet.org/

The Pew Internet & American Life Project produces reports that explore the impact of computers and the Internet. At this site you can access historical and current survey data revealing what Americans do online. You can also take The Internet Typology Test to find out what kind of information technology user you are.

INTERRACIAL MARRIAGE

• Current data

http://www.census.gov/population/www/socdemo/hh-fam/cps2006.html

Here you can access the Census Bureau's detailed tables (FG3 and FG4) from the latest Current Population Survey on the characteristics of husbands by the characteristics of wives—including race and Hispanic origin.

• Historical data

http://www.census.gov/population/www/socdemo/interrace.html
http://www.census.gov/population/www/socdemo/hh-fam.html

The first site takes you to the Census Bureau's gateway to historical statistics on interracial marriage, with data from 1960 through 1992. At the second site, scroll down to the Historical Time Series tables on marital status and download table MS-3 for historical data on interracial marriage through 2002.

IOWA

• State Data Center

http://www.iowadatacenter.org/

At this web site you can access demographic and economic statistics for Iowa, including current population estimates, employment statistics, and 2000 census data. Local area data are also available here.

J

JOB BENEFITS

• Employee Benefit Research Institute

http://www.ebri.org

The Employee Benefit Research Institute is one of the premier sources of information on employment benefits, including analysis of pension coverage, 401(k) account balances, health insurance coverage, and Social Security. EBRI also sponsors the annual Retirement Confidence and Health Confidence surveys, which can be accessed here.

• National Compensation Survey

http://www.bls.gov/ncs/ebs/home.htm

Get the facts about employee benefits from the Bureau of Labor Statistics' National Compensation Survey here. This annual survey examines the entire range of employee benefits provided by the nation's private companies—from vacation days to employee bonuses. Retirement and health care benefits are examined in detail.

JOB TENURE

• Bureau of Labor Statistics

http://www.bls.gov/news.release/tenure.toc.htm

Want to know how long workers have been at their current job? The Bureau of Labor Statistics tracks employee tenure by age, sex, race and Hispanic origin, occupation, and education. Get the numbers here.

JOB TRAINING

• Adult education

http://nces.ed.gov/nhes/

From this page you can access reports with data from the adult education portion of the National Household Education Survey. This survey is fielded every few years to measure participation in educational activities ranging from early childhood programs to work-related adult education courses.

- **Occupational Outlook Handbook**

http://www.bls.gov/oco/home.htm

This is the home page for the *Occupational Outlook Handbook*, the government's continuously updated reference on hundreds of occupations, including training requirements, earnings, and employment projections.

JOBS

- **American Community Survey**

http://factfinder.census.gov/home/saff/main.html?_lang=en

The American Community Survey collects annual data on the labor force. To see the latest information, go to this site—the Census Bureau's Fact Finder Page. Click "get data" under "American Community Survey," then click "Subject Tables." Select your geography, then click "next." Scroll down to the section on employment to retrieve labor force data.

- **Demographics of the labor force**

http://www.bls.gov/cps/home.htm

This site is the federal government's central repository of data on the demographics of the labor force. Here you can access just about everything you would want to know about labor force topics, such as working mothers, the decline in long-term employment, and the characteristics of minimum wage workers. The site also provides access to the Bureau of Labor Statistics' annual average employment tables.

- **Employment statistics from the Current Employment Statistics Program**

http://www.bls.gov/ces/home.htm
http://www.bls.gov/sae/home.htm

Each month the Current Employment Statistics program surveys about 150,000 businesses and government agencies, representing approximately 390,000 individual worksites, in order to provide detailed industry data on employment, hours, and earnings of workers on nonfarm payrolls nationally (available at the first URL), and for all 50 states and over 300 metropolitan areas (available at the second URL).

- **Gateway at the Bureau of Labor Statistics**

http://www.bls.gov/bls/employment.htm

This is the Bureau of Labor Statistics' gateway to its voluminous statistics on employment. Everything you want to know about employment and unemployment can be accessed through this web page.

- **Projections**

http://www.bls.gov/emp/home.htm

Every two years the Bureau of Labor Statistics issues updated employment projections. The latest are available at this site. The projections show big changes on the horizon as the workforce ages.

- **State and local area employment statistics from the Current Population Survey**

http://www.bls.gov/lau/#data

Here you can access local area employment, unemployment, and labor force data from the Current Population Survey, a monthly survey of households. The data are available for regions and divisions, states, counties, metropolitan areas, and many cities.

JOURNEY TO WORK

- **2000 Census**

http://www.census.gov/population/www/socdemo/journey.html

At this site you can access detailed 2000 census data on the journey to work.

- **American Community Survey**

http://factfinder.census.gov/home/saff/main.html?_lang=en

The American Community Survey collects annual data on commuting. To see the latest information, go to this site—the Census Bureau's Fact Finder Page. Click "get data" under "American Community Survey," then click "Subject Tables." Scroll down to table number S0801, "Commuting Characteristics by Sex."

K

KANSAS

• **State Data Center**

http://www.kslib.info/sdc/

At this web site you can access current population estimates, population projections, 2000 census data, and American Community Survey numbers for Kansas. Local area data are also available here.

KENTUCKY

• **State Data Center**

http://ksdc.louisville.edu/

At this web site you can access the range of demographic and economic statistics for Kentucky, including current population estimates, population projections, employment statistics, 2000 census data, and American Community Survey numbers. Local area data are also available here.

L

LABOR FORCE

• American Community Survey

http://factfinder.census.gov/home/saff/main.html?_lang=en

The American Community Survey collects annual data on the labor force. To see the latest information, go to this site—the Census Bureau's Fact Finder Page. Click "get data" under "American Community Survey," then click "Subject Tables." Select your geography, then click "next." Scroll down to the section on employment to retrieve labor force data.

• Demographics of the labor force

http://www.bls.gov/cps/home.htm

This site is the federal government's central repository of data on the demographics of the labor force. Here you can access just about everything you would want to know about labor force topics, such as working mothers, the decline in long-term employment, and the characteristics of minimum wage workers. The site also provides access to the Bureau of Labor Statistics' annual average employment tables.

• Employment statistics from the Current Employment Statistics Program

http://www.bls.gov/ces/home.htm
http://www.bls.gov/sae/home.htm

Each month the Current Employment Statistics program surveys about 150,000 businesses and government agencies, representing approximately 390,000 individual worksites, in order to provide detailed industry data on employment, hours, and earnings of workers on nonfarm payrolls nationally (available at the first URL), and for all 50 states and over 300 metropolitan areas (available at the second URL).

• Gateway at the Bureau of Labor Statistics

http://www.bls.gov/bls/employment.htm

This is the Bureau of Labor Statistics' gateway to its voluminous statistics on employment. Everything you want to know about employment and unemployment can be accessed through this web page.

• Projections

http://www.bls.gov/emp/home.htm

Every two years the Bureau of Labor Statistics issues updated employment projections. The latest are available at this site. The projections show big changes on the horizon as the workforce ages.

- **State and local area employment statistics from the Current Population Survey**

http://www.bls.gov/lau/#data

Here you can access local area employment, unemployment, and labor force data from the Current Population Survey, a monthly survey of households. The data are available for regions and divisions, states, counties, metropolitan areas, and many cities.

LANGUAGE SPOKEN AT HOME

- **2000 Census**

http://www.census.gov/population/www/socdemo/lang_use.html

This site is the Census Bureau's gateway to 2000 census information on language spoken at home.

- **American Community Survey**

http://factfinder.census.gov/home/saff/main.html?_lang=en

The American Community Survey collects annual data on language spoken at home. To see the latest information, go to this site—the Census Bureau's Fact Finder Page. Click "get data" under "American Community Survey," then click "Subject Tables." Select your geography, then click "next." On the Subject Table page, scroll down to the tables on Origins and Language: "Characteristics of People by Language Spoken at Home" and "Language Spoken at Home."

LATINOS

- **2000 Census**

http://www.census.gov/population/www/cen2000/briefs.html

On this page, scroll down to Census 2000 Special Report 18, *We The People: Hispanics in the United States*. This will give you an overview of the Hispanic population as of 2000.

- **Business owners**

http://www.census.gov/csd/sbo/hispanic2002.htm

The Survey of Business Owners, taken every five years as part of the Economic Census, provides details on Hispanic-owned businesses in the United States.

- **Demographics from the American Community Survey**

http://factfinder.census.gov/home/saff/main.html?_lang=en

The American Community Survey provides annual statistics on the population by race and Hispanic origin. To retrieve the information, go to this site—the Census Bureau's Fact Finder page. Click on "get data" under "American Community Survey." On the next page, click on the "Selected Population Profiles" link. On the next page, specify the desired geography (for national totals, just click "add" and "next"). On the following page, select the desired race or Hispanic origin group.

- **Estimates by age**

http://www.census.gov/popest/national/asrh/

To get the latest numbers on the Hispanic population—including estimates of the size of the population by age—visit the Census Bureau's population estimates site.

- **Gateway at the Census Bureau**

http://www.census.gov/population/www/socdemo/hispanic/ho06.html

The Census Bureau has compiled a great deal of data on the Hispanic population and you can access it here. The Current Population Survey tables provide details on Hispanics by age, living arrangement, labor force status, education, income, and more.

- **Health data from the Centers for Disease Control**

http://www.cdc.gov/omhd/Populations/HL/HL.htm

For information on the health of the Hispanic population, this is the place to start. This page has links to a variety of statistics revealing the health of Hispanics, including information on health disparities.

- **Hispanic attitudes**

http://pewhispanic.org/

The Pew Hispanic Center tracks the attitudes of the Hispanic population in surveys exploring language, attitudes toward immigration, socioeconomic status, political orientation, and more.

- **Income data**

http://www.census.gov/hhes/www/income/dinctabs.html

Every March the Current Population Survey collects income data by race and Hispanic origin through the Annual Social and Economic Supplement. The gateway to the data for households, families, and individuals is available here.

- **Poverty data**

http://www.census.gov/hhes/www/poverty/detailedpovtabs.html

Every year, the Census Bureau measures the poverty population by race and Hispanic origin. The poverty estimates are based on income data collected by the Annual Social and Economic Supplement of the March Current Population Survey. The poverty tables are available here.

LEARNING DISABILITIES

- **Census Bureau**

http://www.census.gov/hhes/www/disability/sipp/disable02.html

The Survey of Income and Program Participation produces occasional reports on the disability status of Americans, including estimates of the number of children with learning disabilities. See table 7 for the latest numbers.

- **National Center for Education Statistics**

http://nces.ed.gov/programs/digest/d07/tables_2.asp#Ch2Sub1

Here are the numbers on people aged 3 to 21 in federally supported programs for the disabled, with data spanning three decades.

LEISURE

- **American Time Use Survey**

http://www.bls.gov/tus/home.htm

The Bureau of Labor Statistics' American Time Use Survey collects data on the activities of a representative sample of Americans on a minute-by-minute basis for the past 24 hours. The data are categorized by activity, analyzed by demographic characteristic, and published annually. Americans devote more time to leisure activities, it turns out, than any other activity except sleeping. You can access the time use data here.

- **Federal Reserve Bank of Boston**

http://www.bos.frb.org/economic/wp/wp2006/wp0602.htm

Research from the Federal Reserve Bank of Boston shows that men and women are working less than they once did. Economists from the Bank of Boston and the University of Chicago examine time use over five decades and find that men and women are working less and playing more. Their study, "Measuring Trends in Leisure: The Allocation of Time over Five Decades," is available at this site.

LIFE EXPECTANCY

- **National Center for Health Statistics**

http://www.cdc.gov/nchs/products/pubs/pubd/nvsr/nvsr.htm

If you need life expectancy figures, then visit this site. Download the latest *Deaths: Final Data* report or *United States Life Tables* to find life expectancy numbers by age, sex, and race.

LIVING ALONE

- **Demographics of people who live alone**

http://www.census.gov/population/www/socdemo/hh-fam/cps2006.html

On this web page you can access the range of Census Bureau data on households and families. Many tables include data on the demographic characteristics of people who live alone.

- **Spending of people who live alone**

http://www.bls.gov/cex/home.htm

The Consumer Expenditure Survey collects annual data on household spending, some of it accessible at this site. Scroll down the page until you get to the section on "Current Standard

How Long Do We Live?

Life expectancy is a statistical measure of the average length of life based on age-specific mortality rates in a given year. For babies born in 2005, life expectancy was 78 years, based on the age-specific mortality rates of 2005. Life expectancy at birth has grown enormously over the past century as medical science conquered many infectious diseases. In 1900, newborns could expect to live only 47 years. This does not mean people dropped dead at age 47 (although some did). It means that so many died in infancy and childhood that the average length of life was pulled down to 47.

Life expectancy has increased at older ages as well as at birth—although not by as much. In 1900, life expectancy at age 65 was 12 years. Today, life expectancy at age 65 is 19 years—a gain of 7 years. Should Social Security's retirement age rise by the same amount to reflect those gains? The age of eligibility for full Social Security benefits is already increasing, rising to 67 for people born in 1960 and after—two years later than the traditional Social Security eligibility age of 65. Boosting it much more may not be feasible because there are other issues to consider, such as healthy life expectancy. Just because people live longer does not mean they are able to get up and go to work. In the older age groups, life is lengthening not necessarily because people are healthier, but because they are managing to stay alive despite debilitating chronic conditions.

Tables," and click on the table entitled "Size of consumer unit." This table contains summary spending data by size of household, including people who live alone.

LIVING ARRANGEMENTS

• Census Bureau

http://www.census.gov/population/www/socdemo/hh-fam.html

Everything the government knows about the living arrangements of Americans is here, including marital status, family status, household relationship, average number of people per household, living arrangements of children, and children living with grandparents. The data are based on the Current Population Survey's Annual Social and Economic Supplement.

LIVING STANDARDS

• 100 Years of Spending Data

http://www.bls.gov/opub/uscs/home.htm

This is where you can access the Bureau of Labor Statistics' report *100 Years U.S. Consumer Spending: Data for the Nation, New York City, and Boston*. The report draws on consumer expenditure data and census reports to present a 100-year history of significant changes in consumer spending in the country as a whole, New York City, and Boston.

• Consumer Price Indexes

http://www.bls.gov/cpi/home.htm

On this page you gain access to the government's consumer price indexes over time, item by item. Examine the government's tabulated data or create customized tables.

• Extended Measures of Well-Being

http://www.sipp.census.gov/sipp/p70s/p70s.html

The Census Bureau report series *Extended Measures of Well-Being: Living Conditions in the United States* can be accessed from this page. The reports, based on results from the Survey of Income and Program Participation, examine our standard of living by a variety of measures that go beyond income. These are: ownership of appliances and electronic goods, housing conditions, neighborhood conditions, ability to meet basic needs, and expectation of help should needs arise.

LONG-TERM CARE

• AARP

http://www.aarp.org/research/longtermcare/trends/

AARP conducts research on many topics including long-term care. At this site you can download research reports on long-term care insurance, aging at home, nursing homes, and assisted living facilities. Some reports provide details for states.

LOUISIANA

• State Data Center

http://www.louisiana.gov/wps/wcm/connect/Louisiana.gov/Explore/

At this web site, click on the link Demographics and Geography for Statistics on Louisiana. It will take you to current population estimates, employment statistics, and 2000 census data. Local area data are also available here.

M

MAINE

• State Data Center

http://www.state.me.us/spo/economics/census/

At this web site you can access demographic and economic statistics for Maine, including current population estimates, population projections, employment statistics, and 2000 census data. Local area data are also available here.

MAPPING

• Census Bureau

http://www.census.gov/geo/www/maps/
http://www.census.gov/population/www/cen2000/censusatlas/

At the first URL, you can access the Census Bureau's broad range of mapping products, including maps of the latest metropolitan statistical areas and congressional districts. At the second URL, you can access the *Census 2000 Atlas of the United States*, with nearly 800 maps based on census data.

MARITAL STATUS

• Gateway at the Census Bureau

http://www.census.gov/population/www/socdemo/ms-la.html

This site is your gateway to the Census Bureau's voluminous data on marital status and living arrangements, with current and historical data from the Current Population Survey, links to the American Community Survey, the census, and other relevant sites.

• Marital History

http://www.census.gov/population/www/socdemo/marr-div.html

This address will take you to the Census Bureau's web page devoted to its data on marriage and divorce. Here you can access the report *Number, Timing and Duration of Marriages and Divorces: 2004*, with data on the marital history of Americans including the percentage who have ever divorced.

MARRIAGE

• Demographics of husbands and wives

http://www.census.gov/population/www/socdemo/hh-fam/cps2006.html

Here you can access the Census Bureau's detailed tables on living arrangements. Download tables FG3 and FG4, which cross-tabulate the characteristics of husbands by the characteristics of wives (age, income, education, and race/Hispanic origin). These tables include the most recent data on interracial marriage.

• Earnings of husbands and wives

http://pubdb3.census.gov/macro/032007/faminc/new05_000.htm

This set of tables provides the latest data on the earnings of husbands by the earnings of wives—all by race and Hispanic origin.

• Interracial marriage, current

http://www.census.gov/population/www/socdemo/hh-fam/cps2006.html

Download tables FG3 and FG4, which cross-tabulate the characteristics of husbands by the characteristics of wives (age, income, education, and race/Hispanic origin). These tables include the most recent data on interracial marriage.

• Interracial marriage, historical

http://www.census.gov/population/www/socdemo/interrace.html
http://www.census.gov/population/www/socdemo/hh-fam.html

The first site takes you to the Census Bureau's gateway to historical statistics on interracial marriage, with data from 1960 through 1992. At the second site, scroll down to the Historical Time Series tables on marital status and download table MS-3 for historical data on interracial marriage through 2002.

• National Survey of Family Growth

http://www.cdc.gov/nchs/about/major/nsfg/nsfgcycle6reports.htm

Every few years the National Survey of Family Growth collects information on the family formation behavior—including childbearing, cohabitation, and marriage—of men and women aged 15 to 44. Links to the survey's reports are on this web page.

• Number of marriages

http://www.cdc.gov/nchs/fastats/divorce.htm

Although the word "divorce" appears in the URL, this site is the gateway to the government's statistics on marriage. Find out how many marriages and divorces take place in the United States, including totals by state.

• Wives who earn more

http://www.census.gov/hhes/www/income/histinc/f22.html

This table has data on the number of wives who earn more than their husbands.

MARYLAND

• **State Data Center**

http://www.mdp.state.md.us/msdc/

At this web site you can access the range of demographic and economic statistics for Maryland, including current population estimates, population projections, employment statistics, 2000 census data, and American Community Survey numbers. Local area data are also available here.

MASSACHUSETTS

• **State Data Center**

http://www.massbenchmarks.org/statedata/statedata.htm

At this web site you can access demographic and economic statistics for Massachusetts, including current population estimates, population projections, and 2000 census data. Local area data are also available here.

MEDIA DEMOGRAPHICS

• **Pew Research Center for The People & The Press**

http://www.people-press.org/

Find out what Americans really think at this site. With its many surveys, the Pew Research Center for The People & The Press probes the public's attitudes about a variety of ongoing issues including politics, culture, the media, and current events.

• **Project for Excellence in Journalism**

http://www.journalism.org/

Whether you think the press is too liberal or too conservative, this site will help you sort out its future. Here you will find the Project for Excellence in Journalism, a nonpartisan research center that evaluates the media. The project, which is part of the Pew Research Center, analyzes the content and audience for news on television, in newspapers and magazines, and on the Internet and radio. One of its products is an annual state-of-the-media report.

MEDICAID

• **Centers for Medicare & Medicaid Services**

http://www.cms.hhs.gov/DataCompendium/

To get the latest numbers on the Medicaid health insurance program, download the *Data Compendium* from this site.

MEDICAL EXPENDITURES

- **Coverage statistics from the Current Population Survey**

http://www.census.gov/hhes/www/hlthins/hlthins.html

The Current Population Survey collects data each year on health insurance coverage, including Medicaid. This is the gateway to those data.

- **Medical Expenditure Panel Survey**

http://www.meps.ahrq.gov/mepsweb/data_stats/MEPS_topics.jsp?topicid=9Z-1

The Medical Expenditure Panel Survey collects data on health care spending by source of payment, including Medicaid. At this site you can access the survey's many findings.

MEDICAL EXPENDITURES

- **Kaiser Family Foundation**

http://www.kff.org/insurance/index.cfm

The Kaiser Family Foundation is a nonprofit foundation focusing on how Americans cope with health care issues. Health care costs are one of the issues investigated by Kaiser, and the findings can be accessed here.

- **Medical Expenditure Panel Survey**

http://www.meps.ahrq.gov/mepsweb/survey_comp/household.jsp

The Medical Expenditure Panel Survey collects household spending data for a variety of health care services and conditions. You can access the results from this page by clicking on the Summary Data Table links "Expenditures by Health Care Service" and "Expenditures by Medical Condition."

- **Medicare and Medicaid**

http://www.cms.hhs.gov/DataCompendium/

To get the latest numbers on the cost and benefits of the Medicare and Medicaid programs, download the *Data Compendium* from the Centers for Medicare & Medicaid Services from this site.

- **National Health Expenditures Data**

http://www.cms.hhs.gov/NationalHealthExpendData/

From this Centers for Medicare & Medicaid Services site, you can access historical and projected figures on health care spending in the United States.

MEDICARE

- **Centers for Medicare & Medicaid Services**

http://www.cms.hhs.gov/DataCompendium/

To get the latest numbers on the Medicare health insurance program, download the *Data Compendium* from this site.

Who's Happy with Health Care?

Most think health care in the United States is in trouble. Fully 71 percent of the public believes the health care system has major problems or is in a state of crisis, according to a Gallup survey. Although we have a reputation for having the best health care in the world, most of us no longer believe it. The 54 percent majority of Americans are dissatisfied with the quality of health care in the United States according to the Kaiser Family Foundation Health Care in America Survey.

Clearly, we need to rethink the system. But no one wants to throw out the baby with the bath water. Maybe we should take a look at what works before we start tinkering. One way to do that is by identifying who among us is happiest with their health care. By almost every measure, those happiest with health care are people aged 65 or older. When asked to rate the quality of the health care they received in the past year on a scale from 0 to 10, the 62 percent majority of people aged 65 or older rated their care a 9 or 10, according to the 2005 Medical Expenditure Panel Survey. In contrast, a much smaller 49 percent of people aged 45 to 64 rated their health care that highly. The figure was an even smaller 42 percent among people aged 18 to 44.

The elderly are satisfied with their health care in other ways as well. They are most likely to say they "always" get a doctor's appointment as soon as they want one (64 percent), the doctor "always" spends enough time with them (56 percent), and the doctor "always" listens to them (65 percent). They are least likely to say they had a problem receiving needed medical care in the past year.

The older population is the only one with government-provided universal health care coverage through the Medicare program. Are Americans ready for universal coverage? Maybe so: When the Kaiser survey asked which they would prefer—the current employer-based health insurance system or universal health insurance through a program such as Medicare—the 56 percent majority of the public chose Medicare.

- **Coverage statistics from the Current Population Survey**

http://www.census.gov/hhes/www/hlthins/hlthins.html

The Current Population Survey collects data each year on health insurance coverage, including Medicare. This is the gateway to those data.

- **Medical Expenditure Panel Survey**

http://www.meps.ahrq.gov/mepsweb/data_stats/MEPS_topics.jsp?topicid=9Z-1

The Medical Expenditure Panel Survey collects data on health care spending by source of payment, including Medicare. At this site you can access the survey's many findings.

MEN

- **Estimates by age**

http://www.census.gov/popest/national/asrh/

To get the latest numbers on the male population—including estimates of the male population by age, race, and Hispanic origin—visit the Census Bureau's population estimates site.

- **Fathers of U.S. Children Born in 2001**

http://nces.ed.gov/pubsearch/pubsinfo.asp?pubid=2006002

The report *Fathers of U.S. Children Born in 2001* is based on data collected by the Early Childhood Longitudinal Program, which is tracking a cohort of children born in 2001. The report profiles the demographic characteristics of resident and nonresident biological fathers, the extent of their involvement in pregnancy and birth, their attitudes toward fathering, and their participation in child care.

- **Fertility, Contraception, and Fatherhood report**

http://www.cdc.gov/nchs/pressroom/06facts/fatherhood.htm

This page will take you to the groundbreaking report on men's sexual and reproductive behavior, *Fertility, Contraception, and Fatherhood*. The report is based on the 2002 National Survey of Family Growth, which asked men, for the first time, about their fertility, contraceptive use, and fatherhood status. The NSFG, fielded every few years by the National Center for Health Statistics, typically examines the sexual behavior and fertility status of American women aged 15 to 44. Now men are included too.

- **Income**

http://pubdb3.census.gov/macro/032007/perinc/toc.htm

Taken in March every year, the Current Population Survey's Annual Social and Economic Supplement queries a large, nationally representative sample of Americans about their economic status in the previous year. From this data come the official income and poverty statistics produced by the federal government. The latest statistics on the incomes and earnings of men can be accessed here.

- **Labor force**

http://www.bls.gov/cps/home.htm

This site is the federal government's central repository of data on the demographics of the labor force. Here you can access just about everything you would want to know about men at work. Scroll down for the latest data from the annual average employment tables.

- **Marital history**

http://www.census.gov/population/www/socdemo/marr-div.html

This address will take you to the Census Bureau's web page devoted to its data on marriage and divorce. Here you can access the report *Number, Timing and Duration of Marriages and Divorces: 2004*, with data on the marital history of men including the percentage who have ever divorced.

- **Poverty data**

http://www.census.gov/hhes/www/poverty/detailedpovtabs.html

Every year, the Census Bureau measures the poverty population by sex. The poverty estimates are based on income data collected by the Annual Social and Economic Supplement of the March Current Population Survey. The poverty tables are available here.

MENTAL HEALTH

- **Annual data from the National Center for Health Statistics**

http://www.cdc.gov/nchs/nhis.htm

From this page you can access the annual report *Summary Health Statistics for U.S. Adults* with findings on mental health from the National Health Interview Survey. The survey collects data on mental health status through a series of six questions, probing how often during the past 30 days respondents have experienced feelings of sadness, hopelessness, restlessness, nervousness, worthlessness, or that everything is an effort. The results are broken down by a variety of demographic characteristics.

- **Gateway at the National Institute of Mental Health**

http://www.nimh.nih.gov/health/publications/the-numbers-count-mental-disorders-in-america.shtml

This page links to and provides a summary of what little is known about the demographics of mental health in the United States.

- **Mentally unhealthy days**

http://apps.nccd.cdc.gov/HRQOL/

If you want to know how good—or bad—Americans feel, then this web site is the place to start. The Centers for Disease Control and Prevention has a program in place to measure our health-related quality of life, with handy summary measures of the number of mentally unhealthy days experienced by Americans by age, sex, and race.

METROPOLITAN AREA STATISTICS

• American Community Survey

http://factfinder.census.gov/home/saff/main.html?_lang=en

The American Community Survey collects annual data on metropolitan areas. To see the latest information, go to this site—the Census Bureau's Fact Finder Page. Click "get data" under "American Community Survey," then click "Data Profiles." Select a metropolitan area, and you can retrieve the latest available demographic and socioeconomic data.

• Population estimates

http://www.census.gov/popest/metro.html

Each year the Census Bureau's population estimates program publishes population estimates for all metropolitan and micropolitan statistical areas. The data include estimates of births, deaths, and migration for each area.

• State and Metropolitan Area Data Book

http://www.census.gov/compendia/smadb/

Before the era of the Internet, the *State and Metropolitan Area Data Book* was an eagerly anticipated compendium of facts. Published every few years, it offered metropolitan area demographic and economic data not easily accessible elsewhere. The 2006 edition, which can be downloaded from this site, updates the previous volume published in 1997–98. Since publication of the earlier edition, the *State and Metropolitan Area Data Book* has been upstaged not only by easy access to government data online, but also by the new American Community Survey, which updates state and metropolitan area demographic data every year. Nevertheless, the *State and Metropolitan Area Data Book* still has much to offer. Not only does it include data not collected by the American Community Survey, but it puts all the facts together in one handy place.

MICHIGAN

• State Data Center

http://www.michigan.gov/census

At this web site you can access the range of demographic and economic statistics for Michigan, including current population estimates, employment statistics, 2000 census data, and American Community Survey numbers. Local area data are also available here.

MIGRATION

• 2000 census reports

http://www.census.gov/population/www/cen2000/migration.html

Every ten years the census provides detailed data on the migration of Americans from one area to another. You can access the 2000 census reports here.

- **American Community Survey**

http://factfinder.census.gov/home/saff/main.html?_lang=en

The American Community Survey collects annual data on migration. To see the latest information, go to this site—the Census Bureau's Fact Finder Page. Click "get data" under "American Community Survey," then click "Subject Tables." Select your geography, then click "next." Scroll down to the tables on Mobility and click on "Geographic Mobility" or "Movers between Regions." After you open one of the tables, you can specify a different geography using the links at the top left of the page.

- **Gateway at the Census Bureau**

http://www.census.gov/population/www/socdemo/migrate.html

This is the access point for the Census Bureau's data on geographic mobility, including Current Population Survey and census data.

- **Migration estimates**

http://www.census.gov/popest/estimates.php

The Census Bureau's population estimates program provides annual estimates of national, state, county, and metropolitan area populations. Each round of data includes estimates of net migration into and out of each level of geography. Those numbers can be accessed at this site.

MILITARY DEMOGRAPHICS

- **The Office of Army Demographics**

http://www.armyg1.army.mil/hr/demographics.asp

How many women are in the Army? What percentage of the enlisted is black or Hispanic? The answers can be found at this interesting site dedicated to military demographics. You can link here to data for the Air Force, Coast Guard, Marine Corps, National Guard, and Navy.

MINIMUM WAGE WORKERS

- **Bureau of Labor Statistics**

http://www.bls.gov/cps/minwage2007.htm

Each year the Bureau of Labor Statistics examines the demographics of the minimum wage workforce. This is where you can access the latest statistics.

MINNESOTA

• State Data Center

http://www.demography.state.mn.us/

At this web site you can access the range of demographic and economic statistics for Minnesota, including current population estimates, population projections, employment statistics, 2000 census data, and American Community Survey numbers. Local area data are also available here.

MISSISSIPPI

• State Data Center

http://www.olemiss.edu/depts/sdc/

At this web site you can access 2000 census data for Mississippi, including local areas.

MISSOURI

• State Data Center

http://mcdc2.missouri.edu/

At this web site you can access the range of demographic and economic statistics for Missouri, including current population estimates, population projections, 2000 census data, and American Community Survey numbers. Local area data are also available here.

MOBILITY, ECONOMIC

• Economic Mobility Project

http://economicmobility.org/

The Economic Mobility Project is a nonpartisan collaboration of The Pew Charitable Trusts and four leading policy institutes—the American Enterprise Institute, the Brookings Institution, the Heritage Foundation, and the Urban Institute. Together, these groups analyze economic mobility in the United States and produce reports on the status of the American Dream. At this site you can download reports and access studies of economic mobility.

MOBILITY, GEOGRAPHIC

• 2000 Census

http://www.census.gov/population/www/cen2000/migration.html

Every ten years the census provides detailed data on the migration of Americans from one area to another. You can access the 2000 census reports here.

- **Data from the American Community Survey**

http://factfinder.census.gov/home/saff/main.html?_lang=en

The American Community Survey collects annual data on mobility. To see the latest information, go to this site—the Census Bureau's Fact Finder Page. Click "get data" under "American Community Survey," then click "Subject Tables." Select your geography, then click "next." Scroll down to the tables on Mobility and click on "Geographic Mobility" or "Movers between Regions."

- **Data from the Current Population Survey**

http://www.census.gov/population/www/socdemo/migrate.html

This is the access point for the Census Bureau's data on geographic mobility, including the annual Current Population Survey data and decennial census data.

MONTANA

- **State Data Center**

http://ceic.mt.gov/

At this web site you can access the range of demographic and economic statistics for Montana, including current population estimates, population projections, employment statistics, 2000 census data, and American Community Survey numbers. Local area data are also available here.

MORTALITY DATA

- **Mortality statistics from the National Center for Health Statistics**

http://www.cdc.gov/nchs/deaths.htm

Everything you need to know about mortality statistics can be accessed from this site, which has links to annual reports on deaths by cause as well as life expectancy.

MOTHERS

- **Birth statistics from the National Center for Health Statistics**

http://www.cdc.gov/nchs/fastats/births.htm

The National Center for Health Statistics is the official source of data on births in the United States, collecting and analyzing records from every state. This site is the access point for the information. The annual series *Births: Final Data* provides statistics on childbearing by age, race and Hispanic origin, marital status, and other characteristics.

- **Data from the American Community Survey**

http://factfinder.census.gov/home/saff/main.html?_lang=en

The American Community Survey collects annual data on fertility. To see the latest information, go to this site—the Census Bureau's Fact Finder Page. Click "get data" under "American

Community Survey," then click "Subject Tables." Select your geography, then click "next." Scroll down to the table, "Fertility."

• Data from the Current Population Survey

http://www.census.gov/population/www/socdemo/fertility.html

Every two years the Current Population Survey asks American women about their childbearing experiences, resulting in a report on the fertility of American women. The information includes a profile of the characteristics of women who have had a child in the past year.

• Maternity leave

http://www.census.gov/Press-Release/www/releases/archives/employment_occupations/011536.html

This Census Bureau report, *Maternity Leave and Employment Patterns, 1961–2003*, provides the most comprehensive data available on women's labor force participation before and after giving birth.

• National Survey of Family Growth

http://www.cdc.gov/nchs/products/pubs/pubd/series/sr23/pre-1/sr23_25.htm

This address will take you to the comprehensive report on women's sexual and reproductive behavior, *Fertility, Family Planning, and Reproductive Health of U.S. Women*. The report is based on the 2002 National Survey of Family Growth, which asked women aged 15 to 44 about their sexual behavior, contraceptive use, fertility, and motherhood status. The NSFG, fielded every few years by the National Center for Health Statistics, also examines whether births were wanted or unwanted, maternity leave, and use of family planning services.

MULTIPLE JOB HOLDERS

• Bureau of Labor Statistics

http://www.bls.gov/cps/home.htm

From this page you can access the annual table "Multiple jobholders by selected demographic and economic characteristics." To access the information, scroll down the page to table 36 in the "Annual Averages—Household Data" section.

MUTUAL FUND SHAREHOLDERS

• Investment Company Institute

http://www.ici.org/stats/res/index.html

The Investment Company Institute represents more than 9,000 mutual funds. Its web site offers reports on the demographics of mutual fund shareholders based on the Institute's proprietary surveys.

• Survey of Consumer Finances

http://www.federalreserve.gov/pubs/oss/oss2/scfindex.html

The Federal Reserve Board's Survey of Consumer Finances, taken every three years, can be accessed at this site. The SCF is the only comprehensive source of data on the wealth of Americans at the household level. Here you can download the latest analysis detailing household assets, including stock ownership. Historical data back to 1989 are also available.

N

NATALITY

• Birth statistics from the National Center for Health Statistics

http://www.cdc.gov/nchs/fastats/births.htm

The National Center for Health Statistics is the official source of data on births in the United States, collecting and analyzing records from every state. This site is the access point for the information. The annual series, *Births: Final Data,* provides statistics on childbearing by age, race and Hispanic origin, marital status, and other characteristics.

• Data from the American Community Survey

http://factfinder.census.gov/home/saff/main.html?_lang=en

The American Community Survey collects data on fertility. To see the latest information, go to this site—the Census Bureau's Fact Finder Page. Click "get data" under "American Community Survey," then click "Subject Tables." Select your geography, then click "next." Scroll down to the table, "Fertility."

• Data from the Current Population Survey

http://www.census.gov/population/www/socdemo/fertility.html

Every two years the Current Population Survey asks American women about their childbearing experiences, resulting in a report on the fertility of American women. The information includes a profile of the characteristics of women who have had a child in the past year.

• Maternity leave

http://www.census.gov/Press-Release/www/releases/archives/employment_occupations/011536.html

This Census Bureau report, *Maternity Leave and Employment Patterns, 1961–2003,* provides the most comprehensive data available on women's labor force participation before and after giving birth.

• National Survey of Family Growth

http://www.cdc.gov/nchs/products/pubs/pubd/series/sr23/pre-1/sr23_25.htm

This address will take you to the comprehensive report on women's sexual and reproductive behavior, *Fertility, Family Planning, and Reproductive Health of U.S. Women*. The report is based on the 2002 National Survey of Family Growth, which asked women aged 15 to 44 about their sexual behavior, contraceptive use, fertility, and motherhood status. The NSFG, fielded every few years by the National Center for Health Statistics, also examines whether births were wanted or unwanted, maternity leave, and use of family planning services.

NATIONAL PARKS

• National Park Statistics

http://www.nature.nps.gov/stats/

So you want to know how many people visit the national parks as a whole, or just the number who visit national parks in South Dakota. You can find out this and much more from the National Park Service's Public Use Statistics Office at this site.

NATIVITY

• American Community Survey

http://factfinder.census.gov/home/saff/main.html?_lang=en

The American Community Survey collects annual data on the nativity of the population. To see the latest information, go to this site—the Census Bureau's Fact Finder Page. Click "get data" under "American Community Survey," then click "Subject Tables." Select your geography, then click "next." Scroll down to the section on "Origins and Language," and click on the table "Selected Characteristics of the Native and Foreign-Born Populations."

NEBRASKA

• State Data Center

http://www.unomaha.edu/~cpar/

At this web site you can access the Nebraska Population Report, an annual analysis of state and local population trends. Data from the 2000 census are also available here.

NEIGHBORHOODS

• American Housing Survey

http://www.census.gov/hhes/www/housing/ahs/ahs05/ahs05.html

Here you can access detailed information about American neighborhoods, based on data from the American Housing Survey. Find out what people think about their neighborhood, whether crime is a problem in their neighborhood, and whether their neighborhood borders a four-lane highway or factory. On this page, scroll down to the row labeled "Neighborhood" to access information on the neighborhoods of owners and renters, blacks, Hispanics, or the elderly.

NET WORTH

• Survey of Consumer Finances

http://www.federalreserve.gov/pubs/oss/oss2/scfindex.html

The Federal Reserve Board's Survey of Consumer Finances, taken every three years, can be accessed at this site. The SCF is the only comprehensive source of data on the wealth of Americans at the household level. Here you can download the latest analysis detailing household net worth, assets, and debts. Historical data back to 1989 are also available.

NEVADA

- **State Data Center**

http://dmla.clan.lib.nv.us/docs/nsla/sdc/

At this web site you can access demographic and economic statistics for Nevada, including 2000 census data. Local area data are also available here.

NEW HAMPSHIRE

- **State Data Center**

http://www.nh.gov/oep/programs/DataCenter/index.htm

At this web site you can access demographic and economic statistics for New Hampshire, including current population estimates, population projections, and 2000 census data. Local area data are also available here.

NEW JERSEY

- **State Data Center**

http://lwd.dol.state.nj.us/labor/lpa/content/njsdc_index.html

At this web site you can access the range of demographic and economic statistics for New Jersey, including current population estimates, population projections, employment statistics, 2000 census data, and American Community Survey numbers. Local area data are also available here.

NEW MEXICO

- **State Data Center**

http://www.edd.state.nm.us/

At this web site you can access demographic and economic statistics for New Mexico. Scroll over the "Data Center" link on the left side of the page to view the pop-up window with options such as Fact Book, County Comparison, Census Profiles, More Data (population estimates and projections), and so on.

NEW YORK

• State Data Center

http://www.nylovesbiz.com/nysdc/default.asp

At this web site you can access the demographic and economic statistics for New York, including current population estimates, employment statistics, and 2000 census data. Local area data are also available here.

NON-HISPANIC WHITES

• Demographics from the American Community Survey

http://factfinder.census.gov/home/saff/main.html?_lang=en

The American Community Survey provides annual statistics on the population by race and Hispanic origin. To retrieve the information, go to this site—the Census Bureau's Fact Finder page. Click on "get data" under "American Community Survey." On the next page, click on the "Selected Population Profiles" link. On the next page, specify the desired geography (if you want national totals, just click "add" and "next"). On the following page, select the desired race or Hispanic origin group. One more click and you have the latest demographic profile of non-Hispanic whites.

• Estimates by age

http://www.census.gov/popest/national/asrh/

To get the latest numbers on the non-Hispanic white population—including estimates of the size of the population by age—visit the Census Bureau's population estimates site.

• Health data from the Centers for Disease Control

http://www.cdc.gov/omhd/Populations/White.htm

For information on the health of the white population, this is the place to start. This page has links to a variety of statistics revealing the health of the white population, including information on health disparities.

• Income data

http://www.census.gov/hhes/www/income/dinctabs.html

Every March the Current Population Survey collects income data by race and Hispanic origin through the Annual Social and Economic Supplement. The gateway to the data for households, families, and individuals is available here.

• Poverty data

http://www.census.gov/hhes/www/poverty/detailedpovtabs.html

Every year, the Census Bureau measures the poverty population by race and Hispanic origin. The poverty estimates are based on income data collected by the Annual Social and Economic Supplement of the March Current Population Survey. The poverty tables are available here.

NORTH CAROLINA

• **State Data Center**

http://sdc.state.nc.us/

At this web site you can access the range of demographic and economic statistics for North Carolina, including current population estimates, population projections, 2000 census data, and American Community Survey numbers. Local area data are also available here.

NORTH DAKOTA

• **State Data Center**

http://www.ndsu.nodak.edu/sdc/

At this web site you can access demographic and economic statistics for North Dakota, including current population estimates, population projections, and 2000 census data. Local area data are also available here.

NURSING HOMES

• **National Center for Health Statistics**

http://www.cdc.gov/nchs/nnhs.htm

At this site you can access the federal government's National Nursing Home Survey. Taken only every few years, the latest data are for 2004. Compared with data collected in 1999, the numbers of nursing homes and nursing home residents are declining.

NUTRITION AND DIET

• **Food availability spreadsheets**

http://www.ers.usda.gov/Data/FoodConsumption/FoodAvailIndex.htm

At this site you can access the federal government's food availability spreadsheets, which reveal how much food—item by item—is available for human consumption in the United States. You discover, for example, that 23 pounds of candy per capita disappear from store shelves every year, as do 25 gallons of alcoholic beverages—far more than Americans claim to drink on surveys.

• **Gateway at the Centers for Disease Control**

http://www.cdc.gov/nccdphp/dnpa/nutrition/health_professionals/data/index.htm

From here you can access a variety of reports and statistics on the eating habits of Americans, including the Behavioral Risk Factor Surveillance System, the Pediatric Nutrition Surveillance System, and obesity reports.

O

OBESITY

• Measured weight, historical data

http://www.cdc.gov/nchs/pressroom/04news/americans.htm

Here you can download the eye-opening report *Mean Body Weight, Height, and Body Mass Index*, which tells you just how much weight Americans have gained over the decades. From the early 1960s to 2002, the average weight of both men and women increased by 24 pounds. The data come from the National Health and Nutrition Examination Survey.

• Measured weight, latest data

http://www.cdc.gov/nchs/about/major/nhanes/nhanesmmwrs_obesity.htm

When asked to self-report their weight, most Americans say they weigh less than they really do. At this site you can access the latest data on how much men and women weigh, based on the National Health and Nutrition Examination Survey, which, rather than asking people how much they weigh, actually puts them on the scale and records the numbers.

• Self-reported weight

http://www.cdc.gov/nchs/nhis.htm

In the annual report *Summary Health Statistics for U.S. Adults*, available on this page, you can access tables on body mass index based on self-reported weight and heights by a variety of demographic characteristics. Tables 30 and 31 have the numbers, based on the National Health Interview Survey.

OCCUPATIONS

• Gateway at the Bureau of Labor Statistics

http://www.bls.gov/oes/home.htm

This is the gateway to the Bureau of Labor Statistics' voluminous data on employment by occupation.

• Occupational Outlook Handbook

http://www.bls.gov/oco/home.htm

This is the home page for the *Occupational Outlook Handbook*, the government's continuously updated reference on hundreds of occupations, including training requirements, earnings, and employment projections.

OHIO

• State Data Center

http://www.odod.state.oh.us/research/

At this web site you can access the range of demographic and economic statistics for Ohio, including current population estimates, population projections, employment statistics, 2000 census data, and American Community Survey numbers. Local area data are also available here.

OKLAHOMA

• State Data Center

http://www.okcommerce.gov/data/

At this web site you can access the range of demographic and economic statistics for Oklahoma, including current population estimates, population projections, employment statistics, 2000 census data, and American Community Survey numbers. Local area data are also available here.

OLDER POPULATION

• AARP research

http://www.aarp.org/research/

To lobby for the older population, the AARP must research its needs. At the AARP site you can benefit from its work. This page is your gateway to the AARP's studies and statistics.

• Gateway at the Census Bureau

http://www.census.gov/population/www/socdemo/age.html

This is the Census Bureau's access point to its voluminous data on the age of the American population. Scroll down to the sections on the older (55+) and elderly (65+) populations.

• Health and Retirement Study data book

http://hrsonline.isr.umich.edu/docs/sho_refs.php?hfyle=index&xtyp=7

Here you can access *Growing Older in America: The Health and Retirement Study*, a free pdf download that places some of the University of Michigan's Health and Retirement Study into the hands of the public. The Health and Retirement Study is a longitudinal survey, launched in 1992 and funded by the National Institute on Aging, which tracks a nationally representative sample of Americans aged 50 or older as they age. HRS data are available primarily as datasets, limiting their use to academic researchers. *Growing Older in America* allows the public to review the survey's most important findings.

- **Older Americans: Key Indicators of Well-Being report**

http://www.agingstats.gov/agingstatsdotnet/main_site/default.aspx

Here you can download the summary report *Older Americans 2008*, which provides data on 37 indicators of the socioeconomic status of older Americans.

- **The State of 50+ America report**

http://www.aarp.org/research/reference/statistics/fifty_plus_2006.html

Every two years the AARP analyzes the socioeconomic well being of Americans aged 50 or older in its report *The State of 50+ America*. The report can be downloaded here.

ONLINE ACTIVITIES

- **Pew Internet & American Life Project**

http://www.pewinternet.org/

The Pew Internet & American Life Project produces reports that explore the impact of computers and the Internet. At this site you can access historical and current survey data revealing what Americans do online. You can also take The Internet Typology Test to find out what kind of information technology user you are.

OREGON

- **State Data Center**

http://www.pdx.edu/prc/oregondatacenter.html

At this web site you can access current population estimates for Oregon. Local area data are also available here.

OVERWEIGHT

- **Measured weight, historical data**

http://www.cdc.gov/nchs/pressroom/04news/americans.htm

Here you can download the eye-opening report *Mean Body Weight, Height, and Body Mass Index*, which tells you just how much weight Americans have gained over the decades. From the early 1960s to 2002, the average weight of both men and women increased by 24 pounds. The data come from the National Health and Nutrition Examination Survey.

- **Measured weight, latest data**

http://www.cdc.gov/nchs/about/major/nhanes/nhanesmmwrs_obesity.htm

When asked to self-report their weight, most Americans say they weigh less than they really do. At this site you can access the latest data on how much men and women weigh, based on the National Health and Nutrition Examination Survey, which, rather than asking people how much they weigh, actually puts them on the scale and records the numbers.

OVERWEIGHT

- **Self-reported weight**

http://www.cdc.gov/nchs/nhis.htm

In the annual report *Summary Health Statistics for U.S. Adults,* available on this page, you can access tables on body mass index based on self-reported weight and height by a variety of demographic characteristics. Tables 30 and 31 have the numbers, based on the National Health Interview Survey.

P

PARENTS

• A Child's Day reports

http://www.census.gov/population/www/socdemo/2004_detailedtables.html

This site allows you to access the many tables of data on family life from the Census Bureau's *A Child's Day* series of reports—including whether parents feel angry with their children, whether children participate in sports and after-school activities, and whether a family has rules about television viewing. The data are from the Survey of Income and Program Participation.

• American Community Survey

http://factfinder.census.gov/home/saff/main.html?_lang=en

The American Community Survey collects data on fertility. To see the latest information, go to this site—the Census Bureau's Fact Finder Page. Click "get data" under "American Community Survey," then click "Subject Tables." Select your geography, then click "next." Scroll down to table number S1301, "Fertility."

• Demographics of women giving birth

http://www.census.gov/population/www/socdemo/fertility.html

Every two years the Current Population Survey asks American women about their childbearing experiences, resulting in a report on the fertility of American women. The information includes a profile of the characteristics of women who have had a child in the past year.

• Employed parents

http://www.bls.gov/news.release/famee.toc.htm

Both mother and father are employed in 62 percent of the nation's nuclear families (married couples with children). This is just one of the findings in the Bureau of Labor Statistics' annual Employment Characteristics of Families tabulations, available at this site.

• Fathers of U.S. Children Born in 2001

http://nces.ed.gov/pubsearch/pubsinfo.asp?pubid=2006002

This report, *Fathers of U.S. Children Born in 2001*, is based on data collected by the Early Childhood Longitudinal Program, which is tracking a cohort of children born in 2001. The report profiles the demographic characteristics of resident and nonresident biological fathers, the extent of their involvement in pregnancy and birth, their attitudes toward fathering, and their participation in child care.

- **Fertility, Contraception, and Fatherhood**

http://www.cdc.gov/nchs/pressroom/06facts/fatherhood.htm

This page will take you to the groundbreaking report on men's sexual and reproductive behavior, *Fertility, Contraception, and Fatherhood*. The report is based on the 2002 National Survey of Family Growth, which asked men, for the first time, about their fertility, contraceptive use, fatherhood status, and interaction with children. The NSFG, fielded every few years by the National Center for Health Statistics, typically examines the sexual behavior and fertility status of American women. Now men are included too.

- **Fertility, Family Planning, and Reproductive Health of Women**

http://www.cdc.gov/nchs/products/pubs/pubd/series/sr23/pre-1/sr23_25.htm

This page will take you to the comprehensive report *Fertility, Family Planning, and Reproductive Health of U.S. Women*, which examines the sexual and reproductive behavior of American women. The report is based on the 2002 National Survey of Family Growth, which asked women aged 15 to 44 about their sexual behavior, contraceptive use, fertility, and motherhood status. The NSFG, fielded every few years by the National Center for Health Statistics, also examines whether births were wanted or unwanted, maternity leave, and use of family planning services.

- **Gateway at the National Center for Health Statistics**

http://www.cdc.gov/nchs/fastats/births.htm

The National Center for Health Statistics is the official source of data on births in the United States, collecting and analyzing records from every state. This site is the access point for the information. The annual series *Births: Final Data* provides statistics on childbearing by age, race and Hispanic origin, marital status, and other characteristics.

- **Maternity leave**

http://www.census.gov/Press-Release/www/releases/archives/employment_occupations/011536.html

This Census Bureau report, *Maternity Leave and Employment Patterns, 1961–2003*, provides the most comprehensive data available on women's labor force participation before and after giving birth.

PARKS, NATIONAL

- **National Park Statistics**

http://www.nature.nps.gov/stats/

So you want to know how many people visit the national parks as a whole, or just the number who visit national parks in South Dakota. You can find out this and much more from the National Park Service's Public Use Statistics Office at this site.

PENNSYLVANIA

- **State Data Center**

http://pasdc.hbg.psu.edu/index.html

At this web site you can access the range of demographic and economic statistics for Pennsylvania, including current population estimates, population projections, employment statistics, 2000 census data, and American Community Survey numbers. Local area data are also available here.

PENSIONS

- **Employee Benefit Research Institute**

http://www.ebri.org/

The Employee Benefit Research Institute is a Washington, D.C.–based nonprofit organization devoted to disseminating information about employee benefits, including defined-benefit and defined-contribution pension plans. Here you can download those reports as well as examine results from the annual Retirement Confidence survey.

- **Income data from the Current Population Survey**

http://pubdb3.census.gov/macro/032007/perinc/toc.htm

Want to know how much pension income people receive? Annually updated tables based on the Current Population Survey will tell you. Scroll down to table PINC-08 and click to retrieve income data by age, sex, race, and Hispanic origin.

- **Pension Rights Center**

http://www.pensionrights.org/pubs/reports.html

The Pension Rights Center is an organization dedicated to protecting and promoting retirement security. To that end, it compiles statistics on pensions, wealth, and savings. This page is the gateway to the organization's reports and statistics.

PEOPLE LIVING ALONE

- **Demographics of people who live alone**

http://www.census.gov/population/www/socdemo/hh-fam/cps2006.html

On this web page you can access the range of Census Bureau data on households and families. Many tables include data on the demographic characteristics of people who live alone.

- **Spending of people who live alone**

http://www.bls.gov/cex/home.htm

The Consumer Expenditure Survey collects annual data on household spending, some of it accessible at this site. Scroll down the page until you get to the section on "Current Standard Tables," and click on the table entitled "Size of consumer unit." This table contains summary spending data by size of household, including people who live alone.

PHYSICAL ACTIVITY

• Behavioral Risk Factor Surveillance System

http://www.cdc.gov/nccdphp/dnpa/physical/stats/index.htm

Here you can access physical activity statistics and reports from the Behavioral Risk Factor Surveillance System, a state-by-state telephone survey of a nationally representative sample of Americans.

• Demographics of exercisers

http://www.cdc.gov/nchs/nhis.htm

In the annual report *Summary Health Statistics for U.S. Adults,* available on this page, you can access tables on leisure-time physical activity by a variety of demographic characteristics. Tables 28 and 29 have the numbers, based on the National Health Interview Survey.

• Gateway at the National Center for Health Statistics

http://www.cdc.gov/nchs/fastats/exercise.htm

This is the National Center for Health Statistics gateway to its data on the physical activity of Americans.

• Public school programs

http://nces.ed.gov/pubsearch/pubsinfo.asp?pubid=2006057

This address is the link to *Calories In, Calories Out: Food and Exercise in Public Elementary Schools, 2005,* a report examining the food and physical activity programs available at the nation's public elementary schools.

PHYSICIAN VISITS

• Doctor visit reports

http://www.cdc.gov/nchs/about/major/ahcd/adata.htm

Every year the federal government collects data on the characteristics of people visiting the doctor, based on the National Ambulatory Medical Care Survey. At this site you can access the many reports about those visits.

• Medical Expenditure Panel Survey

http://www.meps.ahrq.gov/mepsweb/survey_comp/household.jsp

On this page, click on the link to the right, "Expenditures by Health Care Service," to see a list of tables showing the demographics of those using a variety of health care services including physician visits.

PLACES OF BIRTH

• **Historical data from the Census Bureau**

http://www.census.gov/population/www/socdemo/foreign/datatbls.html

To access historical data on places of birth of the foreign-born population, this is the site to visit.

• **Latest data from the American Community Survey**

http://factfinder.census.gov/home/saff/main.html?_lang=en

The American Community Survey is the best source of information on the places of birth of the foreign-born population in the United States. To see the latest annual information, go to this site—the Census Bureau's Fact Finder page. Click on "get data" under "American Community Survey." On the next page, click on the "Subject Tables" link for the latest American Community Survey. On the next page, specify your desired geography (if you want national totals, just click "add" and "next." Up pops the list of subject tables. Scroll down to the "Origins and Language" section to access the latest data on region of birth for the foreign-born population.

PLAY

• **American Time Use Survey**

http://www.bls.gov/tus/home.htm

The Bureau of Labor Statistics' American Time Use Survey collects data on the activities of a representative sample of Americans on a minute-by-minute basis for the past 24 hours. The data are categorized by activity, analyzed by demographic characteristic, and published annually. Americans devote more time to leisure and recreational activities, it turns out, than anything else except sleeping. You can access the time use data here.

• **Federal Reserve Bank of Boston**

http://www.bos.frb.org/economic/wp/wp2006/wp0602.htm

Research from the Federal Reserve Bank of Boston shows that men and women are working less than they once did. Economists from the Bank of Boston and the University of Chicago examine time use over five decades and find that men and women are working less and playing more. Their study, "Measuring Trends in Leisure: The Allocation of Time over Five Decades," is available at this site.

POPULATION ESTIMATES

• **Census Bureau**

http://www.census.gov/popest/estimates.php

This site is the gateway to the Census Bureau's population estimates. Here you can access monthly estimates of the total population, as well as annual estimates of the population by

How Much Elbow Room Do We Have?

Last year, the U.S. population topped 300 million. This is a very big number, making us the third most populous country in the world (behind China and India). Yet we still have a long way to go before we are as densely populated as most other countries in the world. In 2007, the United States had 31 people for every square kilometer of land, according to the Population Reference Bureau. Among the 208 nations examined by PRB, we rank 154th in population density.

China, the world's most populous country, has four times our population density at 138 people per square kilometer. In India, the number is much higher, at 344 per square kilometer; Japan is almost as densely packed with 338. Yet even these countries would seem empty in comparison to Bangladesh (1,035) or Singapore (6,785).

Americans have more space per person than most Europeans. France averages 112 people in each of its square kilometers. Germany is much more tightly packed with 230, and the United Kingdom has a density of 251. Some nations, however, are even less crowded than we are, including Brazil (22 people per square kilometer) and Russia (8). Canadians and Australians, whose countries average only 3 people per square kilometer, would feel downright claustrophobic in the United States.

age, sex, race, and Hispanic origin. Estimates by state, county, and metropolitan area are available here.

POPULATION PROJECTIONS

- **Census Bureau**

http://www.census.gov/ipc/www/usinterimproj/

The Census Bureau's latest population projections are available at this site. The projections reflect 2000 census results. Four summary tables show the steady decline of the non-Hispanic white population, to just 50 percent of the nation's 420 million people by 2050. In that year, Hispanics will account for one in four Americans. The site allows users to download an enormous spreadsheet containing single-year-of-age projections for each year between 2000 and 2050 for eight race/Hispanic-origin groups.

- **Pew Research Center**

http://pewresearch.org/pubs/729/

These Pew population projections update the Census Bureau's projections (see above), which underestimate the growth of the Hispanic population. Pew projects the total and Hispanic populations in broad age groups at 10-year intervals through 2050. The projections show the total U.S. population growing to 438 million by 2050 (compared with the Census Bureau's projection of 420 million), with Hispanics accounting for 29 percent of the total (compared with the Census Bureau's 24 percent).

POPULATION, UNITED STATES

- **Census Bureau**

http://www.census.gov/

Want to know how large the United States population is right now? Just visit the Census Bureau's home page and check out the big red number at the upper right corner of the page. That's how large the U.S. population is today. Click on the "Population Clocks" link to get more details about current U.S. and world population totals. This address is also the gateway to the entire range of national, state, and local demographic statistics.

POVERTY

- **Census Bureau**

http://www.census.gov/hhes/www/poverty/poverty.html

This web page is the gateway to the federal government's array of poverty statistics ranging from how poverty is defined to poverty threshold measures, from the current official poverty rate by demographic characteristic to historical statistics back to 1959, the first year for which modern-day poverty estimates are available.

PREGNANCY

- **Birth statistics from the National Center for Health Statistics**

http://www.cdc.gov/nchs/fastats/births.htm

The National Center for Health Statistics is the official source of data on births and pregnancy in the United States, collecting and analyzing records from every state. This site is the access point for the information. The annual series *Births: Final Data* provides statistics on childbearing by age, race and Hispanic origin, marital status, and other characteristics.

- **Data from the American Community Survey**

http://factfinder.census.gov/home/saff/main.html?_lang=en

The American Community Survey collects annual data on fertility. To see the latest information, go to this site—the Census Bureau's Fact Finder Page. Click "get data" under "American Community Survey," then click "Subject Tables." Select your geography, then click "next." Scroll down to the table "Fertility."

- **Data from the Current Population Survey**

http://www.census.gov/population/www/socdemo/fertility.html

Every two years the Current Population Survey asks American women about their childbearing experiences, resulting in a report on the fertility of American women. The information includes a profile of the characteristics of women who have had a child in the past year.

- **Maternity leave**

http://www.census.gov/Press-Release/www/releases/archives/employment_occupations/011536.html

This Census Bureau report, *Maternity Leave and Employment Patterns, 1961–2003*, provides the most comprehensive data available on women's labor force participation before and after giving birth.

- **National Survey of Family Growth**

http://www.cdc.gov/nchs/products/pubs/pubd/series/sr23/pre-1/sr23_25.htm

This address will take you to the comprehensive report on women's sexual and reproductive behavior, *Fertility, Family Planning, and Reproductive Health of U.S. Women*. The report is based on the 2002 National Survey of Family Growth, which asked women aged 15 to 44 about their sexual behavior, contraceptive use, fertility, and motherhood status. The NSFG, fielded every few years by the National Center for Health Statistics, also examines whether births were wanted or unwanted, maternity leave, and use of family planning services.

PRESCRIPTION DRUGS

• **Medical Expenditure Panel Survey**

http://www.meps.ahrq.gov/mepsweb/data_stats/MEPS_topics.jsp?topicid=14Z-1

This site provides access to tables and reports on prescription drug use based on data from the Medical Expenditure Panel Survey.

PRICE INDEX

• **Bureau of Labor Statistics**

http://www.bls.gov/cpi/home.htm

On this page you gain access to the government's Consumer Price Indexes over time, item by item. Examine the government's tabulated data or create customized tables.

PRISON POPULATION

• **Bureau of Justice Statistics**

http://www.ojp.usdoj.gov/bjs/prisons.htm

If you need statistics on prisons or prisoners, then visit this site. Here you can access the Bureau of Justice Statistics' reports on prison populations.

PRIVATE SCHOOLS

• **Digest of Education Statistics**

http://nces.ed.gov/programs/digest/d07/tables_2.asp#Ch2Sub2

The National Center for Education Statistics' annual *Digest of Education Statistics* contains many tables on the nation's private schools. Those tables can be accessed from this site.

• **Private School Survey**

http://nces.ed.gov/surveys/pss/

On this page you can access statistics and reports from the federal government's biennial Private School Survey. You can retrieve data on private schools by size, level, religious orientation, geographic region, community type, and program emphasis. If you want data for a particular private school, use the search function to find out more.

PROJECTIONS, EDUCATION

• **National Center for Education Statistics**

http://nces.ed.gov/programs/projections/projections2016/

If you want to know how many bachelor's degrees will be awarded in 2016, or the number and share of female college students in that year, then take a look at the National Center for Education Statistics' education projections available at this site.

PROJECTIONS, EMPLOYMENT

• Bureau of Labor Statistics

http://www.bls.gov/emp/home.htm

Every two years the Bureau of Labor Statistics issues updated employment projections. The latest are available at this site. The projections show big changes on the horizon as the workforce ages.

PROJECTIONS, POPULATON

• Census Bureau

http://www.census.gov/ipc/www/usinterimproj/

The Census Bureau's latest population projections are available at this site. The projections reflect 2000 census results. Four summary tables show the steady decline of the non-Hispanic white population, to just 50 percent of the nation's 420 million people by 2050. In that year, Hispanics will account for one in four Americans. The site allows users to download an enormous spreadsheet containing single-year-of-age projections for each year between 2000 and 2050 for eight race/Hispanic-origin groups.

• Pew Research Center

http://pewresearch.org/pubs/729/

These Pew population projections update the Census Bureau's projections (see above), which underestimate the growth of the Hispanic population. Pew projects the total and Hispanic populations in broad age groups at 10-year intervals through 2050. The projections show the total U.S. population growing to 438 million by 2050 (compared with the Census Bureau's projection of 420 million), with Hispanics accounting for 29 percent of the total (compared with the Census Bureau's 24 percent).

PUBLIC ASSISTANCE

• Annual data from the Current Population Survey

http://pubdb3.census.gov/macro/032007/pov/toc.htm

On this page you can find data from the latest Current Population Survey on the number and percentage of people who participate in government poverty programs. Click on table POV-26, for example, to see statistics on people who receive food stamps, subsidized housing, and cash assistance by age, sex, and race.

• Participation in government programs

http://www.sipp.census.gov/sipp/p70s/p70s.html

On this page you can access a number of reports from the Census Bureau's Survey of Income and Program Participation. One series collects data on the public's participation in means-tested government programs such as TANF, food stamps, subsidized housing, and

Medicaid. The latest, released in 2006, is entitled *Dynamics of Economic Well-Being: Participation in Government Programs, 2001 Through 2003: Who Gets Assistance?*

PUBLIC SCHOOLS

• Attitudes toward public schools

http://www.pdkintl.org/kappan/kpollpdf.htm

If you want to know what Americans think about public education, visit the Phi Delta Kappa International web site. Phi Delta Kappa International is an association of professional educators committed to public education. Of particular interest is the Phi Delta Kappa/Gallup Poll of the Public's Attitudes Toward the Public Schools, an annual survey the organization has conducted for more than three decades. The polls provide a wealth of current and historical data on attitudes toward public education.

• Digest of Education Statistics

http://nces.ed.gov/programs/digest/d07/tables_2.asp

The National Center for Education Statistics' annual *Digest of Education Statistics* contains hundreds of tables of data on the nation's public elementary and high schools. Those tables can be accessed at this site.

• Local schools

http://nces.ed.gov/ccd/schoolsearch/

If you want data on a specific public school, then visit this National Center for Education Statistics' site and retrieve information on the total number of students in a school as well as the number of students by grade, sex, race, and Hispanic origin. The data come from the federal government's Common Core of Data Program, an annual survey of the nation's public schools.

• School districts

http://nces.ed.gov/surveys/sdds/index.asp

Want to know the demographics of a particular school district? The National Center for Education Statistics' School District Demographics System allows users to retrieve population profiles of school districts for analysis or comparison, based on data from the American Community Survey.

Q

QUALITY OF LIFE

- **Economic**

http://www.sipp.census.gov/sipp/p70s/p70s.html

The Census Bureau report series *Extended Measures of Well-Being: Living Conditions in the United States* can be accessed from this page. The reports, based on results from the Survey of Income and Program Participation, examine our quality of life by a variety of measures that go beyond income. They are ownership of appliances and electronic goods, housing conditions, neighborhood conditions, ability to meet basic needs, and expectation of help should needs arise.

- **Physical**

http://apps.nccd.cdc.gov/HRQOL/

If you want to know how good—or bad—Americans feel, then this National Center for Chronic Disease Prevention and Health Promotion web site is the place to start. Here you can find statistics on our health-related quality of life, with handy summary measures of unhealthy days, both physical and mental.

R

RACE

• Business owners

http://www.census.gov/csd/sbo/

The Survey of Business Owners, taken every five years as part of the Economic Census, provides details on businesses in the United States by race and Hispanic origin of the business owners.

• Demographics from the American Community Survey

http://factfinder.census.gov/home/saff/main.html?_lang=en

The American Community Survey provides annual statistics on the population by race and Hispanic origin. To retrieve the information, go to this site—the Census Bureau's Fact Finder page. Click on "get data" under "American Community Survey." On the next page, click on the "Selected Population Profiles" link. On the next page, specify the desired geography (if you want national totals, just click "add" and "next"). On the following page, select the desired race or Hispanic origin group. One more click and you have the latest demographic profile of the racial or ethnic group.

• Health data from the Centers for Disease Control

http://www.cdc.gov/omhd/Populations/populations.htm

For information on the health of the population by race and Hispanic origin, this is the place to start. This page has links to a variety of statistics, including information on health disparities.

• Historical data

http://www.census.gov/population/www/socdemo/race.html

This is the Census Bureau's gateway to statistics and reports on the race of the population from the 2000 census and earlier censuses.

• Income data

http://www.census.gov/hhes/www/income/dinctabs.html

Every March the Current Population Survey collects income data by race and Hispanic origin through the Annual Social and Economic Supplement. The gateway to the data for households, families, and individuals is available here.

How Are the Races Defined?

It all started with the 2000 census, the first in modern times to allow Americans to identify themselves as belonging to more than one race. By 2003 government surveys were required to go multiracial as well. The bureaucrats and special interest groups behind this Frankenstein probably meant well, but they have devised one of the most complex and confusing systems of racial accounting imaginable. Here is a crash course on how the system works.

Lesson 1, The Census: The 2000 census asked each American to identify him- or herself as belonging to one or more of six racial groups: American Indian and Alaska Native, Asian, black, Native Hawaiian and other Pacific Islander, white, and other. The result is 63 different racial combinations ranging from the largest (white alone, 211 million people) to the smallest (white/black/American Indian/Native Hawaiian/other, 68 people).

Lesson 2, Race: How do you even begin to talk about the new racial categories? To start the discussion, the Census Bureau created three new terms to distinguish one group from another. There is the "race alone" population--people who identify themselves as being of only one race. There is the "race in combination" population—people who are multiracial, identifying themselves as being of more than one race, such as white and black. And there is the "race, alone or in combination" population—which is the two groups combined. If you're wondering how the numbers add up, they don't.

Lesson 3, Hispanic: On censuses and surveys, questions about Hispanic origin are separate from questions about race. This adds another layer of complexity to the accounting of the racial and ethnic make-up of the population. Not only are people white, black, and/or Asian, but they also may (or may not) be Hispanic. While most Hispanics are white, some are black, Asian, American Indian, and/or even Native Hawaiian because the government considers Hispanic to be an ethnicity rather than a race. Many Hispanics disagree, however, and identify themselves as "other" race when they do not find "Hispanic" or "Latino" listed as a race. On the 2000 census, in fact, 42 percent of the nation's Hispanics identified themselves as "other" race. Among the 18 million Americans who identified themselves as "other" race, 90 percent were Hispanic.

Lesson 4, The Multiracial: Among the 7 million Americans who identified themselves as multiracial on the 2000 census, fully 42 percent were under age 18—an age distribution reminiscent of a third-world country. What accounts for this preponderance of youth among the multiracial? The numbers come from parents who are identifying their children as multiracial. When the kids grow up, will they agree?

Final exam: Now it is time to project the new racial and ethnic categories 100 years into the future. That's what the Census Bureau had to do when it produced its population projections based on 2000 census results. How do you project 63 different racial combinations 100 years into the future? What about multiracial children—will they still consider themselves multiracial in 5 or 50 years? Your mission: predict trends in births, deaths, and immigration, and also in the politics and psychology of race.

- **Population estimates**

http://www.census.gov/popest/race.html

To get the latest population estimates by race and Hispanic origin, go to this site. Estimates are available by age and sex, with data for the nation, states, and counties.

- **Poverty data**

http://www.census.gov/hhes/www/poverty/detailedpovtabs.html

Every year, the Census Bureau measures the poverty population by race and Hispanic origin. The poverty estimates are based on income data collected by the Annual Social and Economic Supplement of the March Current Population Survey. The poverty tables are available here.

- **Race and Hispanic origin of husbands and wives**

http://www.census.gov/population/www/socdemo/hh-fam/cps2006.html

For the latest statistics on interracial marriage, go to this page where you can access the Census Bureau's latest detailed tables on living arrangements. Download tables FG3 and FG4, which crosstabulate the characteristics of husbands by the characteristics of wives (age, income, education, and race/Hispanic origin).

- **Race of Hispanics**

http://www.census.gov/popest/national/asrh/

Hispanics are an ethnic group, not a race. This means that Hispanics may be of any race. To see the racial breakdown of Hispanics, go to this page to download the latest population estimates.

RECREATIONAL ACTIVITIES

- **American Time Use Survey**

http://www.bls.gov/tus/home.htm

The Bureau of Labor Statistics' American Time Use Survey collects data on the activities of a representative sample of Americans on a minute-by-minute basis for the past 24 hours. The data are categorized by activity, analyzed by demographic characteristic, and published annually. Americans devote more time to leisure and recreational activities, it turns out, than anything else except sleeping. You can access the time use data here.

- **National Park Statistics**

http://www.nature.nps.gov/stats/

So you want to know how many people visit the national parks as a whole, or just the number who visit national parks in South Dakota. You can find out this and much more from the National Park Service's Public Use Statistics Office at this site.

- **National Sporting Goods Association**

http://www.nsga.org/I4A/pages/index.cfm?pageID=3346

This link takes you to the National Sporting Goods Association's annual sports participation survey. Here you can download the latest data on participation in a variety of sports by children and adults. Trends are also available.

- **U.S. Fish & Wildlife Service**

http://www.census.gov/prod/www/abs/fishing.html

According to the 2006 National Survey of Fishing, Hunting, and Wildlife-Associated Recreation, nearly 88 million Americans fished, hunted, or watched wildlife in 2006. The survey, which has been conducted about every five years since 1955, explores Americans' participation in and spending on fishing, hunting, bird watching, animal feeding, and wildlife photography.

REGIONS

- **American Community Survey**

http://factfinder.census.gov/home/saff/main.html?_lang=en

The American Community Survey collects annual data on regional demographics. To see the latest information, go to this site—the Census Bureau's Fact Finder Page. Click "get data" under "American Community Survey," then "Data Profiles." Select a region and get the latest demographic and socioeconomic profile.

- **Population estimates**

http://www.census.gov/popest/states/

To get the latest regional population estimates, go to this site, which is the access point for the Census Bureau's state estimates. The tables include regional totals as well.

RELIGION

- **American Religious Identification Survey**

http://www.gc.cuny.edu/faculty/research_briefs/aris/aris_index.htm

The American Religious Identification Survey, taken in 2001, can be accessed at this site. Carried out under the auspices of The Graduate Center of the City University of New York, the survey provides an extensive profile of religious identification in the United States, including a variety of demographic breakdowns and trends since an earlier survey was taken in 1990.

- **Gallup**

http://www.gallup.com/

The Gallup organization has been tracking the religious beliefs and practices of Americans for more than 70 years. Go to this site and type "religion" into the search box to explore Gallup's voluminous data.

How Religious Are Americans?

Among the world's developed countries, the United States stands alone in the importance it places on religion. The 59 percent majority of Americans say religion is "very important" in their life, according to a Pew Research Center for the People & the Press survey.

The importance Americans place on religion is one of our distinguishing characteristics, not shared by any other developed country. This characteristic makes us more similar to Pakistan and Turkey than to Canada, Great Britain, or Italy, according to Pew. While the majority of Americans say religion plays a very important role in their life, only 30 percent of Canadians think likewise. In Great Britain, the figure is 33 percent, in Italy 27 percent, and in Japan just 12 percent. In contrast, fully 65 percent of the population of Turkey says religion is very important to them personally. Other countries in which the majority of the population says religion is very important include Brazil, India, Kenya, and Pakistan.

"Religion is much more important to Americans than to people living in other wealthy nations," comments Pew. In an analysis correlating religiosity with per capita income, Pew finds the United States to be the only wealthy country in which religion is considered "very important" by most of the public.

- **General Social Survey**

http://sda.berkeley.edu/cgi-bin32/hsda?harcsda+gss06

If you want to explore religious belief in the United States and are prepared to do a little work, this site allows you to access the data on religion available from the General Social Survey. Religious preferences, belief in the Bible, prayer in public schools, and attendance at religious services are just some of the topics you can explore. To do so, however, you must start with a variable name. Use the search engine on this page to determine variable names, then plug them into the Row field to get results.

- **Pew Forum on Religion & Public Life**

http://pewforum.org/

The Pew Forum on Religion & Public Life, launched in 2001, seeks to promote a deeper understanding of issues at the intersection of religion and public affairs. One way it does this is by surveying the public's attitudes toward religion. The latest such effort is the report *The Religious Landscape of the United States*, which details the changing religious affiliation of Americans.

RENTERS

- **American Community Survey**

http://factfinder.census.gov/home/saff/main.html?_lang=en

The American Community Survey collects annual data on homeowners and renters. To see the latest information, go to this site—the Census Bureau's Fact Finder Page. Click "get data" under "American Community Survey," then click "Subject Tables." Select your geography, then click "next." Scroll down to the three sections of tables on housing.

- **American Housing Survey**

http://www.census.gov/hhes/www/housing/ahs/ahs.html

The American Housing Survey, taken every two years, provides voluminous data on renters including a detailed profile of their houses and neighborhoods.

RETIREMENT

- **AARP research**

http://www.aarp.org/research/work/retirement/

To explore retirement trends in the United States, the AARP is a good place to start. On this page, you can access the AARP's extensive reports and studies on retirement.

- **Employee Benefit Research Institute**

http://www.ebri.org/

No organization does a better job of tracking the retirement preparedness of the U.S. population than the Employee Benefit Research Institute. The organization tracks pension ben-

When Will the Baby-Boom Generation Retire?

The oldest baby boomers, born in 1946, are now in their early sixties and eligible for Social Security benefits. But don't hold your breath waiting for waves of retirees to hit the highways in their RVs. You are more likely to find them stuck in traffic trying to get to work. Because Medicare—the government's health insurance program for the elderly—doesn't kick in until age 65, few aging boomers will give up their employer-provided health insurance and opt for early retirement until they are eligible for the federal government's universal health insurance program.

The latest set of labor force projections from the Bureau of Labor Statistics, published in the November 2007 *Monthly Labor Review*, shows the baby-boom generation retiring much more slowly than its parents did. Labor force participation rates are projected to rise substantially among older men as boomers adapt to a declining standard of living relative to today's retirees. The BLS lists five reasons, some of them troubling, for the rising labor force participation rate among older Americans:

• Longer, healthier lives. The BLS is right about living longer, but the assumption that we also will be healthier is dubious. Some studies show that today's middle aged are not as healthy as preceding generations at the same age.

• Better educated. The more educated a person, the higher the likelihood of his or her labor force participation. Because boomers are well educated, they should remain on the job longer than their parents did.

• The substitution of defined-contribution savings plans for defined-benefit pensions. This shift has reduced the potential retirement income of individual boomers by thousands of dollars a year. Many will work well into old age to make up the difference.

• Later eligibility. The age at which older Americans can receive full Social Security benefits is rising from 65 to 67, forcing many to stay on the job.

• Health insurance. With fewer employers offering health insurance for their early retirees, most boomers will have to wait for Medicare.

If boomers were to retire at the same age as their parents did, by 2016 the nation would have 61 million retirees aged 55 or older looking for something fun to do. Because boomers will work much longer than their parents, the retirement market will be smaller than was once anticipated, with only 50 million retirees aged 55 or older in 2016. For businesses eagerly awaiting the expansion of the retiree market there is good news—the number of retirees will grow because of the large size of the baby-boom generation. But the increase will be smaller than what was once projected, and many retirees will be struggling to make ends meet.

efits and coverage in a variety of reports and studies. Want to know what has happened to defined benefit pension plans, or how much money workers have in their 401(k) accounts? You can find out here.

- **Health and Retirement Study data book**

http://hrsonline.isr.umich.edu/docs/sho_refs.php?hfyle=index&xtyp=7

Here you can access *Growing Older in America: The Health and Retirement Study*, a free pdf download that places some of the University of Michigan's Health and Retirement Study into the hands of the public. The Health and Retirement Study is a longitudinal survey, launched in 1992 and funded by the National Institute on Aging, which tracks a nationally representative sample of Americans aged 50 or older as they age. HRS data are available primarily as datasets, limiting their use to academic researchers. *Growing Older in America* allows the public to review the survey's most important findings.

- **Retirement Confidence Survey**

http://www.ebri.org/surveys/rcs/

The Retirement Confidence Survey, sponsored by the Employee Benefit Research Institute and Mathew Greenwald & Associates, can be accessed at this site. The survey of 1,000 nationally representative people aged 25 or older has been conducted annually since 1996. It provides a snapshot of attitudes toward retirement and the status of retirement planning.

- **Social Security Administration**

http://www.ssa.gov/policy/

This is the portal to the Social Security Administration's statistical information on Social Security, the nation's most important retirement income program. At this site you can access the *Annual Statistical Supplement*, with data on beneficiaries and average monthly benefits by age, sex, race, and more.

- **Survey of Consumer Finances**

http://www.federalreserve.gov/pubs/oss/oss2/2004/scf2004home.html

The Federal Reserve Board's triennial Survey of Consumer Finances is the best source of information on household wealth, which reveals how well households are preparing for retirement. At this site you access data from the latest (2004) survey, which includes estimates of the size of retirement accounts owned by households.

RHODE ISLAND

- **State Data Center**

http://www.planning.ri.gov/census/ri2000.htm

At this web site you can access demographic and economic statistics for Rhode Island including current population estimates, population projections, 2000 census data, and American Community Survey numbers. Local area data are also available here.

RURAL POPULATION

- **USDA Economic Research Service**

http://www.ers.usda.gov/Briefing/Population/

Did you know that most of the rural population lives in a metropolitan area? If this doesn't make sense, then find out more about the nation's rural population at this site. Here you can access statistics on rural Americans, find out how "rural" is defined, and learn how the rural population is changing.

S

SAVINGS

• 401(k) savings

http://www.ebri.org/

For the most up-to-date analysis of how much workers have saved in 401(k)-type plans, the Employee Benefit Research Institute has the numbers. In reports such as *401(k) Plan Asset Allocation, Account Balances, and Loan Activity in 2006*, EBRI reveals that the median 401(k) account balance was $66,650 at the end of 2006. EBRI reports include analysis of retirement savings by demographic characteristic.

• Retirement Confidence Survey

http://www.ebri.org/surveys/rcs/

For information about retirement savings, the Retirement Confidence Survey, sponsored by the Employee Benefit Research Institute and Mathew Greenwald & Associates, can be accessed at this site. The survey of 1,000 nationally representative people aged 25 or older has been conducted annually since 1996. It provides some data on retirement plans, amount saved for retirement, and concern about having saved enough.

• Survey of Consumer Finances

http://www.federalreserve.gov/pubs/oss/oss2/scfindex.html

The Federal Reserve Board's Survey of Consumer Finances, taken every three years, can be accessed at this site. The SCF is the only comprehensive source of data on the wealth of Americans at the household level. Here you can download the latest data on household savings, including overall net worth and financial and nonfinancial assets by type including stock ownership and retirement savings accounts. Historical data back to 1989 are also available.

SCHOOL ENROLLMENT

• Digest of Education Statistics

http://nces.ed.gov/programs/digest/d07/tables_2.asp#Ch2Sub1

The *Digest of Education Statistics* provides enrollment data for public and private schools from prekindergarten through graduate school and adult education programs. The *Digest*'s enrollment data can be accessed here.

- **Gateway at the Census Bureau**

http://www.census.gov/population/www/socdemo/school.html

This site is the gateway to the Census Bureau's data on school enrollment from the Current Population Survey.

SCHOOL, PRIVATE

- **Digest of Education Statistics**

http://nces.ed.gov/programs/digest/d07/tables_2.asp#Ch2Sub2

The National Center for Education Statistics' annual *Digest of Education Statistics* contains many tables on the nation's private elementary and high schools. Those tables can be accessed here.

- **Private School Survey**

http://nces.ed.gov/surveys/pss/

On this page you can access statistics and reports from the federal government's biennial Private School Survey. You can retrieve data on private schools by size, level, religious orientation, geographic region, community type, and program emphasis. If you want data for a particular private school, use the search function to find out more.

SCHOOL, PUBLIC

- **Attitudes toward public schools**

http://www.pdkintl.org/kappan/kpollpdf.htm

If you want to know what Americans think about public education, visit the Phi Delta Kappa International web site. Phi Delta Kappa International is an association of professional educators committed to public education. Of particular interest is the Phi Delta Kappa/Gallup Poll of the Public's Attitudes Toward the Public Schools, an annual survey the organization has conducted for more than three decades. The polls provide a wealth of current and historical data on attitudes toward public education.

- **Digest of Education Statistics**

http://nces.ed.gov/programs/digest/d07/tables_2.asp

The National Center for Education Statistics' annual *Digest of Education Statistics* contains hundreds of tables of data on the nation's public elementary and high schools. Those tables can be accessed from this site.

- **Local schools**

http://nces.ed.gov/ccd/schoolsearch/

If you want data on a specific public school, then visit this National Center for Education Statistics' site and retrieve information on the total number of students in a school as well as the number of students by grade, sex, race, and Hispanic origin. The data come from the federal government's Common Core of Data Program, an annual survey of the nation's public schools.

• School districts

http://nces.ed.gov/surveys/sdds/index.asp

Want to know the demographics of a particular school district? The National Center for Education Statistics' School District Demographics System allows users to retrieve population profiles of school districts for analysis or comparison, based on data from the American Community Survey.

SCHOOLS, GENERAL STATISTICS

• Digest of Education Statistics

http://nces.ed.gov/programs/digest/

The *Digest of Education Statistics* is the comprehensive source of statistics on education in the United States, from prekindergarten through graduate school. Updated annually, the *Digest* covers a variety of topics, including school enrollment, SAT scores, high school graduates, college degrees awarded, as well as data on schools, teachers, and school finances.

SCHOOLS, SATISFACTION WITH

• American Housing Survey

http://www.census.gov/hhes/www/housing/ahs/ahs05/ahs05.html

Want to know how many parents of children under age 13 are satisfied with their local public elementary school? Want to know how many are so bothered by the poor quality of the local school that they want to move? Visit the online tables of the American Housing Survey at this address and scroll down to the Neighborhood tables (tables 2-8 to 6-8). Click on one of these tables and scroll to the tab "Public elementary school" for data on school satisfaction.

• Public school survey

http://www.pdkintl.org/

If you want to know what Americans think about public education, visit the Phi Delta Kappa International web site. Phi Delta Kappa International is an association of professional educators committed to public education. Of particular interest is the Phi Delta Kappa/Gallup Poll of the Public's Attitudes Toward the Public Schools, an annual survey the organization has conducted for more than three decades. The polls provide a wealth of current and historical data on attitudes toward public education.

SELF-EMPLOYMENT

• Annual data

http://www.bls.gov/cps/home.htm

For the latest annual numbers on self-employment, visit this web site, which is the Bureau of Labor Statistics gateway to official employment and unemployment statistics from the Current Population Survey. Scroll down to the "Annual Averages—Household Data" section and click on tables 12 and 13 (the self-employed by race and Hispanic origin), 15 (age and sex), 16 (industry and sex), and 21 (usual full- or part-time work).

• Independent contractors

http://www.bls.gov/news.release/conemp.toc.htm

Every few years the Bureau of Labor Statistics collects data on the nontraditional workforce, which includes independent contractors—or the nation's self-employed. The data can be accessed at this site.

SEXUAL BEHAVIOR

• National Survey of Family Growth

http://www.cdc.gov/nchs/about/major/nsfg/nsfgcycle6reports.htm

Every few years the federal government fields the National Survey of Family Growth, which probes the sexual behavior and family formation practices of Americans aged 15 to 44. The reports from the latest (2002) survey are available at this site. They cover such topics as sexual behavior, teenage sexual activity, the family formation behavior of men and women, and trends in contraceptive use.

SHIFT WORK

• Bureau of Labor Statistics

http://www.bls.gov/news.release/flex.toc.htm

Fifteen percent of full-time wage and salary workers usually work a shift other than a daytime schedule. Among black workers, the figure is an even larger 21 percent. These are some of the findings from the latest Workers on Flexible and Shift Schedules tabulations available at this Bureau of Labor Statistics site.

SHOPPING

• American Time Use Survey

http://www.bls.gov/tus/home.htm

This is the home page of the American Time Use Survey, a government initiative that measures the amount of time people spend doing everything from sleeping to working and shopping during an average day. The survey results, released annually, show how much

Does Religion Influence Sexual Behavior?

Does religious belief influence sexual attitudes and behavior? Most would call this question a no brainer—of course it does. But human nature being what it is, religious belief has less influence on behavior than on attitudes.

This becomes clear in an examination of the National Survey of Family Growth, a survey taken every few years by the National Center for Health Statistics. The NSFG probes the attitudes and behavior of a representative sample of Americans aged 15 to 44 toward sexuality and reproduction. An examination of the results suggests that religious belief affects the talk much more than the walk.

Religious belief shapes attitudes toward premarital sex: The percentage of women who think it is all right for unmarried 18-year-olds to have sexual relations if they have strong affection for one another ranges from a high of 74 percent among women with no religion to a low of 29 percent among fundamentalist Protestants.

But it delays first sexual intercourse by only a few months: Among women aged 15 to 44 with no religion, average age at first sexual intercourse was 16.4 years. Fundamentalist Protestants said no to sex for only a few more months, with an average age at first sexual intercourse of 16.9 years.

And it has little impact on "saving oneself" for marriage: Among women with no religion, only 12 percent waited until marriage before having sex. The proportion was a slightly higher 17 percent among fundamentalist Protestants.

Religious belief drives attitudes toward out-of-wedlock childbearing: Among women with no religion, fully 86 percent think it is OK for an unmarried woman to have a child. Among fundamentalist Protestants, only 49 percent agree.

But it has almost no effect on out-of-wedlock childbearing itself: The percentage of mothers aged 15 to 44 who have had a child out-of-wedlock is about the same regardless of religion. Among mothers with no religion, 49 percent had a child out-of-wedlock. Among fundamentalist Protestants, the figure is 47 percent.

time people spend shopping by a variety of demographic characteristics. It also reveals differences in the amount of time devoted to shopping on weekdays versus weekends.

SICK LEAVE

- **Bureau of Labor Statistics**

http://www.bls.gov/ncs/ebs/home.htm

Get the facts about employee benefits, including sick leave, from the Bureau of Labor Statistics' National Compensation Survey here. This annual survey examines the entire range of employee benefits provided by the nation's private companies. Retirement and health care benefits are examined in detail.

SINGLE-PERSON HOUSEHOLDS

- **Demographics of people who live alone**

http://www.census.gov/population/www/socdemo/hh-fam/cps2006.html

On this web page you can access the range of Census Bureau data on households and families. Many tables include data on the demographic characteristics of people who live alone.

- **Spending of people who live alone**

http://www.bls.gov/cex/home.htm

The Consumer Expenditure Survey collects annual data on household spending, some of it accessible at this site. Scroll down the page until you get to the section on "Current Standard Tables" and click on the table entitled "Size of consumer unit." This table contains summary spending data by size of household, including people who live alone.

SLEEP

- **American Time Use Survey**

http://www.bls.gov/tus/home.htm

This is the home page of the American Time Use Survey, a government initiative that measures the amount of time people spend doing everything from sleeping to watching television during an average day. The survey results, released annually, show how much people sleep by a variety of demographic characteristics. It also reveals differences in the amount of time devoted to sleep on weekdays versus weekends.

- **National Sleep Foundation**

http://www.sleepfoundation.org/

Each year since 1995, the nonprofit National Sleep Foundation has surveyed the sleep habits of Americans. The latest findings from the Sleep in America poll are available here.

How Much Time Do We Spend Shopping?

How about working, sleeping, or eating? We know how much time we spend on these activities thanks to the American Time Use Survey. In taking the survey, government researchers interview a representative sample of Americans aged 15 or older, asking them what they did, minute by minute, during the past 24 hours. The results reveal how the public balances work and family, how husbands and wives share household chores, how much time parents spend caring for children, and whether people spend more time reading books or playing on the computer. Some of the survey's findings:

- **Shopping:** During an average weekend day, 45 percent of people aged 15 or older shop for consumer goods. The shoppers spend an average of two hours in stores, online, or thumbing through catalogs.

- **Sleeping:** The average person sleeps 8.3 hours on weekdays and 9.3 hours on weekends.

- **Eating:** Teenagers spend the least time eating and drinking, an average of 1.07 hours per day. People aged 75 or older spend the most time eating and drinking, 1.50 hours a day.

- **Working:** Employed men work 8.04 hours per day on average. Employed women work 7.04 hours per day.

- **Child care:** In households with preschoolers, mothers average 2.58 hours a day caring for children; fathers devote 1.22 hours to caring for children.

- **Television:** On an average weekend day, people aged 65 or older spend more than 4 hours watching television. Teenagers average only 2.45 hours.

The government examines time use by sex, age, employment status, and presence and age of children at home. The American Time Use Survey is an important contribution to our national self-image.

SMOKING

• Behavioral Risk Factor Surveillance System

http://www.cdc.gov/brfss/

This annual survey collects data nationally and by state on the health behaviors of adults, including tobacco use.

• Gateway at the Centers for Disease Control

http://www.cdc.gov/tobacco/data_statistics/index.htm

This is the Centers for Disease Control's gateway to government information on tobacco use, with links to many surveys and statistics.

• High school students

http://www.monitoringthefuture.org/

The annual Monitoring the Future survey fielded by the Institute for Social Research at the University of Michigan tracks the behavior and attitudes of American 8th, 10th, and 12th graders toward alcohol, drugs, and tobacco.

• Summary Health Statistics reports

http://www.cdc.gov/nchs/nhis.htm

In the annual report *Summary Health Statistics for U.S. Adults*, available on this page, you can access tables on cigarette smoking by a variety of demographic characteristics. Tables 24 and 25 have the numbers, based on the National Health Interview Survey.

• Youth Risk Behavioral Surveillance System

http://www.cdc.gov/HealthyYouth/yrbs/

Every two years the Youth Risk Behavioral Surveillance System examines the behavior of 9th through 12th graders nationally and by state. Drug, tobacco, and alcohol use are examined.

SOCIAL SECURITY

• AARP research

http://www.aarp.org/research/socialsecurity/

AARP is one of the best sources of information about the Social Security program. This address is the gateway to the AARP's Social Security surveys, reports, and fact sheets.

• Employee Benefit Research Institute

http://www.ebri.org/media/findings/index.cfm?fa=ssFindings

This address is the access point to the Employee Benefit Research Institute's many studies and analysis of the Social Security system. It also contains links to other sources of information about Social Security.

- **Retirement Confidence Survey**

http://www.ebri.org/surveys/rcs/

The Retirement Confidence Survey, sponsored by the Employee Benefit Research Institute and Mathew Greenwald & Associates, can be accessed at this site. The survey of 1,000 nationally representative people aged 25 or older has been conducted annually since 1996. Each year the survey probes people's attitudes toward Social Security and asks workers how important they think Social Security income will be in retirement.

- **Social Security Administration**

http://www.ssa.gov/policy/

What better place to explore the facts about Social Security than the program's official web site. This is the portal to the Social Security Administration's statistical information on Social Security. At this site you can access the *Annual Statistical Supplement*, with data on beneficiaries and average monthly benefits by age, sex, race, and more.

SOUTH CAROLINA

- **State Data Center**

http://www.ors.state.sc.us/

At this web site you can access the range of demographic and economic statistics for South Carolina, including current population estimates, population projections, 2000 census data, and American Community Survey numbers. Local area data are also available here.

SOUTH DAKOTA

- **State Data Center**

http://www.usd.edu/sdsdc/

At this web site you can access demographic and economic statistics for South Dakota, including current population estimates, population projections, and 2000 census data. Local area data are also available here.

SPANISH, SPOKEN AT HOME

- **American Community Survey**

http://factfinder.census.gov/home/saff/main.html?_lang=en

The American Community Survey collects annual data on language spoken at home. To see the latest information, go to this site—the Census Bureau's Fact Finder Page. Click "get data" under "American Community Survey," then click "Subject Tables." Select your geography, then click "next." On the Subject Table page, scroll down to the tables on Origins and Language: "Characteristics of People by Language Spoken at Home" and "Language Spoken at Home."

- **Gateway at the Census Bureau**

http://www.census.gov/population/www/socdemo/lang_use.html

This site is the Census Bureau's gateway to information on language spoken at home.

- **Hispanic attitudes toward language**

http://pewhispanic.org/

The Pew Hispanic Center tracks the attitudes of the Hispanic population. One topic explored by the organization is language. The analysis *English Usage among Hispanics in the United States*, for example, explores the fluency of immigrants and native-born Hispanics by generation.

SPENDING

- **100 Years of Consumer Spending**

http://www.bls.gov/opub/uscs/home.htm

This is where you can access the Bureau of Labor Statistics report *100 Years of U.S. Consumer Spending: Data for the Nation, New York City, and Boston*. The report draws on a wide range of consumer expenditure data to present a 100-year history of significant changes in consumer spending in the country as a whole, New York City, and Boston.

- **Consumer Expenditure Survey**

http://www.bls.gov/cex/

This is the site of the Bureau of Labor Statistics Consumer Expenditure Survey (CEX), which releases annual data on household spending. Summary statistics back to 1984 are available here. The data are shown by a variety of demographic characteristics such as age of householder, household type, and household income. Detailed spending data from the CEX are available only by special request.

SPORTS

- **National Sporting Goods Association**

http://www.nsga.org/i4A/pages/index.cfm?pageid=3346

This link takes you to the National Sporting Goods Association's annual sports participation survey. Here you can download the latest data on participation in a variety of sports by children and adults. Trends are also available.

STANDARD OF LIVING

- **100 Years of Consumer Spending**

http://www.bls.gov/opub/uscs/home.htm

This is where you can access the Bureau of Labor Statistics report *100 Years U.S. Consumer Spending: Data for the Nation, New York City, and Boston*. The report draws on consumer

How Much Does Gasoline Matter?

The price of gasoline is frequently in the news because gasoline is one of the biggest items in the household budget—and that was true even before prices soared. Gasoline is more costly to the average household than clothing, federal income tax, or health insurance. According to the Consumer Expenditure Survey, here are the top ten expenditures for the average household in 2006 (the latest data available):

1. Social Security deductions ($3,811)

2. Mortgage interest ($3,461) or rent ($2,437)

3. Vehicle purchases ($3,417)

4. Groceries ($2,785)

5. Restaurant meals ($2,249)

6. Gasoline ($2,227)

7. Clothes ($1,874)

8. Federal income tax ($1,711)

9. Property tax ($1,649)

10. Health insurance ($1,465)

Gasoline ranks a lofty sixth—and that was in 2006, when the average price of one gallon of gasoline was still below $3.00. Ouch.

expenditure data and census reports to present a 100-year history of significant changes in consumer spending in the country as a whole, New York City, and Boston.

- **Consumer Price Indexes**

http://www.bls.gov/cpi/home.htm

On this web page you gain access to the government's consumer price indexes over time, item by item. Examine the government's tabulated data or create custom tables.

- **Extended Measures of Well-Being**

http://www.sipp.census.gov/sipp/p70s/p70s.html

The Census Bureau report series *Extended Measures of Well-Being: Living Conditions in the United States* can be accessed from this page. The reports, based on results from the Survey of Income and Program Participation, examine our standard of living by a variety of measures that go beyond income. They are ownership of appliances and electronic goods, housing conditions, neighborhood conditions, ability to meet basic needs, expectation of help should needs arise.

STATE DEMOGRAPHICS

- **American Community Survey**

http://factfinder.census.gov/home/saff/main.html?_lang=en

The American Community Survey collects annual data by state. To see the latest information, go to this site—the Census Bureau's Fact Finder Page. Click "get data" under "American Community Survey," then click "Data Profiles." Select a state, and you can retrieve the latest available demographic and socioeconomic data.

- **Population estimates**

http://www.census.gov/popest/states/

Each year the Census Bureau's population estimates program publishes population estimates for states. The data include estimates of births, deaths, and migration.

- **State and County QuickFacts**

http://quickfacts.census.gov/qfd

This link takes you to an interactive map of the United States where you click on a state and pull up a demographic snapshot of the state based on the range of Census Bureau data. Comparisons with national totals are shown alongside the state data. Once on a state page, you can select a county or city within the state. Comparisons with state totals are shown alongside the local data.

- **State and Metropolitan Area Data Book**

http://www.census.gov/compendia/smadb/

Before the era of the Internet, the *State and Metropolitan Area Data Book* was an eagerly anticipated compendium of facts. Published every few years, it offered metropolitan area demographic and economic data not easily accessible elsewhere. The 2006 edition, which can be downloaded from this site, updates the previous volume published in 1997-98. Since publication of the earlier edition, the *State and Metropolitan Area Data Book* has been upstaged not only by easy access to government data online, but also by the new American Community Survey, which updates state and metropolitan area demographic data every year. Nevertheless, the *State and Metropolitan Area Data Book* still has much to offer. Not only does it include data not collected by the American Community Survey, but it puts all the facts together in one handy place.

- **State Data Centers**

http://www.census.gov/sdc/www/

Through this Census Bureau web site you can access its network of State Data Centers, which are repositories of state and local demographic and economic information. Just click on a state to retrieve its data center links. The first-listed center is the primary repository.

STATISTICS, DEMOGRAPHIC

- **Census Bureau**

http://www.census.gov/

Love demographics but don't know quite what you're looking for? Then stop by the Census Bureau's home page, where the entire range of demographic data is at your fingertips.

- **Statistical Abstract**

http://www.census.gov/compendia/statab/

The premier book of numbers, the *Statistical Abstract of the United States*, is at this site, which provides direct access to the latest and earlier editions of the *Abstract* (all the way back to 1878). The *Abstract* is the authoritative and comprehensive summary of statistics on the social, political, and economic organization of the United States. Use the *Abstract* as a convenient volume for statistical reference and as a guide to sources of more information both in print and on the web.

STOCKS

- **Investment Company Institute**

http://www.ici.org/stats/res/index.html

The Investment Company Institute represents more than 9,000 mutual funds. Its web site offers reports on the demographics of mutual fund shareholders based on the Institute's proprietary surveys.

- **Survey of Consumer Finances**

http://www.federalreserve.gov/pubs/oss/oss2/scfindex.html

The Federal Reserve Board's Survey of Consumer Finances, taken every three years, can be accessed at this site. The SCF is the only comprehensive source of data on the wealth of Americans at the household level. Here you can download the latest analysis detailing household assets, including stock ownership. Historical data back to 1989 are also available.

STUDENTS, ATTITUDES OF

- **The American Freshman Survey**

http://www.gseis.ucla.edu/heri/heri.html

At this site you can order results from the latest American freshman survey. Sponsored by the Higher Education Research Institute at UCLA's Graduate School of Education and Information Studies, the well-known survey of college freshmen has been taken annually for more than 40 years. The site itself does not offer a lot of data, but you can download the press release and a few charts from the most recent survey. For $25 you can order the annual publication *The American Freshman: National Norms*.

SUBSTANCE ABUSE

- **Gateway at the National Center for Health Statistics**

http://www.cdc.gov/nchs/fastats/druguse.htm

This page is a gateway to the government's many statistics on illegal drug use.

- **High school students**

http://www.monitoringthefuture.org/

The Monitoring the Future Survey fielded by the Institute for Social Research at the University of Michigan tracks the behavior and attitudes of American 8th, 10th, and 12th graders toward alcohol, drugs, and tobacco.

- **National Survey on Drug Use and Health**

http://oas.samhsa.gov/nsduh.htm

This annual survey of illegal drug use by Americans aged 12 or older provides detailed data by drug and by demographic characteristic.

- **Youth Risk Behavioral Surveillance System**

http://www.cdc.gov/HealthyYouth/yrbs/

Every two years the Youth Risk Behavioral Surveillance System examines the behavior of 9th through 12th graders nationally and by state. Alcohol, drug, and tobacco use are examined.

T

TAXES

• Internal Revenue Service

http://www.irs.gov/taxstats/index.html

The Internal Revenue Service's Tax Stats web site shows you the numbers behind the headaches, with statistics on individual as well as business and nonprofit tax returns. The IRS allows you to search for information by topic (estate tax returns, sole proprietorships, etc.) or by tax form (1040, Schedule C, etc.). Some tax data are available for geographic areas as small as individual zip codes.

TECHNOLOGY

• Cell-phone-only households

http://www.cdc.gov/nchs/nhis.htm

Sometimes the most interesting bits of information come from unlikely places. The National Health Interview Survey is a source of information on cell-phone only households. Scroll down this page, which lists reports from the NHIS, to *Wireless Substitution: Estimates from the National Health Interview Survey* for the latest numbers. The survey tracks cell-phone-only use because of the growing difficulty of surveying Americans by landline phone.

• Historical data on computer ownership

http://www.census.gov/population/www/socdemo/computer.html

For historical data on household computer ownership and use, the Census Bureau has data that can be accessed here.

• Pew Internet & American Life Project

http://www.pewinternet.org/

The Pew Internet & American Life Project produces reports that explore the impact of computers and the Internet. At this site you can access historical and current survey data revealing what Americans do online. You can also take The Internet Typology Test to find out what kind of information technology user you are.

TEENAGERS

• Drug, alcohol, and tobacco use

http://www.monitoringthefuture.org/

The annual Monitoring the Future Survey by the Institute for Social Research at the University of Michigan tracks the behavior and attitudes of American 8th, 10th, and 12th graders toward alcohol, drugs, and tobacco.

• Family life

http://www.census.gov/population/www/socdemo/2004_detailedtables.html

This site allows you to access the many tables of data on the family life of children from the Census Bureau's series entitled *A Child's Day*. Most of the tables examine teenagers (aged 12 to 17) separately from younger children. Topics include subjects such as enrollment in honors classes, participation in after-school sports and clubs, and parents' feelings toward their children. The data are from the Census Bureau's Survey of Income and Program Participation.

• Youth Indicators

http://nces.ed.gov/programs/youthindicators/

Every few years the National Center for Education Statistics publishes a comprehensive analysis of the state of American youth. The first report was published in 1988 and the latest in 2005, examining the demographics, school-related characteristics, employment-related characteristics, and extracurricular activities of people aged 14 to 24. You can access those reports here.

• Youth labor force

http://www.bls.gov/news.release/youth.toc.htm

Every year the Bureau of Labor Statistics takes a look at the summertime youth labor force. For tables with the most current statistics and trends, go to this site.

• Youth Risk Behavioral Surveillance System

http://www.cdc.gov/HealthyYouth/yrbs/

Every two years the Youth Risk Behavioral Surveillance System examines the behavior of 9th through 12th graders nationally and by state. Alcohol, drug, and tobacco use are examined.

TELEPHONES

• Cell-phone-only households

http://www.cdc.gov/nchs/nhis.htm

Sometimes the most interesting bits of information come from unlikely places. The National Health Interview Survey is a source of information on cell-phone-only households. Scroll down this page, which lists reports from the NHIS, to *Wireless Substitution: Estimates from the*

National Health Interview Survey for the latest numbers. The survey tracks cell-phone-only use because of the growing difficulty of surveying Americans by landline phone.

- **Occasional surveys from Pew**

http://www.pewinternet.org/index.asp

The Pew Internet & American Life Project, one of the eight Pew Research Center groups, surveys the public about its computer and Internet use. Occasionally, it produces reports on cell phone use, which you can find here.

TELEVISION AUDIENCE

- **Project for Excellence in Journalism**

http://www.journalism.org/by_the_numbers/

The Project for Excellence in Journalism collects and analyzes statistics on the audience for network, cable, and local television. Choose your sector and see the demographic trends including the audience for morning and evening news and the median age of viewers.

TEMPORARY WORKERS

- **Bureau of Labor Statistics**

http://www.bls.gov/news.release/conemp.nr0.htm

Temporary workers are included under "contingent and alternative workers." They are defined as those who do not expect their jobs to last or who reported that their jobs were temporary. The Current Population Survey has been collecting data on these workers since 1995 and the results can be found at this Bureau of Labor Statistics' site.

TENNESSEE

- **State Data Center**

http://cber.bus.utk.edu/

At this web site you can access demographic and economic statistics for Tennessee, including current population estimates, population projections, employment statistics, and 2000 census data. Local area data are also available here.

TENURE, JOB

- **Bureau of Labor Statistics**

http://www.bls.gov/news.release/tenure.toc.htm

Want to know how long workers have been at their current job? The Bureau of Labor Statistics tracks employee tenure by age, sex, race and Hispanic origin, occupation, and education. Get the numbers here.

TEXAS

• State Data Center

http://txsdc.utsa.edu/

At this web site you can access demographic statistics for Texas, including current population estimates, population projections, and 2000 census data. Local area data are also available here.

TIME USE

• American Time Use Survey

http://www.bls.gov/tus/home.htm

This is the home page of the American Time Use Survey, a government initiative that measures the amount of time people spend doing everything from sleeping to watching television during an average day. The survey results, released annually, show how people spend their time by demographic characteristics such as age, sex, education, presence of children, and marital and labor force statuses. It also examines time use on weekdays and weekends.

TOBACCO USE

• Behavioral Risk Factor Surveillance System

http://www.cdc.gov/brfss/

This annual survey collects data nationally and by state on the health behaviors of adults, including tobacco use.

• Gateway at the Centers for Disease Control

http://www.cdc.gov/tobacco/data_statistics/index.htm

This is the Centers for Disease Control's gateway to the government's information on tobacco use, with links to many surveys and statistics.

• High school students

http://www.monitoringthefuture.org/

The annual Monitoring the Future survey fielded by the Institute for Social Research at the University of Michigan tracks the behavior and attitudes of American 8th, 10th, and 12th graders toward alcohol, drugs, and tobacco.

• Summary Health Statistics reports

http://www.cdc.gov/nchs/nhis.htm

In the annual report, *Summary Health Statistics for U.S. Adults*, available on this page, you can access tables on cigarette smoking by a variety of demographic characteristics. Tables 24 and 25 have the numbers, based on the National Health Interview Survey.

Who Does the Laundry?

Most women now work, and consequently men are doing more around the house. But women still shoulder the burden of household chores. Which chores are most likely to be done by women?

Number one is the laundry. On an average day, a substantial 26 percent of women do the laundry. This compares with only 7 percent of men, according to an analysis of the American Time Use Survey. Women are four times more likely than men to do the laundry. Which women are most often in the laundry room? Not surprisingly, women aged 35 to 44—the ones with the most children at home. On an average day, 33 percent of women aged 35 to 44 are doing the laundry, making it one of the most time consuming activities for women in the age group. Those doing the laundry spend more than an hour washing, drying, folding, and ironing clothes.

Other chores predominantly shouldered by women are housecleaning and kitchen cleanup. On an average day, 36 percent of women and 13 percent of men clean the house. Thirty-two percent of women and 11 percent of men clean up in the kitchen.

Some household chores are more likely to be tackled by men, such as lawn care. On an average day, 12 percent of men and 9 percent of women care for their lawn, garden, or houseplants. Men are still more likely than women to work at a paying job. Fifty-three percent of men and 41 percent of women work on an average day.

- **Youth Risk Behavioral Surveillance System**

http://www.cdc.gov/HealthyYouth/yrbs/

Every two years the Youth Risk Behavioral Surveillance System examines the behavior of 9th through 12th graders nationally and by state. Drug, tobacco, and alcohol use are examined.

TRACT DATA (CENSUS)

- **Census Bureau**

http://www.census.gov/geo/www/tractez.html

If you need demographic data by census tract, this is the place to start. This site explains how to determine a census tract number from a street address and guides you in retrieving the demographic information.

TRAINING, JOB

- **Adult education**

http://nces.ed.gov/nhes/

From this page you can access reports with data from the adult education portion of the National Household Education Survey. This survey is fielded every few years to measure participation in educational activities ranging from early childhood programs to work-related adult education courses.

- **Occupational Outlook Handbook**

http://www.bls.gov/oco/home.htm

This is the home page for the *Occupational Outlook Handbook*, the government's continuously updated reference on hundreds of occupations, including training requirements, earnings, and employment projections.

TRANSPORTATION

- **American Public Transportation Association**

http://www.apta.com/research/stats/factbook/index.cfm

Each year the American Public Transportation Association publishes the *Public Transportation Fact Book* with statistics on the use of public transportation in the United States.

- **Bureau of Transportation Statistics**

http://www.bts.gov/

The Bureau of Transportation Statistics web site has the latest on the nation's transportation system, from cars and trains to ships and planes. Occasional reports have some demographic breakdowns.

TRAVEL

- **National Household Travel Survey**

http://www.bts.gov/programs/national_household_travel_survey/

This is the home page for the National Household Travel Survey, sponsored by the Bureau of Transportation Statistics and the Federal Highway Administration. The survey, taken in 2001, collected information on both long-distance and local travel by Americans and extensive demographic detail is available.

- **Office of Travel & Tourism Industries**

http://tinet.ita.doc.gov/

Here you can retrieve the government's official statistics on travel and tourism to and from the United States. While many of the reports listed here are for sale, some free data are available. There are few breakdowns of travelers by demographic characteristic, however.

- **Travel Industry Association**

http://www.tia.org/pressmedia/domestic_a_to_z.html

This web page, Travel Trends from A to Z, contains an alphabetical listing of interesting findings about travel based on the many surveys and studies done by the Travel Industry Association. Those studies are available for sale on the site.

TRAVEL TO WORK

- **2000 Census**

http://www.census.gov/population/www/socdemo/journey.html

At this site you can access detailed census data on the journey to work.

- **American Community Survey**

http://factfinder.census.gov/home/saff/main.html?_lang=en

The American Community Survey collects annual data on commuting. To see the latest information, go to this site—the Census Bureau's Fact Finder Page. Click "get data" under "American Community Survey," then click "Subject Tables." Scroll down to the section on Transportation and download the table "Commuting Characteristics by Sex."

TRIBES, AMERICAN INDIAN

- **2000 Census**

http://www.census.gov/population/www/cen2000/briefs.html

On this page, scroll down to Census 2000 Special Report 28, *We The People: American Indians and Alaskan Natives in the United States*. This will give you an overview of the American Indian population by tribe as of 2000.

How Many Own a Vacation Home?

You are not the only one without a vacation home retreat after a hard week of work. The percentage of Americans who own a vacation home is tiny, and contrary to expectations, the vacation home market has not swelled with customers as boomers have entered the peak owning age groups. For the past 50 years, vacation homes have accounted for the same small share of the nation's housing stock—just 3 percent.

On any given day, 18 million housing units sit vacant across the country—enough empty space to house the populations of the nation's three largest metropolitan areas (New York, Los Angeles, and Chicago) with room to spare. Most of these vacant units are for sale or rent. Only 4 million are what the government calls "seasonal"—occupied only a few weeks a year. These are the nation's vacation homes.

To the disappointment of the real estate industry, the vacation home market has not expanded as was expected with the aging of the population. The demographics promised much but, so far, have delivered little. The percentage of households that own a vacation home rises with age of householder to a peak of 6 percent in the 55-to-64 age group, which is now filling with the large baby-boom generation. But no crush of buyers has appeared so far, forcing real estate pundits to massage the numbers by adding investment properties and timeshares to the mix when reporting on the trends.

Why such a lackluster showing? Many of the middle aged are too squeezed by stagnant wages and rising costs to even think about taking on another mortgage payment. But if they did, where would they be most likely to find such a retreat? Not at the Hamptons or South Beach. The three states in which vacation homes account for the largest percentage of housing units are Maine (16 percent), Vermont (15 percent), and New Hampshire (10 percent).

TUITION, COLLEGE

- **American Community Survey**

http://factfinder.census.gov/home/saff/main.html?_lang=en

The American Community Survey provides annual statistics on the population by Indian tribe. To retrieve the information, go to this site—the Census Bureau's Fact Finder page. Click on "get data" under "American Community Survey." On the next page, click on the "Selected Population Profiles" link. On the next page, specify the desired geography (for national totals, just click "add" and "next"). On the following page, select the desired American Indian tribe. One more click and you have the latest demographic profile. You can also create custom tables of American Community Survey data via the "Custom Table" link.

TUITION, COLLEGE

- **College Board**

http://www.collegeboard.com/student/pay/add-it-up/4494.html

On this page you can access the College Board's annual publication *Trends in College Pricing*, with the latest available data on college costs by type of institution. Historical data are also included in the publication.

- **National Center for Education Statistics**

http://nces.ed.gov/pubsearch/pubsinfo.asp?pubid=2006186

Everyone knows college costs are in the stratosphere and rising. But few pay full freight to go to school. This report from the National Center for Education Statistics, *Student Financing of Undergraduate Education: 2003–04*, reveals how much families actually pay, out of pocket, to send their kids to school—or what the NCES calls the net price of attendance.

TURNOVER (LABOR)

- **Bureau of Labor Statistics**

http://www.bls.gov/jlt/

The results of the Job Openings and Labor Turnover Survey, which produces data on job openings, hires, and separations (or turnover), are available here.

U

UNEMPLOYMENT

- **National statistics**

http://www.bls.gov/cps/

This is the gateway to the federal government's voluminous statistics on employment and unemployment, based on data from the Current Population Survey. The CPS is a monthly survey of households whose primary purpose is to provide official data on the labor force. On this page you can find links to the latest monthly, quarterly, and annual data on unemployment. For a detailed look at the demographics of the unemployed, scroll down to the "Annual Averages—Household Data" section entitled "Characteristics of the Unemployed."

- **Employment statistics from the Current Employment Statistics Program**

http://www.bls.gov/ces/home.htm
http://www.bls.gov/sae/home.htm

Each month the Current Employment Statistics program surveys about 150,000 businesses and government agencies, representing approximately 390,000 individual worksites, in order to provide detailed industry data on employment, hours, and earnings of workers on nonfarm payrolls nationally (available at the first URL), and for all 50 states and over 300 metropolitan areas (available at the second URL).

- **State and local area employment statistics from the Current Population Survey**

http://www.bls.gov/lau/#data

Here you can access local area employment, unemployment, and labor force data from the Current Population Survey, a monthly survey of households. The data are available for regions and divisions, states, counties, metropolitan areas, and many cities.

UNION MEMBERS

- **Bureau of Labor Statistics**

http://stats.bls.gov/news.release/union2.toc.htm

Annual data on union membership are available at this site. Not only can you download the latest data on the union affiliation of employed wage and salary workers by demographic characteristic, but also their median weekly earnings.

UNMARRIED PARTNERS

• Current statistics

http://www.census.gov/population/www/socdemo/hh-fam/cps2006.html

This site will provide you with the latest numbers on unmarried couples from the Census Bureau's Current Population Survey. Scroll down to the bottom of the page and download tables H3, UC1, UC2, and UC3 for the numbers.

• Historical statistics

http://www.census.gov/population/www/socdemo/hh-fam.html

Here you can find historical data on the number of unmarried couples in the United States. Scroll down to the Historical Time Series Tables on the living arrangements of adults, and download table UC-1 for the numbers.

URBAN

• Census Bureau

http://www.census.gov/geo/www/ua/ua_2k.html

Urban is not the same as metropolitan. If you need to know the definition of urban and access data on urban areas, then this site will give you the information you need.

UTAH

• State Data Center

http://www.governor.utah.gov/dea/sdc.html

At this web site you can access demographic and economic statistics for Utah, including current population estimates, population projections, employment statistics, and 2000 census data. Local area data are also available here.

V

VACATION DAYS

• Bureau of Labor Statistics

http://www.bls.gov/ncs/ebs/home.htm

Get the facts about employee benefits, including vacation days, from the Bureau of Labor Statistics' National Compensation Survey here. This annual survey examines the entire range of employee benefits provided by the nation's private companies. Retirement and health care benefits are examined in detail.

VEHICLES

• American Community Survey

http://factfinder.census.gov/home/saff/main.html?_lang=en

The Census Bureau's annual American Community Survey has national, state, and local information on vehicles available to workers and households by a variety of characteristics. To see the latest information, go to this site—the Census Bureau's Fact Finder Page. Click "get data" under "American Community Survey," then select "Custom Table." On the next page, select your desired geography, and on the following page choose a table "By Keyword" and use "vehicle" as the keyword. You can then select from among a number of tables on vehicle availability.

VERMONT

• State Data Center

http://crs.uvm.edu/census/

At this web site you can access demographic and economic statistics for Vermont, including current population estimates and 2000 census data. Local area data are also available here.

VETERANS

• Department of Veterans Affairs

http://www1.va.gov/vetdata/page.cfm?pg=15

This address will take you to the Veteran's Administration site that provides a variety of current and projected demographics of the nation's veterans. You can download national, state, and county data on veterans by age, sex, period of service, race, disability status, etc. Projections of the number of veterans to 2036 are also available at this site.

Who Is the Average Voter?

Politicians on both sides of the aisle try to portray themselves as in touch with the average American. In truth, however, they only need to be in touch with the average voter—who is different from the average American. Here is a look at some of those differences.

The average voter is older. The median age of voters is 48, well above the median age of 36 for the average American. Voters are older because young adults are least likely to vote. In the 2004 presidential election, only 39 percent of 18-year-olds went to the polls (the lowest turnout among age groups). In contrast, 73 percent of 74-year-olds voted (the highest turnout).

The average voter is more likely to be white. Among voters in the 2004 presidential election, 79 percent were non-Hispanic white. Among the U.S. population as a whole, a smaller 67 percent are non-Hispanic white. Non-Hispanic whites account for a larger share of voters because they are more likely to vote than blacks or Hispanics.

The average voter is richer. Among voters in 2004, median family income stood at $69,242. This was 31 percent greater than the $52,680 median of all families in 2004.

- **Employment**

http://www.bls.gov/news.release/vet.toc.htm

Here you can examine detailed data on the employment of veterans by a variety of demographic characteristics.

VIRGINIA

- **State Data Center**

http://www.vec.virginia.gov/vecportal/index.cfm

At this web site you can access demographic and economic statistics for Virginia, including population projections, employment statistics, and 2000 census data. Local area data are also available here.

VITAL STATISTICS

- **National Center for Health Statistics**

http://www.cdc.gov/nchs/nvss.htm

Everything you could possibly want to know about the nation's births, deaths, and life expectancy is available from the federal government's official repository of such information. Links to reports and statistics on births and deaths as well as information about how the data are collected and categorized are all here.

VOLUNTEERING

- **Bureau of Labor Statistics**

http://www.bls.gov/news.release/volun.toc.htm

This is the place to go for the latest data on volunteering. The data come from a Bureau of Labor Statistics' supplement to the Current Population Survey, which asks respondents whether they had volunteered in the past year, how many hours they volunteered, the type of organization(s) for which they volunteered, the type of work performed, and why they volunteered. Those who did not volunteer were asked why not. The data are available by sex, age, race and Hispanic origin, education, marital status, presence of children, and employment status.

VOTING

- **Census Bureau**

http://www.census.gov/population/www/socdemo/voting.html

Every two years, after each national election, the Census Bureau surveys Americans to determine who voted. At this site you can access those data, which break down voters by age, sex, race and Hispanic origin, citizenship status, education, and more. The Census Bureau also examines how many did not vote, and it asks why people did not vote. The biggest single reason: they were too busy.

W

WAGES

• Annual earnings

http://pubdb3.census.gov/macro/032007/perinc/toc.htm

The latest annual earnings data from the Current Population Survey can be accessed at this site by downloading tables PINC-03 to PINC-07. The data are available by sex, race, and other demographic characteristics.

• Wage Statistics from the Current Employment Statistics Program

http://www.bls.gov/ces/home.htm

Each month the Current Employment Statistics program surveys about 150,000 businesses and government agencies, representing approximately 390,000 individual worksites, in order to provide detailed industry data on employment, hours, and earnings of workers on nonfarm payrolls nationally.

• Wage statistics from the Occupational Employment Statistics survey

http://www.bls.gov/bls/blswage.htm

From this site you can retrieve wage data from the Bureau of Labor Statistics' Occupational Employment Statistics Survey. The OES is a survey of the nation's business establishments, producing detailed estimates of earnings by occupation for the nation, regions, states, and metropolitan areas.

• Weekly earnings

http://www.bls.gov/cps/home.htm

This page is the gateway to accessing the latest labor force characteristics from the Current Population Survey, including median weekly earnings. Scroll down to "Annual Averages—Household Data" and click on tables 37, 38, and 39 for median weekly earnings data, including earnings by detailed occupation.

• Wives who earn more

http://www.census.gov/hhes/www/income/histinc/f22.html

This table has data on the number of wives who earn more than their husbands.

WASHINGTON

• **State Data Center**

http://www.ofm.wa.gov/pop/sdc/default.asp

At this web site you can access demographic and economic statistics for Washington, including current population estimates, employment statistics, and 2000 census data. Local area data are also available here.

WEALTH

• **Survey of Consumer Finances**

http://www.federalreserve.gov/pubs/oss/oss2/scfindex.html

The Federal Reserve Board's Survey of Consumer Finances, taken every three years, can be accessed at this site. The SCF is the only comprehensive source of data on the wealth of Americans at the household level. Here you can download the latest analysis detailing household net worth, assets, and debts. Historical data back to 1989 are also available.

WEEKENDS

• **Bureau of Labor Statistics**

http://www.bls.gov/tus/home.htm

This is the home page of the American Time Use Survey, a government initiative that measures the amount of time people spend doing everything from sleeping to watching television during an average day. The survey results, released annually, show how people spend their time by demographic characteristic such as age, sex, education, presence of children, and marital and labor force statuses. It also examines time use on weekdays and weekends.

WEIGHT

• **Measured weight, historical data**

http://www.cdc.gov/nchs/pressroom/04news/americans.htm

Here you can download the eye-opening report *Mean Body Weight, Height, and Body Mass Index*, which tells you just how much weight Americans have gained over the decades. From the early 1960s to 2002, the average weight of both men and women increased by 24 pounds. The data come from the National Health and Nutrition Examination Survey.

• **Measured weight, latest data**

http://www.cdc.gov/nchs/about/major/nhanes/nhanesmmwrs_obesity.htm

When asked to self-report their weight, most Americans say they weigh less than they really do. At this site you can access the latest data on how much men and women weigh, based on the National Health and Nutrition Examination Survey, which, rather than asking people how much they weigh, actually puts them on the scale and records the numbers.

Who Has Put on the Most Pounds?

Why have Americans gained so much weight? Many researchers are trying to answer that question. Perhaps the most interesting attempt at an explanation is a study by the National Bureau of Economic Research showing the more restaurants per capita, the greater a population's weight gain over the past 25 years (Working Paper 11584). The researchers cannot pinpoint exactly why weight gain is associated with restaurant density, but here's a theory: As fast food became part of the daily diet, and as the number of fast-food restaurants proliferated, Americans ate out more often and consumed more food when they ate out. The fierce competition among restaurants has created an arms race of sorts, boosting portion size. Average daily caloric intake has grown from 1,854 calories in the mid-1970s to 2,002 calories in the mid-1990s, say the NBER researchers.

According to the National Center for Health Statistics, the average woman gained 19 pounds and the average man gained 17 pounds between 1976–80 and 1999–2002. If you examine weight change by cohort, however, the trend is even more alarming. The middle aged have put on more weight than older Americans.

In 1976–80, the average man in his twenties weighed 168 pounds. By 1999–2002, the same man (now in his forties or early fifties) weighed 196 pounds. During those years, he gained a whopping 28 pounds. Now look at his older counterpart. A man in his forties in 1976–80 had gained only 12 additional pounds by 1999–2002.

For women, it gets worse. Women in their twenties in 1976–80 had gained an average of 33 pounds by the time they were in their forties and early fifties in 1999–2002—a greater weight gain than among men and more than double the increase experienced by older women. Women in their forties in 1976–80 had gained only 16 additional pounds by 1999–02.

Why have the middle aged gained more weight than older Americans over the past quarter century? One reason could be that women's rising labor fore participation rate results in more restaurant meals. Unfortunately, struggles with weight appear to be intensifying. The average woman now in her twenties weighs 21 pounds more than today's middle-aged women had weighed as young adults. The average man now in his twenties weighs 16 pounds more than his middle-aged counterpart had at the same age. If young adults gain weight at the same rate as the middle aged did over the past few decades, then the obesity epidemic has only just begun.

- **Self-reported weight**

http://www.cdc.gov/nchs/nhis.htm

In the annual report *Summary Health Statistics for U.S. Adults*, available on this page, you can access tables on body mass index based on self-reported weight and height by a variety of demographic characteristics. Tables 30 and 31 have the numbers, based on the National Health Interview Survey.

WELFARE

- **Annual data from the Current Population Survey**

http://pubdb3.census.gov/macro/032007/pov/toc.htm

On this page you can find data from the latest Current Population Survey on the number and percentage of people who participate in government poverty programs. Click on table POV-26, for example, to see statistics on people who receive food stamps, subsidized housing, and cash assistance by age, sex, and race.

- **Participation in government programs**

http://www.sipp.census.gov/sipp/p70s/p70s.html

On this page you can access a number of reports from the Census Bureau's Survey of Income and Program Participation. One series collects data on the public's participation in means-tested government programs such as TANF, food stamps, subsidized housing, and Medicaid. The latest, released in 2006, is entitled *Dynamics of Economic Well-Being: Participation in Government Programs, 2001 Through 2003: Who Gets Assistance?*

WELL-BEING

- **Economic**

http://www.sipp.census.gov/sipp/p70s/p70s.html

The Census Bureau report series *Extended Measures of Well-Being: Living Conditions in the United States* can be accessed from this page. The reports, based on results from the Survey of Income and Program Participation, examine our standard of living by a variety of measures that go beyond income. They are ownership of appliances and electronic goods, housing conditions, neighborhood conditions, ability to meet basic needs, expectation of help should needs arise.

- **Physical**

http://apps.nccd.cdc.gov/HRQOL/

If you want to know how good—or bad—Americans feel, then this web site is the place to start. The Centers for Disease Control and Prevention has a program in place to measure our health-related quality of life, with handy summary measures of unhealthy days, both physical and mental.

WEST VIRGINIA

• State Data Center

http://www.wvdo.org/business/statedatacenter.html

At this web site you can access demographic statistics for West Virginia from the 2000 census data. Local area data are also available here.

WHITES

• Demographics from the American Community Survey

http://factfinder.census.gov/home/saff/main.html?_lang=en

The American Community Survey provides annual statistics on the population by race and Hispanic origin. To retrieve the information, go to this site—the Census Bureau's Fact Finder page. Click on "get data" under "American Community Survey." On the next page, click on the "Selected Population Profiles" link. On the next page, specify the desired geography (if you want national totals, just click "add" and "next"). On the following page, select the desired race or Hispanic origin group. One more click and you have the latest demographic profile of whites.

• Estimates by age

http://www.census.gov/popest/national/asrh/

To get the latest numbers on the white population—including estimates of the size of the population by age—visit the Census Bureau's population estimates site.

• Health data from the Centers for Disease Control

http://www.cdc.gov/omhd/Populations/White.htm

For information on the health of the white population, this is the place to start. This page has links to a variety of statistics revealing the health of the white population, including information on health disparities.

• Income data

http://www.census.gov/hhes/www/income/dinctabs.html

Every March the Current Population Survey collects income data by race and Hispanic origin through the Annual Social and Economic Supplement. The gateway to the data for households, families, and persons is available here.

• Poverty data

http://www.census.gov/hhes/www/poverty/detailedpovtabs.html

Every year the Census Bureau measures the poverty population by race and Hispanic origin. The poverty estimates are based on income data collected by the Annual Social and Economic Supplement of the March Current Population Survey. The poverty tables are available here.

WIDOWS

- **Census Bureau**

http://www.census.gov/population/www/socdemo/marr-div.html

This address will take you to the Census Bureau's web page devoted to its data on marriage and divorce. Here you can access the report, *Number, Timing and Duration of Marriages and Divorces: 2004*, with data on the marital history of Americans including the percentage who have ever been widowed.

WILDLIFE-ASSOCIATED RECREATION

- **U.S. Fish & Wildlife Service**

http://www.census.gov/prod/www/abs/fishing.html

According to the 2006 National Survey of Fishing, Hunting, and Wildlife-Associated Recreation, nearly 88 million Americans fished, hunted, or watched wildlife in 2006. The survey, which has been conducted about every five years since 1955, explores Americans' participation in and spending on fishing, hunting, bird watching, animal feeding, and wildlife photography.

WISCONSIN

- **State Data Center**

http://www.doa.state.wi.us/section_detail.asp?linkcatid=11&linkid=64&locid=9

At this web site you can access demographic statistics for Wisconsin, including current population estimates, population projections, and 2000 census data. Local area data are also available here.

WOMEN

- **Business owners**

http://www.census.gov/csd/sbo/women2002.htm

The Survey of Business Owners, taken every five years as part of the Economic Census, provides details on women-owned businesses in the United States.

- **Educational opportunity**

http://nces.ed.gov/pubsearch/pubsinfo.asp?pubid=2005016

On this page you can access the report *Trends in Educational Equity of Girls & Women: 2004*. The report examines the extent to which males and females have access to the same educational opportunities, avail themselves equally of these opportunities, perform at similar levels throughout schooling, succeed at similar rates, and reap the same benefits from their educational experiences.

- **Estimates by age**

http://www.census.gov/popest/national/asrh/

To get the latest numbers on the female population, including estimates of the female population by age, race, and Hispanic origin, visit the Census Bureau's population estimates site.

- **Fertility, Family Planning, and Reproductive Health of Women**

http://www.cdc.gov/nchs/products/pubs/pubd/series/sr23/pre-1/sr23_25.htm

This page will take you to the comprehensive report *Fertility, Family Planning, and Reproductive Health of U.S. Women*, which examines the sexual and reproductive behavior of American women. The report is based on the 2002 National Survey of Family Growth, which asked women aged 15 to 44 about their sexual behavior, contraceptive use, fertility, and motherhood status. The NSFG, fielded every few years by the National Center for Health Statistics, also examines whether births were wanted or unwanted, maternity leave, and use of family planning services.

- **Health**

http://www.cdc.gov/nchs/fastats/womens_health.htm

This National Center for Health Statistics web page has links that take you to a variety of government sources with information about women's health, including their health status, risk factors, health care utilization, access to health care, mortality rates, etc.

- **Income**

http://pubdb3.census.gov/macro/032007/perinc/toc.htm

Taken in March every year, the Current Population Survey's Annual Social and Economic Supplement queries a large, nationally representative sample of Americans about their economic status in the previous year. From this data come the official income and poverty statistics produced by the federal government. The latest statistics on the incomes and earnings of women can be accessed here.

- **Labor force statistics, current**

http://www.bls.gov/cps/home.htm

This site is the federal government's central repository of data on the demographics of the labor force. Here you can get the latest data on women in the labor force, based on the Current Population Survey.

- **Labor force statistics, historical**

http://www.bls.gov/cps/wlf-databook2007.htm

On this page you can access the Bureau of Labor Statistics' report *Women in the Labor Force: A Databook*, a comprehensive guide to women's evolving employment situation. The report compiles a variety of labor force statistics on women including historical tables on women's labor force participation.

- **Marital history**

http://www.census.gov/population/www/socdemo/marr-div.html

This address will take you to the Census Bureau's web page devoted to its data on marriage and divorce. Here you can access the report *Number, Timing and Duration of Marriages and Divorces: 2004*, with data on the marital history of women including the percentage who have ever divorced.

- **Maternity leave**

http://www.census.gov/Press-Release/www/releases/archives/employment_occupations/011536.html

This Census Bureau report, *Maternity Leave and Employment Patterns, 1961–2003*, provides the most comprehensive data available on women's labor force participation before and after giving birth.

- **Poverty data**

http://www.census.gov/hhes/www/poverty/detailedpovtabs.html

Every year, the Census Bureau measures the poverty population by sex. The poverty estimates are based on income data collected by the Annual Social and Economic Supplement of the March Current Population Survey. The poverty tables are available here.

- **Women's earnings report**

http://www.bls.gov/cps/home.htm

On this page, scroll down to the report *Highlights of Women's Earnings in 2006*, a detailed profile of women's earnings in 2006 with comparisons to men's earnings by state, occupation, and a variety of demographic characteristics.

WORK

- **American Community Survey**

http://factfinder.census.gov/home/saff/main.html?_lang=en

The American Community Survey collects annual data on the labor force. To see the latest information, go to this site—the Census Bureau's Fact Finder Page. Click "get data" under "American Community Survey," then click "Subject Tables." Select your geography, then click "next." Scroll down to the section on employment to retrieve labor force data.

- **Demographics of the labor force**

http://www.bls.gov/cps/home.htm

This site is the federal government's central repository of data on the demographics of the labor force. Here you can access just about everything you would want to know about labor force topics, such as working mothers, the decline in long-term employment, and the characteristics of minimum wage workers. The site also provides access to the Bureau of Labor Statistics' annual average employment tables.

- **Employment statistics from the Current Employment Statistics Program**

http://www.bls.gov/ces/home.htm
http://www.bls.gov/sae/home.htm

Each month the Current Employment Statistics Program surveys about 150,000 businesses and government agencies, representing approximately 390,000 individual worksites, in order to provide detailed industry data on employment, hours, and earnings of workers on nonfarm payrolls nationally (available at the first URL), and for all 50 states and over 300 metropolitan areas (available at the second URL).

- **Gateway at the Bureau of Labor Statistics**

http://www.bls.gov/bls/employment.htm

This is the Bureau of Labor Statistics' gateway to its voluminous statistics on employment. Everything you want to know about employment and unemployment can be accessed through this web page.

- **Projections**

http://www.bls.gov/emp/home.htm

Every two years the Bureau of Labor Statistics issues updated employment projections. The latest are available at this site. The projections show big changes on the horizon as the workforce ages.

- **State and local area employment statistics from the Current Population Survey**

http://www.bls.gov/lau/#data

Here you can access local area employment, unemployment, and labor force data from the Current Population Survey, a monthly survey of households. The data are available for regions and divisions, states, counties, metropolitan areas, and many cities.

WORK ARRANGEMENTS

- **Bureau of Labor Statistics**

http://www.bls.gov/news.release/conemp.toc.htm

Every few years the Bureau of Labor Statistics collects data on the nontraditional workforce, which includes independent contractors, temporary workers, on-call workers, and contract workers. The data can be accessed at this site.

WORK-AT-HOME POPULATION

- **Bureau of Labor Statistics**

http://www.bls.gov/news.release/homey.toc.htm

For the government's most detailed data on the work-at-home population, visit this page. The latest numbers (for 2004) show that 15 percent of the nonagricultural workforce works at home at least once a week. The data are broken down by age, sex, occupation, industry, and reason for working at home.

WORK EXPERIENCE

• Demographics of full- and part-time workers

http://www.bls.gov/news.release/work.toc.htm

Here you can download tables showing hours of work for both full- and part-time workers. The data are shown by sex, race, and Hispanic origin.

• Earnings of full- and part-time workers

http://pubdb3.census.gov/macro/032007/perinc/toc.htm

The Current Population Survey collects data on earnings by full- and part-time work status. Go to this web page and click on table PINC-05.

WORK SCHEDULES

• Bureau of Labor Statistics

http://www.bls.gov/news.release/flex.toc.htm

More than 27 million full-time wage and salary workers had flexible work schedules that allowed them to vary the time they begin or end their work. This is one of the findings in the Workers on Flexible and Shift Schedules tabulations from the Bureau of Labor Statistics available at this site.

WORK TIME

• American Time Use Survey

http://www.bls.gov/tus/home.htm

This is the home page of the American Time Use Survey, a government initiative that measures the amount of time people spend doing everything from watching television to working during an average day. The survey results, released annually, show how people spend their time by demographic characteristic such as age, sex, education, presence of children, and marital and labor force statuses.

WORKING MOTHERS

• Employed parents

http://www.bls.gov/news.release/famee.toc.htm

Both mother and father are employed in 62 percent of the nation's nuclear families (married couples with children). This is just one of the findings in the Bureau of Labor Statistics' annual Employment Characteristics of Families tabulations, available at this site.

- **Maternity leave**

http://www.census.gov/Press-Release/www/releases/archives/employment_occupations/011536.html

This Census Bureau report, *Maternity Leave and Employment Patterns, 1961–2003*, provides the most comprehensive data available on women's labor force participation before and after giving birth.

- **Women in the Labor Force: A Databook**

http://www.bls.gov/cps/wlf-databook2007.htm

On this page you can access the Bureau of Labor Statistics' report *Women in the Labor Force: A Databook*, a comprehensive guide to women's evolving employment situation. The report compiles a variety of labor force statistics, including the labor force participation of women with children.

WORKING POOR

- **A Profile of the Working Poor**

http://www.bls.gov/cps/home.htm

On this page, scroll down to the report *A Profile of the Working Poor: 2005* for a detailed demographic profile of people with incomes below poverty level despite their participation in the workforce.

- **Poverty rate of full-time workers**

http://pubdb3.census.gov/macro/032007/pov/toc.htm

On this page you can find a number of tables on the working poor. Click on table POV-22 to download the percentage of full-time workers by age, sex, and race whose incomes are below poverty level.

WORKING, REASONS FOR NOT

- **Current Population Survey**

http://pubdb3.census.gov/macro/032007/pov/toc.htm

On this page you can find a number of tables on the working poor. Click on table POV-24 to download tables showing the reasons people did not work by sex, age, race, Hispanic origin, and type of family.

WORLD POPULATION

- **Central Intelligence Agency**

https://www.cia.gov/library/publications/the-world-factbook/index.html

If you want up-to-date demographic and political information on any nation in the world, check out the Central Intelligence Agency's *The World Factbook*. The online edition of the factbook is updated periodically throughout the year, and provides national-level data for countries, territories, and dependencies.

- **International Database at the Census Bureau**

http://www.census.gov/ipc/www/idb/

To access population statistics for just about any country, this is the place to start—the Census Bureau's International Database. The database is a computerized data bank containing statistical tables of demographic and socioeconomic information for 227 countries and areas of the world. Just pick a country and get the data, including population projections.

- **Population Reference Bureau**

http://www.prb.org/Datafinder.aspx

Here you can access the Population Reference Bureau's database of international demographic statistics. Select a country and a topic, and retrieve the numbers you need.

WYOMING

- **State Data Center**

http://eadiv.state.wy.us/

At this web site you can access the range of demographic and economic statistics for Wyoming, including current population estimates, population projections, employment statistics, 2000 census data, and American Community Survey numbers. Local area data are also available here.

Y

YOUTH

- **Drug, alcohol, and tobacco use**

http://www.monitoringthefuture.org/

The annual Monitoring the Future Survey by the Institute for Social Research at the University of Michigan tracks the behavior and attitudes of American 8th, 10th, and 12th graders toward alcohol, drugs, and tobacco.

- **Family life**

http://www.census.gov/population/www/socdemo/2004_detailedtables.html

This site allows you to access the many tables of data on the family life of children from the Census Bureau's series entitled *A Child's Day*. Most of the tables examine teenagers (aged 12 to 17) separately from younger children. Topics include subjects such as enrollment in honors classes, participation in after-school sports and clubs, and parents' feelings toward their children. The data are from the Census Bureau's Survey of Income and Program Participation.

- **Youth Indicators**

http://nces.ed.gov/programs/youthindicators/

Every few years the National Center for Education Statistics publishes a comprehensive analysis of the state of American youth. The first report was published in 1988 and the latest in 2005, examining the demographics, school-related characteristics, employment-related characteristics, and extracurricular activities of people aged 14 to 24. You can access those reports here.

- **Youth labor force**

http://www.bls.gov/news.release/youth.toc.htm

Every year the Bureau of Labor Statistics takes a look at the summertime youth labor force. For tables with the most current statistics and trends, go to this site.

- **Youth Risk Behavioral Surveillance System**

http://www.cdc.gov/HealthyYouth/yrbs/

Every two years the Youth Risk Behavioral Surveillance System examines the behavior of 9th through 12th graders nationally and by state. Alcohol, drug, and tobacco use are examined.

Z

ZIP CODE DEMOGRAPHICS

- **Census Bureau**

http://www.census.gov/epcd/www/zipstats.html

For those who need to know the demographics of zip codes, this Census Bureau web page will guide you to the 2000 census data. Here you can retrieve population, labor force, housing, and income data at these U.S. Post Office–defined areas. Business statistics by zip code from the 2002 Economic Censuses are also available here.

Appendix A

Major Demographic Surveys

Below is a list of major government, nonprofit, and proprietary surveys or data collection efforts that provide demographic information about the U.S. population. The data from these surveys are either freely available to the public or available for a nominal charge. This directory links users to results from all of these surveys.

American Community Survey

http://www.census.gov/acs/www/

The American Community Survey is an ongoing nationwide survey of 250,000 households per month, providing detailed demographic data at the community level. Designed to replace the census "long form" questionnaire, the ACS includes more than 60 questions that formerly appeared on the long form, such as ones concerning language spoken at home, income, and education. ACS data are available for areas as small as census tracts.

American Freshman Survey

http://www.gseis.ucla.edu/heri/cirpoverview.php

Each year the Higher Education Research Institute of the University of California–Los Angeles surveys approximately 400,000 entering freshmen during orientation or registration at 700 two-year colleges and four-year colleges and universities. The survey covers a wide range of student characteristics: parental income and education, ethnicity, and other demographic items; financial aid; secondary school achievement and activities; educational and career plans; and values, attitudes, beliefs, and self-concept. The survey has been conducted annually since 1966.

American Housing Survey

http://www.census.gov/hhes/www/housing/ahs/ahs.html

The American Housing Survey collects national and metropolitan-level data on the characteristics of the nation's housing, including apartments, single-family homes, and mobile homes. The Census Bureau conducts the nationally representative survey, based on a sample of 55,000 homes, for the Department of Housing and Urban Development every other year. The survey collects data on the physical characteristics of housing units and neighborhoods, the financial characteristics of mortgages, and the demographic characteristics of homeowners and renters.

American Religious Identification Survey

http://www.gc.cuny.edu/faculty/research_briefs/aris/aris_index.htm

The 2001 American Religious Identification Survey, sponsored by the Graduate Center of the City University of New York, was a random telephone survey of 50,281 households in the continental United States. Interviewers asked respondents aged 18 or older for their demographic characteristics and their religion. The 2001 ARIS updates the 1990 National Survey of Religious Identification.

American Time Use Survey

http://www.bls.gov/tus/home.htm

Under contract with the Bureau of Labor Statistics, the Census Bureau collects American Time Use Survey data, revealing how people spend their time. The ATUS sample is drawn from households completing their final month of interviews for the Current Population Survey. One individual from each selected household is chosen to participate. Respondents are interviewed by telephone about their time use during the previous 24 hours. About 26,300 households are included in the sample, with 13,300 completed interviews.

Behavioral Risk Factor Surveillance System

http://www.cdc.gov/brfss/

The Behavioral Risk Factor Surveillance System is a collaborative project of the Centers for Disease Control and Prevention and the states and territories of the United States. It is an ongoing data collection program designed to measure behavioral risk factors in the population aged 18 or older. All 50 states, three territories, and the District of Columbia take part in the survey, making the BRFSS the primary source of information on the health-related behaviors of Americans.

Census of Population and Housing

http://www.census.gov/main/www/cen2000.html

Every ten years, in years ending in 0, the Census Bureau conducts the Census of Population and Housing. Every household in the United States receives a census form by mail which it is required by law to fill out and return. In taking the 2000 census, some households received a "short form," which asked a limited number of questions (including sex, age, race and Hispanic origin, household relationship, and housing tenure). Other households received a "long form" which included the same short form questions plus additional ones about place of birth, educational attainment, ancestry, income, labor force participation, housing characteristics, and so on. The 2010 census will include only the short form questions because the American Community Survey now asks the "long form" questions on an annual basis.

Common Core of Data Program

http://nces.ed.gov/ccd/

The Common Core of Data program is the Department of Education's primary database on public elementary and secondary education in the United States. The program collects annual data—fiscal and nonfiscal—from every public school (approximately 97,000), public school district (approximately 18,000), and state education agency in the United States. The data are supplied by state education agency officials and include information that describes schools and school districts, including name, address, and phone number; descriptive information about students and staff, including demographics; and fiscal data, including revenues and current expenditures.

Consumer Expenditure Survey

http://www.bls.gov/cex/home.htm

The Consumer Expenditure Survey is an ongoing study of the day-to-day spending of American households administered by the Bureau of Labor Statistics. The CEX includes an interview survey and a diary survey. A separate, nationally representative sample is used for each survey. For the interview survey, about 7,500 consumer units are interviewed on a rotating panel basis each quarter for five consecutive quarters. For the diary survey, 7,500 consumer units keep weekly diaries of spending for two consecutive weeks.

Current Employment Statistics Survey

http://www.bls.gov/ces/home.htm
http://www.bls.gov/sae/home.htm

Each month the Bureau of Labor Statistics' Current Employment Statistics program surveys about 150,000 businesses and government agencies, representing approximately 390,000 individual worksites, in order to provide detailed industry data on employment, hours, and earnings of workers on nonfarm payrolls nationally (first URL), for all 50 states, the District of Columbia, Puerto Rico, the Virgin Islands, and over 300 metropolitan areas and divisions (second URL).

Current Population Survey

http://www.census.gov/hhes/www/income/dinctabs.html

The Current Population Survey is a nationally representative survey of the civilian noninstitutional population aged 15 or older. The Census Bureau takes it monthly for the Bureau of Labor Statistics, collecting information on employment and unemployment from more than 50,000 households. In March of each year, the survey includes the Annual Social and Economic Supplement (formerly called the Annual Demographic Survey), which is the source of most national data on the characteristics of Americans, such as educational attainment, living arrangements, incomes, and poverty.

Early Childhood Longitudinal Study

http://nces.ed.gov/ecls/

The Early Childhood Longitudinal Study program includes two overlapping cohorts: a birth cohort and a kindergarten cohort. The birth cohort follows a sample of children from birth through kindergarten entry. The kindergarten cohort follows a sample of children from kindergarten through the eighth grade. The ECLS provides national data on children's status at birth and at various points thereafter; children's transitions to nonparental care, early education programs, and school; and children's experiences and growth through the eighth grade.

Economic Census

http://www.census.gov/econ/census02/

The Economic Census provides a detailed portrait of the nation's economy from the national to the local level once every five years in years ending in 2 and 7. Censuses of agriculture and governments are conducted at the same time. In taking the census, forms are mailed to the universe of the nation's businesses (more than 5 million in 2002). Some very small firms do not receive a census form, and their statistics are estimated using administrative records. There are over 600 versions of the census form, each customized to a particular industry. Businesses are required by law to return the forms. The series of reports from the economic census includes industry statistics, geographic statistics, nonemployer statistics (businesses without employees), the Survey of Business Owners, and special topics.

General Social Survey

http://www.norc.org/GSS+Website

The General Social Survey is a biennial survey of the attitudes of Americans taken by the University of Chicago's National Opinion Research Center. The GSS is conducted through face-to-face interviews with an independently drawn, representative sample of 3,000 to 4,000 noninstitutionalized people aged 18 or older in the United States.

Health and Retirement Study

http://hrsonline.isr.umich.edu/

The University of Michigan Health and Retirement Study is a longitudinal survey of health, retirement, and aging funded by the National Institute on Aging. Every two years since 1992, more than 22,000 nationally representative Americans aged 50 or older are interviewed, painting a portrait of an aging America's physical and mental health, insurance coverage, financial status, family support systems, labor market status, and retirement planning. Because it is a longitudinal survey, cohorts can be followed over time to determine how aging affects wellbeing.

Health Confidence Survey

http://www.ebri.org/surveys/hcs/

The Health Confidence Survey is sponsored by the Employee Benefit Research Institute and Mathew Greenwald & Associates, a Washington, DC-based market research firm. Since 1998, this annual survey has tracked a broad spectrum of health care issues, including Americans' satisfaction with health care, their confidence in the health care system of today, the future of the health care system and the Medicare program, and their attitudes toward health care reform. It is conducted through telephone interviews with a sample of 1,000 Americans aged 21 or older.

HIV/AIDS Surveillance

http://www.cdc.gov/hiv/topics/surveillance/index.htm

All 50 states, the District of Columbia, and U.S. dependent areas report AIDS cases to the Centers for Disease Control using a uniform surveillance case definition and case report form. During the 1980s, AIDS cases alone provided an adequate picture of HIV trends because the time between infection with HIV and progression to AIDS was predictable. This predictability diminished beginning in 1996, when highly active antiretroviral therapy became available. Access, adherence, and response to such therapy affect whether or when HIV progresses to

AIDS. Thus, trends in AIDS cases alone no longer accurately reflect trends in HIV infection. By April 2004, all states had adopted some system for reporting HIV diagnoses to CDC.

Housing Vacancy Survey

http://www.census.gov/hhes/www/housing/hvs/hvs.html

The Housing Vacancy Survey is a supplement to the Current Population Survey, providing quarterly and annual data on rental and owned-home vacancy rates, characteristics of units available for occupancy, and homeownership rates by age, household type, region, state, and metropolitan area. The Current Population Survey sample includes approximately 50,000 occupied housing units and 9,000 vacant units.

Integrated Postsecondary Education Data System

http://nces.ed.gov/ipeds/

The Integrated Postsecondary Education Data System is the postsecondary data collection program of the National Center for Education Statistics. IPEDS encompasses all institutions and educational organizations whose primary purpose is to provide postsecondary education in the United States. IPEDS is built around a series of interrelated surveys to collect institution-level data in areas such as enrollment, program completion, faculty, staff, finances, and academic libraries.

Investment Company Institute

http://www.ici.org/shareholders/index.html

The Investment Company Institute is the primary source of statistical data on the investment industry. It conducts an annual survey to determine household and individual ownership of mutual funds. These surveys identify the characteristics, trends, behaviors, and needs of fund owners. For the 2007 survey, the Institute surveyed 3,977 randomly selected households in the United States.

Job Openings and Labor Turnover Survey

http://www.bls.gov/jlt/

The Bureau of Labor Statistics' Job Openings and Labor Turnover Survey collects data on job openings, hires, quits, layoffs, discharges, and other work separations. It provides an economic indicator of the unmet demand for labor and is an important measure of the tightness of job markets, paralleling the unemployment rate. JOLT Survey data are collected monthly from a sample of approximately 16,000 U.S. business establishments that represent all nonagricultural industries in the public and private sectors.

Kaiser Family Foundation

http://www.kff.org/

The Kaiser Family Foundation runs the largest public opinion research program in health. It undertakes original research working either independently or in partnership with media organizations and academic institutions. For its Health Care in America survey, a nationally representative survey of 1,201 adults conducted in September, 2006, it partnered with ABC

News and *USA Today* to explore the public's views and experiences related to health care costs and quality, as well as attitudes toward possible policy solutions.

Medical Expenditure Panel Survey

http://www.meps.ahrq.gov/mepsweb/

The Medical Expenditure Panel Survey is a nationally representative survey that collects detailed information on the health status, access to care, health care use, health care expenses, and health insurance coverage of the civilian noninstitutionalized population of the United States and nursing home residents. MEPS comprises four component surveys: the Household Component, the Medical Provider Component, the Insurance Component, and the Nursing Home Component. The Household Component is the core survey. It is conducted each year and includes 15,000 households and 37,000 people.

Monitoring the Future Project

http://monitoringthefuture.org/

The University of Michigan Survey Research Center administers the Monitoring the Future survey to approximately 50,000 students in 420 public and private secondary schools every year. High school seniors have been surveyed annually by MTF since 1975. Students in 8th and 10th grade have been surveyed annually since 1991.

National Ambulatory Medical Care Survey

http://www.cdc.gov/nchs/about/major/ahcd/ahcd1.htm

The National Ambulatory Medical Care Survey is an annual survey of visits to nonfederally employed office-based physicians who are primarily engaged in direct patient care. NAMCS data are collected from physicians rather than patients, with each physician assigned a one-week reporting period. During that week, the physician or the office staff records a systematic random sample of visit characteristics.

National Compensation Survey

http://www.bls.gov/ncs/home.htm

The Bureau of Labor Statistics' National Compensation Survey collects annual data on the incidence and detailed provisions of selected employee benefit plans in small, medium, and large private establishments, and in state and local governments. Interviewers collect the data by visiting a representative sample of establishments across the country and asking questions about the establishment, its employees, and their benefits.

National Crime Victimization Survey

http://www.ojp.usdoj.gov/bjs/cvict.htm

The National Crime Victimization Survey collects data each year on nonfatal crimes against people aged 12 or older, including those reported and those not reported to the police, from a nationally representative sample of 42,000 households and 76,000 persons in the United States. The NCVS provides information about victims, offenders, and criminal offenses.

National Health and Nutrition Examination Survey

http://www.cdc.gov/nchs/nhanes.htm

The National Health and Nutrition Examination Survey is a continuous survey of a representative sample of the U.S. civilian noninstitutionalized population. Respondents are interviewed at home about their health and nutrition, and the interview is followed up by a physical examination in mobile examination centers. The physical examination measures such attributes as height and weight, providing a more accurate determination of Americans' weight status than self-reports.

National Health Interview Survey

http://www.cdc.gov/nchs/nhis.htm

The National Health Interview Survey is an ongoing nationwide sample survey of the civilian noninstitutional population of the United States conducted by the Census Bureau for the National Center for Health Statistics. In interviews, data are collected from more than 100,000 people about their illnesses, injuries, impairments, chronic and acute conditions, activity limitations, and use of health services.

National Home and Hospice Care Survey

http://www.cdc.gov/nchs/nhhcs.htm

The National Home and Hospice Care Survey is a series of surveys of a nationally representative sample of home and hospice care agencies in the United States, sponsored by the National Center for Health Statistics. Data on the characteristics of patients and on services provided are collected through personal interviews with administrators and staff.

National Hospital Ambulatory Medical Care Survey

http://www.cdc.gov/nchs/about/major/ahcd/ahcd1.htm

The National Hospital Ambulatory Medical Care Survey, sponsored by the National Center for Health Statistics, is an annual national probability sample survey of visits to emergency departments and outpatient departments at nonfederal, short-stay, and general hospitals. Hospital staff collects the data from patient records.

National Hospital Discharge Survey

http://www.cdc.gov/nchs/about/major/hdasd/nhds.htm

This survey, which has been conducted annually since 1965, collects nationally representative data on the characteristics of inpatients discharged from nonfederal, short-stay hospitals in the United States. Using a national sample of about 500 hospitals, the survey collects data from approximately 270,000 inpatient records.

National Household Education Survey

http://nces.ed.gov/nhes/

The National Household Education Survey, sponsored by the National Center for Education Statistics, provides descriptive data on the educational activities of the U.S. population, including after-school care and adult education. The NHES is a system of telephone surveys of a representative sample of 45,000 to 60,000 households in the United States.

National Household Travel Survey

http://www.bts.gov/programs/national_household_travel_survey/

The 2001 National Household Travel Survey is the nation's inventory of daily and long-distance travel. National surveys of daily travel have been taken previously in 1969, 1977, 1983, 1990, and 1995. Long-distance travel information has been collected previously in 1977 and 1995. The 2001 survey was the integration of two previous national travel surveys: the Nationwide Personal Transportation Survey and the American Travel Survey. For the 2001 survey, approximately 66,000 households were asked to keep a diary of their travel in a designated 24-hour period.

National Immunization Survey

http://www.cdc.gov/nis/

The National Immunization Survey is a random-digit-dialed telephone survey followed by a mailed survey to children's immunization providers that began in 1994 to monitor childhood immunization. The target population is children aged 19 to 35 months living in the United States at the time of the interview. Vaccinations included in the survey are diphtheria, tetanus, and pertussis vaccine; poliovirus vaccine; measles vaccine; Haemophilus influenzae type b vaccine; hepatitis B vaccine; varicella zoster vaccine; pneumococcal conjugate vaccine; hepatitis A vaccine; and influenza vaccine.

National Nursing Home Survey

http://www.cdc.gov/nchs/nnhs.htm

This is a series of national sample surveys of nursing homes, their residents, and staff conducted at various intervals since 1973–74 and sponsored by the National Center for Health Statistics. The latest survey was taken in 2004. Data for the survey are obtained from a sample of about 1,500 facilities through personal interviews with administrators and staff.

National Prisoner Statistics

http://www.ojp.usdoj.gov/bjs/prisons.htm

Begun in 1926 under a mandate from Congress, the National Prisoner Statistics program collects statistics on prisoners at midyear and at the end of the year. In this effort, the Census Bureau serves as the data collection agent for the Bureau of Justice Statistics. Data collection depends entirely upon the voluntary participation of state departments of corrections and the Federal Bureau of Prisons.

National Sporting Goods Association

http://www.nsga.org

The National Sporting Goods Association's annual survey of sports participation is based on a questionnaire mailed to 10,000 nationally representative households in the continental United States. The questionnaire asks the male and female heads of households and up to two other household members who are at least seven years of age to indicate their age, the sports in which they participated in the previous year, and the number of days of participation.

National Survey of Family Growth

http://www.cdc.gov/nchs/nsfg.htm

The 2002 National Survey of Family Growth, sponsored by the National Center for Health Statistics, is a nationally representative survey of the civilian noninstitutional population aged 15 to 44. In-person interviews were completed with 12,571 men and women, collecting data on marriage, divorce, contraception, and infertility. The 2002 survey updates previous NSFG surveys taken in 1973, 1976, 1988, and 1995.

National Survey of Fishing, Hunting, and Wildlife-Associated Recreation

http://wsfrprograms.fws.gov/Subpages/NationalSurvey/National_Survey.htm

The National Survey of Fishing, Hunting, and Wildlife-Associated Recreation has been conducted about every five years since 1955. It collects information on the number of anglers, hunters, and wildlife watchers, how often they participate, and how much they spend on their activities in the United States. For the 2006 survey, interviews were completed with 21,938 anglers and hunters and 11,279 wildlife watchers.

National Survey on Drug Use and Health

http://www.oas.samhsa.gov/nhsda.htm

The National Survey on Drug Use and Health was formerly called the National Household Survey on Drug Abuse. It is sponsored by the Substance Abuse and Mental Health Services Administration, and has been conducted since 1971. It is the primary source of information on the use of illegal drugs by the U.S. population. Each year, a nationally representative sample of about 70,000 individuals aged 12 or older are surveyed in the 50 states and the District of Columbia.

National Vital Statistics System

http://www.cdc.gov/nchs/nvss.htm

The National Vital Statistics System is the mechanism by which the National Center for Health Statistics collects and disseminates the nation's official vital statistics. In the United States, legal authority for the registration of these events resides individually with the 50 States and 2 cities (Washington, DC, and New York City). The NCHS contracts with each of these jurisdictions to provide data on vital events—births, deaths, marriages, divorces, and fetal deaths. The NCHS compiles and analyzes the data in a series of reports and online databases.

Occupational Employment Statistics Survey

http://www.bls.gov/OES/

The Occupational Employment Statistics Survey is a semi-annual mail survey designed to produce estimates of employment and wages for specific occupations. The OES program collects data on wage and salary workers in nonfarm establishments in order to produce employment and wage estimates for about 800 occupations. Data from self-employed persons are neither collected nor included in the estimates. The OES survey includes approximately 200,000 establishments per panel (every six months), so that it takes three years to collect the data from the full sample of 1.2 million establishments.

Phi Delta Kappa/Gallup Poll of the Public's Attitudes toward the Public Schools

http://www.pdkintl.org/kappan/kpollpdf.htm

The annual Phi Delta Kappa/Gallup Poll of the Public's Attitudes toward the Public Schools has been chronicling the growth and changes in K–12 schooling for nearly four decades. Since the first poll was conducted in 1969, it has served as a source of information for those shaping educational policy. The survey's results are based on telephone interviews with a representative sample of about 1,000 people aged 18 or older in the United States.

Private School Survey

http://nces.ed.gov/surveys/pss/

The Private School Survey generates biennial data on the total number of private schools and their teachers and students. It has been conducted every two years since 1989–90. Private schools are defined as schools that are not supported primarily by public funds, and provide instruction for one or more of grades K–12 or comparable ungraded levels, and have one or more teachers. Organizations or institutions that provide support for home schooling without offering classroom instruction for students are excluded. The PSS consists of a single survey that is completed by administrative personnel in private schools. Information collected includes data on religious orientation, level of school, size of school, length of school year and length of school day, total enrollment (K–12), number of high school graduates, whether a school is single-sexed or coeducational, enrollment by sex, and number of teachers employed.

Residential Energy Consumption Survey

http://www.eia.doe.gov/emeu/recs/

The Residential Energy Consumption Survey provides information on the use of energy in residential housing units in the United States. The information collected includes the physical characteristics of housing units, the demographic characteristics of households, appliance ownership and use, and energy consumption and expenditure data by type of fuel used. RECS is a national area-probability sample survey conducted through 45-minute in-person interviews. First conducted in 1978, the 2005 survey is the 12th, collecting data from 4,381 households that represent all occupied housing units in the United States.

Retirement Confidence Survey

http://www.ebri.org/surveys/rcs/

The Retirement Confidence Survey, sponsored by the Employee Benefit Research Institute and Mathew Greenwald & Associates, a Washington, DC-based market research firm, is an annual survey of a nationally representative sample of 1,000 people aged 25 or older. Respondents are asked a core set of questions that have been asked since 1996, measuring attitudes and behavior toward retirement. Additional questions are also asked about current retirement issues such as 401(k) participation.

School Survey on Crime and Safety

http://nces.ed.gov/surveys/ssocs/

The School Survey on Crime and Safety is the primary source of school-level data on crime and safety for the National Center for Education Statistics. The SSOCS is a nationally representative cross-sectional survey of about 3,000 public elementary and secondary schools. Designed to provide estimates of school crime, discipline, disorder, programs and policies, the SSOCS is administered to public primary, middle, high, and combined school principals in the spring of even-numbered school years.

Sleep in America Poll

http://www.sleepfoundation.org

The National Sleep Foundation sponsors the annual Sleep in America survey to explore the quality of sleep for different groups of Americans. The poll is conducted through interviews with a random sample of 1,000 people aged 18 or older living in the continental United States. The 2008 poll examines the sleep habits of workers.

Survey of Business Owners

http://www.census.gov/csd/sbo/

The Survey of Business Owners is part of the Economic Census, taken in years ending in 2 and 7. The 2002 SBO was conducted by mail, with census forms sent to a random sample of more than 2 million businesses selected from a list of all firms operating during 2002 with receipts of $1,000 or more. The 2002 SBO examined businesses in which at least 51 percent of the stock or equity was owned by American Indians and Alaska Natives, Asians, blacks, Hispanics, Native Hawaiians and other Pacific Islanders, or women.

Survey of Construction

http://www.census.gov/const/www/

The Survey of Construction provides monthly estimates of housing units authorized but not started, housing starts, housing units under construction, and housing completions. The SOC is comprised of two parts: (1) Survey of Use of Permits, which estimates the amount of new construction in areas that require a building permit; and (2) Nonpermit Survey, which estimates the amount of new construction in areas that do not require a building permit. Less than 3 percent of all new construction takes place in nonpermit areas. Census Bureau field representatives collect data for both parts of the SOC. For the Survey of Use of Permits, they visit a sample of permit offices and select a sample of permits issued for new housing. Researchers then follow these permits to see when projects were started, completed, and sold. Each project is also surveyed to collect information on the characteristics of the structure. For the Nonpermit Survey, roads in sampled nonpermit land areas are driven at least once every three months to see if there is any new construction. When new residential construction is found, it is followed up in the same way as the Survey of Use of Permits.

Survey of Consumer Finances

http://www.federalreserve.gov/pubs/oss/oss2/scfindex.html

The Survey of Consumer Finances is a triennial survey sponsored by the Federal Reserve Board. It collects data on the assets (financial and nonfinancial), debts, and net worth of American households. For the 2004 SCF, the Federal Reserve Board interviewed a representative sample of 4,522 households.

Survey of Income and Program Participation

http://www.sipp.census.gov/sipp/

The Census Bureau conducts the Survey of Income and Program Participation, which is designed to measure the effectiveness of existing federal, state, and local programs; to estimate future costs and coverage for government programs, such as food stamps; and to provide improved statistics on the distribution of income and measures of economic well-being in the United States. The survey design is a continuous series of national panels, with sample size ranging from approximately 14,000 to 36,700 interviewed households. The duration of each panel ranges from 2 ½ years to 4 years.

Uniform Crime Reporting Program

http://www.fbi.gov/ucr/ucr.htm

The Uniform Crime Reporting Program is an FBI-run effort that collects crime statistics from jurisdictions across the United States. The International Association of Chiefs of Police started the program in 1929 to meet the need for reliable, uniform crime statistics for the nation. In 1930, the FBI took over collecting, publishing, and archiving the statistics. Today, several annual statistical publications, such as the comprehensive *Crime in the United States* are produced from data provided to the FBI by nearly 17,000 law enforcement agencies across the United States. To ensure the data are uniformly reported, the FBI provides contributing law enforcement agencies with a handbook that explains how to classify and score offenses and provides uniform crime offense definitions.

Youth Risk Behavior Surveillance System

http://www.cdc.gov/HealthyYouth/yrbs/

The Youth Risk Behavior Surveillance System was created by the Centers for Disease Control to monitor health risks being taken by young people at the national, state, and local level. The national survey is taken every two years based on a nationally representative sample of 16,000 students in 9th through 12th grade in public and private schools.

Appendix B:

Mailing Addresses, Telephone Numbers, and Web Sites

AARP
601 E Street, N.W.
Washington, DC 20049
(888) 687-2277
www.aarp.org

Agency for Healthcare Research and Quality
540 Gaither Road
Rockville, MD 20850
(301) 427-1364
www.ahrq.gov

American Public Transportation Association
1666 K Street, N.W.
Washington, DC 20006
(202) 496-4800
www.apta.com

Bureau of Labor Statistics
Postal Square Building
2 Massachusetts Avenue, N.E.
Washington, DC 20212-0001
(202) 691-5200
www.bls.gov

Bureau of Transportation Statistics
1200 New Jersey Avenue, S.E.
Washington, DC 20590
(800) 853-1351
www.bts.gov

Census Bureau
4600 Silver Hill Road
Washington, DC 20233
(301) 763-INFO or (800) 923-8282
www.census.gov

Centers for Disease Control and Prevention
1600 Clifton Road
Atlanta, GA 30333
(404) 498-1515 or (800) 311-3435
www.cdc.gov

Centers for Medicare & Medicaid Services
7500 Security Boulevard
Baltimore, MD 21244
(877) 267-2323
www.cms.hhs.gov

Central Intelligence Agency
Office of Public Affairs
Washington, D.C. 20505
(703) 482-0623
www.cia.gov

Child Welfare Information Gateway
Children's Bureau/ACYF
1250 Maryland Avenue, S.W., 8th Floor
Washington, DC 20024
(703) 385-7565 or (800) 394-3366
www.childwelfare.gov

College Board
45 Columbus Avenue
New York, NY 10023
Phone: (212) 713-8000
www.collegeboard.com

U.S. Department of Homeland Security
Washington, DC 20528
(202) 282-8000
www.dhs.gov

Economic Mobility Project
The Pew Charitable Trusts
1025 F Street, N.W., Suite 900
Washington, DC 20004
(202) 552-2144
www.economicmobility.org

Economic Research Service
1800 M Street N.W.
Washington, DC 20036
(202) 694-5050
www.ers.gov

Employee Benefit Research Institute
1100 13th Street, N.W., Suite 878
Washington, DC 20005
(202) 659-0670
www.ebri.org

Energy Information Administration
1000 Independence Avenue, S.W.
Washington, DC 20585
(202) 586-8800
www.eia.doe.gov

Federal Bureau of Investigation
J. Edgar Hoover Building
935 Pennsylvania Avenue, N.W.
Washington, DC 20535-0001
(202) 324-3000
www.fbi.gov

Federal Reserve Bank of Boston
600 Atlantic Avenue
Boston, MA 02210
(617) 973-3000
www.bos.frb.org

Federal Reserve Board
20th Street and Constitution Avenue, N.W.
Washington, DC 20551
(202) 452-3693
www.federalreserve.gov

Gallup
The Gallup Building
901 F Street, N.W.
Washington, D.C. 20004
(202) 715-3030
www.gallup.com

General Social Survey
National Opinion Research Center
University of Chicago
1155 East 60th Street
Chicago, IL 60637
(773)256-6288
www.norc.org/GSS+website

Guttmacher Institute
• New York
125 Maiden Lane, 7th floor
New York, NY 10038
(212) 248-1111 or (800) 355-0244

• Washington, DC
1301 Connecticut Avenue N.W., Suite 700
Washington, DC 20036
(202) 296-4012 or (877) 823-0262
www.guttmacher.org

Harris Interactive
60 Corporate Woods
Rochester, NY 14623-1457
(585) 272-8400 or (800) 866-7655
www.harrisinteractive.com

Higher Education Research Institute
University of California, Los Angeles
3005 Moore Hall
Box 951521
Los Angeles, CA 90095-1521
(310) 825-1925
www.gseis.ucla.edu/heri

Internal Revenue Service
1111 Constitution Avenue. N.W.
Washington, DC 20224
(202) 283-8710
www.irs.gov

Investment Company Institute
1401 H Street, N.W., Suite 1100
Washington, DC, 20005
(202) 326-5800
www.ici.org

Joint Center for Housing Studies
Harvard University
1033 Massachusetts Avenue, 5th Floor
Cambridge, MA 02138
(617) 495-7908
www.jchs.harvard.edu

Kaiser Family Foundation
2400 Sand Hill Road
Menlo Park, CA 94025
(650) 854-9400
www.kff.org

Monitoring the Future
Institute for Social Research
The University of Michigan
426 Thompson Street
Ann Arbor, MI 48106-1248
(734) 764-8354
www.monitoringthefuture.org

National Association of Realtors
430 North Michigan Avenue
Chicago, IL 60611
(800) 874-6500
www.realtor.org

National Bureau of Economic Research
1050 Massachusetts Avenue
Cambridge, MA 02138
(617) 868-3900
www.nber.org

National Center for Complementary and Alternative Medicine
National Institutes of Health
9000 Rockville Pike
Bethesda, MD 20892
(888) 644-6226 or (301) 519-3153
www.nccam.nih.gov

National Center for Education Statistics
1990 K Street, N.W.
Washington, DC 20006
(202) 502-7300
www.nces.ed.gov

National Endowment for the Arts
1100 Pennsylvania Avenue N.W.
Washington, DC 20506-0001
(202) 682-5400
www.nea.gov

National Institute of Mental Health
6001 Executive Boulevard
Room 8184, MSC 9663
Bethesda, MD 20892-9663
(301) 443-4513
www/nimh.nih.gov

National Oceanic and Atmospheric Admin.
1401 Constitution Avenue, N.W., Room 6217
Washington, DC 20230
(202) 482-6090
www.noaa.gov

National Park Service
Department of the Interior
1849 C Street, N.W.
Washington DC 20240
(970) 225-3554
www.nps.gov

National Sleep Foundation
1522 K Street, N.W., Suite 500
Washington, DC 20005
(202) 347-3471
www.sleepfoundation.org

National Sporting Goods Association
1601 Feehanville Drive, Suite 300
Mt. Prospect, IL 60056
(847) 296-6742
www.nsga.org

Office of Justice Programs
U.S. Department of Justice
810 Seventh Street N.W.
Washington, DC 20531
(800) 458-0786
www.ojp.usdoj.gov

Office of Travel & Tourism Industries
14th & Constitution Avenues. N.W., Room 1003
Washington, DC 20230
(202) 482-0140
http://tinet.ita.doc.gov

Pension Rights Center
1350 Connecticut Avenue, N.W., Suite 206
Washington, DC 20036-1739
(202) 296-3776
www.pensionrights.org

Pew Research Center
1615 L Street, N.W., Suite 700
Washington, DC 20036
(202) 419-4300
www.pewresearch.org

Phi Delta Kappa International
408 N. Union Street
Bloomington, IN 47402-0789
(812) 339-1156
www.pdkintl.org

Population Association of America
8630 Fenton Street, Suite 722
Silver Spring, MD 20910
(301) 565-6710
www.popassoc.org

Population Reference Bureau
1875 Connecticut Avenue, N.W., Suite 520
Washington, DC 20009-5728
(800) 877-9881
www.prb.org

Project for Excellence in Journalism
1615 L Street, N.W.
Washington, DC 20036
(202) 419-3650
www.journalism.org

Roper Center for Public Opinion Research
University of Connecticut
Homer Babbidge Library
369 Fairfield Way, Unit 2164
Storrs, CT 06269-2164
(860) 486.4440
www.ropercenter.uconn.edu

Social Security Administration
Office of Public Inquiries
Windsor Park Building
6401 Security Boulevard
Baltimore, MD 21235
(800) 772-1213
www.ssa.gov

Substance Abuse and Mental Health Services Administration
P.O. Box 2345
Rockville, MD 20847-2345
(877) 726-4727
www.samhsa.gov/shin

Travel Industry Association
1100 New York Avenue, N.W., Suite 450
Washington, DC 20005-3934
(202) 408-8422
www.tia.org

Veterans Administration
1722 I Street, N.W.
Washington, DC 20006
(202) 429-0180
www.va.gov

World Public Opinion
Global Public Opinion on International Affairs
1779 Massachusetts Avenue, N.W., Suite 510
Washington, DC 20036
(202) 232-7500
www.worldpublicopinion.org

Appendix C:

Glossary of Demographic Terms

adjusted for inflation Income or a change in income that has been adjusted for the rise in the cost of living, or the consumer price index (CPI-U-RS).

American Indians In most government data, American Indians include Alaska Natives, unless otherwise noted.

Asian In most government data, the term "Asian" includes Native Hawaiians and other Pacific Islanders unless those groups are shown separately.

baby boom Americans born between 1946 and 1964.

baby bust Americans born between 1965 and 1976, also known as Generation X.

births, out of wedlock Out-of-wedlock births are defined as births occurring in the 12-month period preceding the survey date to women who were currently divorced, widowed, or never married at the time of the interview.

black The black racial category includes those who identified themselves as "black" or "African American."

child support Data on award of child support payments are collected from people 15 years or older with children under 21 years of age whose other parent is not living in the household.

children All persons under age 18, excluding people who maintain households, families, or subfamilies as a reference person or spouse. *See also* Own children and Related children.

children ever born The question "How many babies has...ever had, if any? (Do not count stillbirths)" is asked of all women aged 15 to 44. When asking about children ever born, interviewers are instructed to include children born to women before her present marriage, children no longer living, and children away from home as well as those still living in the home.

citizenship status There are five categories of citizenship status: 1) born in the United States; 2) born in Puerto Rico or another outlying area of the U.S.; 3) born abroad of U.S. citizen parents; 4) naturalized citizens; and 5) non-citizens.

college enrollment Anyone enrolled in college at any time during the current term or school year, except those who have left for the remainder of the term. Regular college enrollment includes people attending a two-year or four-year college, university, or professional school (such as medical or law school) in courses that may advance the student toward a recognized college or university degree (e.g., BA or MA). Attendance may be either full time or part time, during the day or night. The college student need not be working toward a degree, but he/she must be enrolled in a class for which credit would be applied toward a degree. College students are regarded as attending college full time if they are taking 12 or more hours of classes during the average school week, and part time if they are taking less than 12 hours of classes during the average school week.

consumer unit Consumer units are used in the Bureau of Labor Statistics' Consumer Expenditure Survey. A consumer unit is all related members of a household, or financially independent members of a household. Consumer units are similar to households, but a household may include more than one consumer unit.

disability Disability is defined differently depending on the survey. The National Health Interview Survey estimates the number of people aged 18 or older who have difficulty in physical functioning, probing whether respondents could perform nine activities by themselves without using special equipment. The categories are walking a quarter mile; standing for two hours; sitting for two hours; walking up 10 steps without resting; stooping, bending, kneeling; reaching over one's head; grasping or handling small objects; carrying a 10-pound object; and pushing/pulling a large object. Adults who reported that any of these activities was very difficult or they could not do it at all were defined as having physical difficulties. The Current Population Survey identifies people aged 15 and older as having a disability in a communication, mental, or physical domain. They were classified as having a communication disability if they had difficulty seeing, hearing, or speaking. People were identified as having a disability in a physical domain if they used a wheelchair, cane, crutches, or walker or had difficulty with one or more functional activities. People were identified as having a disability in a mental domain if they had any mental or emotional condition that seriously interfered with everyday activities. The American Community Survey defines the disabled as the those who are blind, deaf, or had severe vision or hearing impairments, and/or had a condition that substantially limited one or more basic physical activities such as walking, climbing stairs, reaching, lifting, or carrying. It also included people who, because of a physical, mental, or emotional condition lasting six months or more, have difficulty functioning.

dual-earner couple A married couple in which both the householder and the householder's spouse are in the labor force.

earnings A type of income, earnings are the amount of money a person receives from his or her job. *See also* Income.

educational attainment Educational attainment applies only to progress in "regular" schools. Such schools include graded public, private, and parochial elementary and high schools (both junior and senior high schools), colleges, universities, and professional schools, whether day schools or night schools. Schooling in other than regular schools is counted only if the credits obtained are regarded as transferable to a school in the regular school system.

employed All civilians who did any work as a paid employee or farmer/self-employed worker, or who worked 15 hours or more as an unpaid farm worker or in a family-owned business, during the reference period. All those who have jobs but who are temporarily absent from their jobs due to illness, bad weather, vacation, labor management dispute, or personal reasons are considered employed.

ethnic origin In the census and government surveys, Hispanic origin is identified in a question that is separate from the question about race. Hispanics may be of any race.

expenditure The transaction cost including excise and sales taxes of goods and services acquired during the survey period. The full cost of each purchase is recorded even though full payment may not have been made at the date of purchase. Average expenditure figures may be artificially low for infrequently purchased items such as cars because figures are calculated using all consumer units within a demographic segment rather than just purchasers. Expenditure estimates include money spent on gifts for others.

family A family is a group of two or more people (one of whom is the householder) related by birth, marriage, or adoption and residing together; all such people (including related subfamily members) are considered members of one family. The number of families is equal to the number of family households. But the count of family members differs from the count of family household members because family household members include any non-relatives living in the household.

family group A family group is any two or more people (not necessarily including a householder) residing together, and related by birth, marriage, or adoption. A household may be composed of one such group, more than one, or none at all. The count of family groups includes family households, related subfamilies, and unrelated subfamilies.

family household A family household is a household maintained by a householder who is in a family (as defined above), and includes any unrelated people (unrelated subfamily members and/or secondary individuals) who may be residing there. The number of family households is equal to the number of families. The count of family household members differs from the count of family members, however. Family household members include all people living in a household, while family members include only the householder and his or her relatives. *See also* Family.

female/male householder A woman or man who maintains a household without a spouse present. May head family or nonfamily households.

foreign-born population People who are not U.S. citizens at birth.

full-time employment Full-time is 35 or more hours of work per week during a majority of the weeks worked.

full-time, year-round Indicates 50 or more weeks of full-time employment during the previous calendar year.

Generation X Americans born between 1965 and 1976, also known as the baby-bust generation.

group quarters Noninstitutional living arrangements for groups not living in conventional housing units, or groups living in housing units containing ten or more unrelated people or nine or more people unrelated to the person in charge. Examples of people in group quarters include a person residing in a rooming house, in staff quarters at a hospital, or in a halfway house.

health insurance coverage A person is considered covered by health insurance in the Current Population Survey if, at some time during the year, he or she was covered by at least one of the following types of coverage: employer/union, privately purchased (not related to employment), Medicare, Medicaid, military health care (military, CHAMPUS, CHAMPVA, VA, Indian Health Services), someone outside the household, or other. An individual can have more than one type of health insurance coverage.

Hispanic Because Hispanic is an ethnic origin rather than a race, Hispanics may be of any race. While most Hispanics are white, there are black, Asian, American Indian, and even Native Hawaiian Hispanics.

household A household consists of all the people who occupy a housing unit. A house, an apartment or other group of rooms, or a single room, is regarded as a housing unit when it is occupied or intended for occupancy as separate living quarters; that is, when the occupants do not live and eat with any other persons in the structure and there is direct access from the outside or through a common hall. A household includes the related family members and all the unrelated people, if any, such as lodgers, foster children, wards, or employees who share the housing unit. A person living alone in a housing unit, or a group of unrelated people sharing a housing unit such as partners or roomers, is also counted as a household. The count of households excludes group quarters. There are two major categories of households, "family" and "nonfamily."

household, size of The term "size of household" includes all the people occupying a housing unit. "Size of family" includes the family householder and all other people in the living quarters who are related to the householder by birth, marriage, or adoption.

household, nonfamily A nonfamily household consists of a householder living alone (a one-person household) or a householder who shares the home exclusively with people to whom he/she is not related.

household, race/ethnicity of Households are categorized according to the race or ethnicity of the householder only.

householder The householder is the person (or one of the people) in whose name the housing unit is owned or rented (maintained) or, if there is no such person, any adult member, excluding roomers, boarders, or paid employees. If the house is owned or rented jointly by a married couple, the householder may be either the husband or the wife. The person designated as the householder is the "reference person" to whom the relationship of all other household members, if any, is recorded. The number of householders is equal to the number of households. Also, the number of family householders is equal to the number of families.

householder, age of The age of the householder is used to categorize households into age groups. Married couples, for example, are classified according to the age of either the husband or wife, depending on which one identified him or herself as the householder.

head versus householder The Bureau of the Census discontinued the use of the terms "head of household" and "head of family" in 1980. Instead, the terms "householder" and "family householder" are used.

housing unit A housing unit is a house, an apartment, a group of rooms, or a single room occupied or intended for occupancy as separate living quarters. Separate living quarters are those in which the occupants do not live and eat with any other persons in the structure and that have direct access from the outside of the building or through a common hall that is used or intended for use by the occupants of another unit or by the general public. The occupants may be a single family, one person living alone, two or more families living together, or any other group of related or unrelated persons who share living arrangements.

housing value The respondent's estimate of how much his or her house and lot would sell for if it were for sale.

immigration The relatively permanent movement (change of residence) of people into the country of reference.

income On the Current Population Survey, the government's official measure, income is defined as money received in the preceding calendar year by each person aged 15 or older from each of the following sources: 1) earnings from longest job or self-employment), 2) earnings from jobs other than longest job, 3) unemployment compensation, 4) workers' compensation, 5) Social Security, 6) Supplemental Security income, 7) public assistance, 8) veterans' payments, 9) survivor benefits, 10) disability benefits, 11) retirement pensions, 12) interest, 13) dividends, 14) rents and royalties or estates and trusts, 15) educational assistance, 16) alimony, 17) child support, 18) financial assistance from outside the household, and other periodic income. Income is reported in several ways. Household income is the combined income of all household members. Income of persons is all income accruing to a person from all sources. Earnings are the money a person receives from his or her job.

job tenure The length of time a person has been employed continuously by the same employer.

labor force The labor force includes both the employed and the unemployed (people who are looking for work).

labor force participation rate The percent of the civilian noninstitutional population that is in the civilian labor force, which includes both the employed and the unemployed.

marital status The marital status classification identifies four major categories: never married, married, widowed, and divorced. These terms refer to marital status at the time of the census or survey. The category "married" is further divided into "married, spouse present," "separated," and "other married, spouse absent." A person was classified as "married, spouse present" if the husband or wife was reported as a member of the household, even though he or she may have been temporarily absent on business or on vacation, visiting, in a hospital, etc., at the time of the census or survey. People reported as separated include those with legal separations, those living apart with intentions of obtaining a divorce, and other people permanently or temporarily separated because of marital discord. The group "other married, spouse absent" includes married people living apart because either the husband or wife was employed and living at a considerable distance from home, was serving away from home in the Armed Forces, had moved to another area, or had a different place of residence for any other reason except separation as defined above.

married couple A married couple, as defined for census purposes, is a husband and wife enumerated as members of the same household. The married couple may or may not have children living with them. The expression "husband-wife" or "married-couple" before the term "household," "family," or "subfamily" indicates that the household, family, or subfamily is maintained by a husband and wife. The number of married couples equals the count of married-couple families plus related and unrelated married-couple subfamilies.

married couples with or without children under age 18 Refers to married couples with or without own children under age 18 living in the same household. Couples without children under age 18 may be parents of grown children who live elsewhere, or they could be childless couples.

mean (average) income Mean (average) income is the amount obtained by dividing the total aggregate income of a group by the number of units in that group. The means for households, families, and unrelated individuals are based on all households, families, and unrelated individuals, respectively. The means (averages) for people are based on people 15 years old and over with income.

median income Median income is the amount that divides the income distribution into two equal groups, half having incomes above the median, half having incomes below the median. The medians for households, families, and unrelated individuals are based on all households, families, and unrelated individuals, respectively. The medians for people are based on people 15 years old and over with income.

metropolitan–nonmetropolitan residence The general concept of a metropolitan area is one of a large population nucleus, together with adjacent communities that have a high degree of economic and social integration with the nucleus. The metropolitan classification is a statistical standard defined by the Federal Office of Management and Budget, following a set of official published standards. These standards were developed with the aim of producing definitions that are as consistent as possible for all metropolitan areas nationwide. Each area must contain either a place with a minimum population of 50,000 or a Census Bureau-defined urbanized area and a total population of at least 100,000 (75,000 in New England). A metropolitan area is comprised of one or more central counties, and it may also include one or more outlying counties that have close economic and social relationships with the central county. An outlying county must have a specified level of commuting to the central counties and also must meet certain standards regarding metropolitan character, such as population density, urban population, and population growth. In New England, metropolitan areas are composed of cities and towns rather than whole counties. The metropolitan category is subdivided into "inside principal city" and "outside principal city." The area outside metropolitan areas is referred to as "nonmetropolitan."

millennial generation Americans born between 1977 and 1994.

mobility status The mobility status of each individual is determined by comparing his current place of residence with his place of residence one year earlier.

moving, reasons for Reasons for moving are collected from the householder and others who were living in a different house/apartment one year earlier. People who moved into the household during the year are assigned the reason of the householder.

native-born Native-born people are citizens at birth. All people with the following citizenship statuses are native born: 1) born in the United States; 2) born in Puerto Rico or an outlying area; or 3) born abroad of American parents. All other people are foreign born.

nativity There are two categories of nativity, native-born and foreign-born.

nonfamily household A household maintained by a householder who lives alone or who lives with people to whom he or she is not related.

nonfamily householder A householder who lives alone or with nonrelatives.

non-Hispanic People who do not identify themselves as Hispanic are classified as non-Hispanic. Non-Hispanics may be of any race.

non-Hispanic white People who identify their race as white and who do not indicate a Hispanic origin.

occupation Occupational classification is based on the kind of work a person did at his or her job during the previous calendar year. If a person changed jobs during the year, the data refer to the occupation of the job held the longest during that year.

occupied housing units A housing unit is classified as occupied if a person or group of people is living in it or if the occupants are only temporarily absent—on vacation, for example. By definition, the count of occupied housing units is the same as the count of households.

own children Own children are sons and daughters, including stepchildren and adopted children, of the householder. Similarly, "own" children in a subfamily are sons and daughters of the married couple or parent in the subfamily. The count of "own children under age 18" is limited to never-married children; however, "own children under age 25" and "own children of any age," include all children regardless of marital status. The counts include never-married children living away from home in college dormitories.

owner occupied A housing unit is "owner occupied" if the owner lives in the unit, even if it is mortgaged or not fully paid for. A cooperative or condominium unit is "owner occupied" only if the owner lives in it. All other occupied units are classified as "renter occupied."

part-time employment Part-time is less than 35 hours of work per week in a majority of the weeks worked during the year.

per capita income Per capita income is the average income computed for every man, woman, and child in a particular group. The Census Bureau derives per capita income by dividing the total income of a particular group by the total population in that group (excluding patients or inmates in institutional quarters).

percent change The change (either positive or negative) in a measure that is expressed as a proportion of the starting measure. When median income changes from $20,000 to $25,000, for example, this is a 25 percent increase.

percentage point change The change (either positive or negative) in a value which is already expressed as a percentage. When a labor force participation rate changes from 70 percent of 75 percent, for example, this is a 5 percentage point increase.

poverty The Census Bureau uses a set of money income thresholds that vary by family size and composition to detect who is poor. If a family's total income is less than that family's threshold, then that family, and every individual in it, is considered poor. The poverty thresholds do not vary geographically, but they are updated annually for inflation using the consumer price index. The official poverty definition counts money income before taxes and excludes capital gains and noncash benefits (such as public housing, Medicaid, and food stamps). Poverty statistics are based on a definition developed by Mollie Orshansky of the Social Security Administration in 1964. At the core of the definition of poverty was the economy food plan, the least costly of four nutritionally adequate food plans designed by the Department of Agriculture. It was determined from the Department of Agriculture's 1955 Household Food Consumption Survey that families of three or more people spent approximately one-third of their after-tax money income on food; accordingly, poverty thresholds for families of three or more people were set at three times the cost of the economy food plan. The poverty thresholds have been increased each year by the same percentage as the annual average consumer price index.

proportion or share The value of a part expressed as a percentage of the whole. If there are 4 million people aged 25 and 3 million of them are white, then the white proportion is 75 percent.

race Race is self-reported on the census and most surveys. The 2000 census and government surveys (beginning in 2003) recognize six racial groups: American Indian, Asian, black, Native Hawaiian, white, and other. Because respondents are now allowed to identify themselves as belonging to more than one racial group, the federal government defines three broad racial categories: The "race alone" population comprises people who identify themselves as only one race. The "race in combination" population comprises people who identify themselves as more than one race, such as white and black. The "race, alone or in combination" population includes both those who identify themselves as one race and those who identify themselves as more than one race. Census and survey data collected before 2000 define race differently. Check table footnotes for those definitions.

reference person The reference person is the person to whom the relationship of other people in the household is recorded. The household reference person is the person listed as the householder. The subfamily reference person is either the single parent or the husband/wife in a married-couple situation.

regions, geographic The four major regions of the United States for which data are presented represent groups of states as follows:

• *Northeast* Connecticut, Maine, Massachusetts, New Hampshire, New Jersey, New York, Pennsylvania, Rhode Island, Vermont.

• *Midwest* Illinois, Indiana, Iowa, Kansas, Michigan, Minnesota, Missouri, Nebraska, North Dakota, Ohio, South Dakota, Wisconsin.

• *South* Alabama, Arkansas, Delaware, District of Columbia, Florida, Georgia, Kentucky, Louisiana, Maryland, Mississippi, North Carolina, Oklahoma, South Carolina, Tennessee, Texas, Virginia, West Virginia.

• *West* Alaska, Arizona, California, Colorado, Hawaii, Idaho, Montana, Nevada, New Mexico, Oregon, Utah, Washington, Wyoming.

• *Sunbelt* Consists of 13 states plus one county in Nevada and nine counties in California. The states that are entirely inside the Sunbelt are: North Carolina, South Carolina, Georgia, Florida, Alabama, Mississippi, Louisiana, Tennessee, Arkansas, Oklahoma, Texas, New Mexico, and Arizona. Also included are Clark County, Nevada, and Imperial, Kern, Los Angeles, Orange, Riverside, San Bernardino, San Diego, Santa Barbara, and Ventura Counties in California.

related children Related children include own children and all other children under age 18 in a household (regardless of their marital status) who are related to the householder by birth, marriage, or adoption.

renter occupied *See* Owner occupied.

rounding In most of the demographic statistics published by the federal government, percentages are rounded to the nearest tenth of a percent; therefore, the percentages in a distribution do not always add to exactly 100.0 percent.

school enrollment School enrollment includes anyone enrolled at any time during the current term or school year in any type of public, parochial, or other private school in the *regular* school system. Such schools include nursery schools, kindergartens, elementary schools, high schools, colleges, universities, and professional schools. Attendance may be on either a full-time or part-time basis and during the day or night. Regular schooling is that which may advance a person toward an elementary or high school diploma, a college, university, or professional school degree. Enrollment in schools that are not in the regular school system, such as trade schools, business colleges, and schools for the mentally handicapped, which do not advance students to regular school degrees, is not included. People enrolled in classes that do not require physical presence in school, such as correspondence courses or other courses of independent study, and in training courses given directly on the job, are also excluded from the count of those enrolled in school, unless such courses are being counted for credit at a regular school.

school, level of The statistics on level of school indicate the number of people enrolled at each of five levels—nursery school, kindergarten, elementary school (1st to 8th grades), high school (9th to 12th grades), and college or professional school. The last group includes graduate students in colleges or universities. People enrolled in elementary, middle school, intermediate school, or junior high school through the eighth grade are classified as in elementary school. All people enrolled in 9th through 12th grade are classified as in high school.

school, nursery A nursery school is defined as a group or class that is organized to provide educational experiences for children during the year or years preceding kindergarten. It includes instruction as an important and integral phase of its program of child care. Private homes in which essentially custodial care is provided are not considered nursery schools. Children enrolled in Head Start or similar programs are counted as in nursery school.

school, public or private A public school is defined as any educational institution operated by publicly elected or appointed school officials and supported by public funds. Private schools include educational institutions established and operated by religious bodies, as well as those that are under other private control. In cases where enrollment is in a school or college that is both publicly and privately controlled or supported, enrollment is counted according to whether it is primarily public or private.

self-employment In the Current Population Survey, from which the government's official labor statistics are derived, a person is categorized as self-employed if he or she was self-employed in the job held longest during the reference period. Persons who report self-employment from a second job are excluded, but those who report wage-and-salary income from a second job are included. Unpaid workers in family businesses are excluded. Self-employment statistics include only nonagricultural workers and exclude people who work for themselves in incorporated business.

sex ratio The number of men per 100 women.

step-family A step-family is a married-couple household with at least one child under age 18 who is a stepchild (i.e., a son or daughter through marriage, but not by birth) of the householder. This definition, used in the Current Population Survey and many others, undercounts the true number of step-families in instances where the parent of the natural born or biological child is the householder and that parent's spouse is not the child's parent, as biological or step-parentage is not ascertained for both parents.

subfamily A subfamily is a married couple with or without children, or a single parent and her/his never-married children under age 18, who live in a household maintained by someone else. A *related subfamily* is related to the householder, such as a young married couple sharing the home of the husband's or wife's parents. The number of related subfamilies is not included in the count of families. An *unrelated subfamily* is not related to the householder. An unrelated subfamily may include people such as guests, partners, roommates, or resident employees and their spouses and/or children. The number of unrelated subfamily members is included in the total number of household members, but is not included in the count of family members.

tenure A housing unit is "owned" if the owner or co-owner lives in the unit, even if it is mortgaged or not fully paid for. A cooperative or condominium unit is "owned" only if the owner or co-owner lives in it. All other occupied units are classified as "rented," including units rented for cash rent and those occupied without payment of cash rent.

undocumented immigrants or illegal aliens Because all residents of the United States living in households are represented in the sample of households included in most government surveys, many undocumented immigrants or illegal aliens are included in the government's demographic data. Because most government surveys make no attempt to ascertain the legal status of respondents (if they did, many undocumented immigrants simply would not respond), illegal aliens cannot be identified by census or survey data.

unemployed The unemployed are those who have no employment but are available and looking for work. Those who were laid off from their jobs and are waiting to be recalled are also classified as unemployed.

units in structure In the determination of the number of units in a structure, all housing units—both occupied and vacant—are counted. The statistics are presented in terms of the number of occupied housing units in structures of specified size, not in terms of the number of residential structures.

unmarried couple An unmarried couple is composed of two unrelated adults of the opposite sex (one of whom is the householder) who share a housing unit. Unmarried couple households contain only two adults.

unrelated individuals Unrelated individuals are people of any age who are not members of families or subfamilies.

vocational school enrollment Vocational school enrollment includes enrollment in business, vocational, technical, secretarial, trade, or correspondence courses which are not counted as regular school enrollment and are not for recreation or adult education classes. College courses are not vocational.

voter, reported participation Voter participation data are derived from replies to the following question asked of people (excluding noncitizens) of voting age: "In any election some people are not able to vote because they are sick or busy, or have some other reason, and others do not want to vote. Did (this person) vote in the election held on November (date varies)?" Those of voting age are classified as "voted" or "did not vote." In most tables, the "did not vote" class includes those who reported "did not vote" and "do not know," as well as noncitizens and nonrespondents.

white The "white" racial category includes many Hispanics (who may be of any race) unless the term "non-Hispanic white" is used.

work experience A person with work experience is one who, during the preceding calendar year, did any work for pay or profit or worked without pay on a family-operated farm or business at any time during the year, on a part-time or full-time basis. A full-time worker is one who worked 35 hours or more per week during the majority of weeks worked during the preceding calendar year. A year-round worker is one who worked for 50 weeks or more during the preceding calendar year. A full-time, year-round worker is a person who worked full time (35 or more hours per week) for 50 or more weeks during the previous calendar year.

Index

100 Years of U.S. Consumer Spending Data, 32, 59, 104, 163
401(k) Plan Asset Allocation, Account Balances, and Loan Activity in 2006, 154
2000 Census
    adoption, 3, 23
    American Indians, 9–10, 145, 174
    ancestry, 10
    Asians, 11, 145
    blacks, 4, 18, 145
    children's living arrangements, 24
    commuting, 30, 95, 174
    definition of race, 146
    geographical mobility, 69, 114, 116
    Hispanics, 78, 100, 145
    Internet home page, 22
    language spoken at home, 100
    non-Hispanic whites, 145
    surname file, 67
AARP
    aging research, 6, 54–55, 128–129
    baby-boom studies, 15
    caregivers, 21
    long-term care, 104
    retirement, 150
    Social Security, 161
abortion, 3
adoption, 3
adult education, 3
African Americans, 4–5
after-school programs, 5
age, 5–6
aging, 6–7
AIDS, 8
Alabama, 8
Alaska, 8
alcohol consumption, 8–9
alternative
    medicine, 9
    workers, 9
American Community Survey
    age data, 5
    American Indians, 10, 145, 176
    Asians, 11, 145
    births, 17
    blacks, 4, 145
    children, 24
    citizenship, 27
    city demographics, 27
    commuting, 30, 95, 174
    county demographics, 36
    employment, 56, 94, 99, 190
    English, ability to speak, 58
    fertility, 64, 117, 121, 131, 138
    foreign-born population, 65
    geographical mobility, 69, 115, 117
    group quarters population, 70
    Hispanics, 80, 100, 145
    homeownership, 81
    housing, 85
    incomes, 88
    language spoken at home, 100
    metropolitan areas, 114
    nativity, 122
    non-Hispanic whites, 124, 145
    place of birth, 135
    poverty program participation, 186
    regions, 148
    renters, 150
    school district demographics, 54
    Spanish spoken at home, 162
    state demographics, 165
    vehicle ownership, 179
    whites, 187
The American Freshman: National Norms, 30, 51, 167
American Freshman Survey, 30, 51, 167
American Housing Survey, 82–83, 85, 122, 150, 156
American Indians, 9–10, 174–175
American Public Transportation Association, 173
American Religious Identification Survey, 148
American Time Use Survey, 102, 135, 147, 157, 159–160, 171–172, 184, 192
America's Children: Key National Indicators of Well-Being, 26

ancestry, 10
Annual Statistical Supplement (SSA), 152, 162
apparel, spending on, 164
appliance ownership, 143
Arizona, 10
Arkansas, 11
arts participation, 11–12
Asians, 11, 13
assets, 13, 118, 166–167
attitudes, 13–14
   of college students, 30, 167
   of Hispanics, 80, 101, 163
   toward education, 51–53, 141, 155–156
   toward health, 75–77, 113 186
   toward health care, 73, 111, 143

Baby-Boom generation, 7, 15, 84, 151, 185
behavior, 15–16
Behavioral Risk Factor Surveillance System
   alcohol consumption, 8, 44
   food consumption, 65, 125
   health behavior, 15, 72
   health status, 76–77
   physical activity, 59, 134
   smoking, 26, 161, 171
benefits (employee), 16
birth control, 16
births, 17, 63
Births: Final Data, 17, 117, 121, 132, 138
blacks, 18–19
body mass index, 20
books, 11–12
Boston College Center of Wealth and Philanthropy, 22
business owners, 4, 9, 11, 18, 20, 80, 100, 145, 188

California, 21
Calories In, Calories Out: Food and Exercise in Public Elementary Schools, 59, 134
careers, 21
caregivers, 21
cell phone demographics, 21
census
   of population and housing, 22
   tract demographics, 22
Census 2000 Atlas of the United States, 67, 107

charitable giving, 22
Charitable Giving Indices: Social Indicators of Philanthropy by State, 22
child care arrangements, 22, 160
child support, 23
children
   adopted and step, 23
   after-school activities, 23
   by race and Hispanic origin, 25
   family life, 23–24
   health, 24
   in poverty, 24
   living arrangements, 24
   socioeconomics, 24, 26
A Child's Day, 5, 23, 62, 131, 169, 195
chronic conditions, 26
cigarette smoking, 26–27
citizenship, 27
city demographics, 27–28
College Board, 28–29, 176
college
   costs, 28–29
   debt, 29
   degrees awarded, 28
   enrollment, 28
   student attitudes, 30
   student employment, 30
Colorado, 30
Common Core of Data Program, 54, 141, 155–156
commuting, 30
compensation, 31
Complementary and Alternative Medicine Use Among Adults, 9
computer use, 31, 168
Congressional demographics, 31
Connecticut, 31
construction statistics, 32
Consumer Expenditure Survey, 12, 32, 60, 102, 133, 159, 163–164
consumer
   expenditures, 12, 32, 60, 102, 104, 133, 159, 163–165
   finances, 13, 32, 40–41, 119, 122–123, 152, 154, 167, 184
   price index, 33–34, 104, 139, 165
contingent workers, 34

contraceptive use, 34
counties, coastal, 34–35
County and City Data Book, 28, 36
county demographics, 34–36
credit card debt, 41
crime, 36–37
Crime in the United States, 36
Current Employment Statistics Program
    earnings, 49, 183
    employment, 57, 89, 94, 99, 191
    unemployment, 177
Current Population Survey
    Asians, 13, 145
    blacks, 4–5, 18, 20, 145
    college enrollment, 28, 78
    dual-income couples, 47
    earnings, 49, 183, 192
    educational attainment, 54
    employment, 57, 89, 95, 100, 157, 189, 191
    fertility, 17, 64, 118, 121, 131, 138
    geographical mobility, 69, 115, 117
    health insurance, 74, 90
    Hispanics, 80, 101, 145
    households, 83
    incomes, 4, 13, 18, 77, 80, 88, 101, 112, 124, 147, 187, 189
    interracial marriage, 92
    living arrangements, 24, 104
    Medicaid coverage, 110
    Medicare coverage, 112
    non-Hispanic whites, 124, 145
    pensions, 133
    poverty, 5, 13, 20, 24, 81, 101, 113, 124, 137, 147, 187, 190
    public assistance, 140
    school enrollment, 54, 58, 155
    temporary workers, 170
    unemployment, 177
    unmarried partners, 178
    volunteering, 181
    whites, 187
    working poor, 193
Custodial Mothers and Fathers and Their Child Support, 23

Data Compendium, 73–74, 91, 109–110
day care, 39
daytime population, 39
deaths, 39
Deaths: Final Data, 102
debt, 40–41
degrees awarded, 40
Delaware, 40
demographic data,
    general, 40
    historical, 42
demography, 42
dental care, 42
diet and nutrition, 42
Digest of Education Statistics, 28, 40, 51–52, 58, 69, 78, 139, 141, 154–156
disability, 43
discouraged workers, 43
diseases, 43
District of Columbia, 44
divorce, 44–45
doctor visits, 44
drinking, 44, 46
drug use
    illegal, 46–47
    prescription, 47
dual earners, 47
Dynamics of Economic Well–Being: Participation in Government Programs, 141, 186

Early Childhood Longitudinal Program, 62, 112, 131
earnings, 49, 190
eating, time spent, 160
Economic Census, 145, 197
    American Indian-owned businesses, 9
    Asian-owned businesses, 11
    Black-owned businesses, 4, 18
    Hispanic-owned businesses, 80, 100
    women-owned businesses, 188
economic
    indicators, 50
    mobility, 50
Economic Mobility Project, 50, 89, 116
economic trends, 50
education
    adult, 50
    attitudes toward, 51–53, 141, 155–156
    general statistics, 51

homeschooling, 51
private schools, 52
projections, 52
public schools, 52–54
school enrollment, 54
educational attainment, 54
elderly, 54–55
emergency department visits, 55
Employee Benefit Research Institute, 16, 56, 74, 90, 93, 133, 150–151, 154, 161–162
employee
benefits, 56
compensation, 56
tenure, 56
employment, 30, 56–57
employment projections, 57, 151
energy consumption, 58
English, ability to speak, 58
English Usage among Hispanics in the United States, 163
enrollment, school, 58
Estimates of the Unauthorized Immigrant Population, 87
estimates, population, 59
exercise, 59
expenditures, 59–60
Extended Measures of Well–Being: Living Conditions in the United States, 104, 143, 165, 186

families, employment of, 61
family
formation, 61
planning, 61
statistics, 62
fathers, 62, 112, 131–132
Fathers of U.S. Children Born in 2001, 62, 112, 131
fertility, 62–64, 158
Fertility, Contraception, and Fatherhood, 62, 112, 132
Fertility, Family Planning, and Reproductive Health of U.S. Women, 64, 118, 121, 132, 138, 189
fishing, 64
flextime, 65
Florida, 65

food
consumption, 65, 160
spending on, 164
foreign-born population, 65–66

Gallup Poll, 13, 51–53, 148, 155–156
gasoline, spending on, 164
gays and lesbians, 67–68
genealogy, 67
General Social Survey, 12, 14, 150
Generation X, 7
generations, 7
geographic products, 67
geographical mobility, 69
Georgia, 69
graduation rates, 69
grandparents, 69
group-quarters population, 70
Growing Older in America: The Health and Retirement Study, 6, 55, 71, 128, 152
Guttmacher Institute, 3

Harris Poll, 14
Hawaii, 71
health and aging, 71
health and nutrition, 72
Health and Retirement Study, 6, 55, 71, 128, 152
health behavior, 72
health care costs, 73
health care system, attitudes toward, 73
health conditions, 74
Health Confidence Survey, 16, 56, 73–74, 91
health insurance, 74, 164
health-related quality of life, 75, 113, 186
health statistics, 4, 10, 13, 18, 75–77, 80, 101, 124, 145, 187, 189
health status, self–reported, 75–77, 113 186
high-income households, 77
Highlights of Women's Earnings in 2006, 190
high school graduates, 78
higher education, 78
Hispanics, 78–81
historical demographic statistics, 81
HIV, 81
home and hospice care, 81

A TO Z GUIDE TO AMERICAN CONSUMERS 227

homeownership, 81–82, 175
homeschooling, 82
homosexuality, 68, 82
hospital
    emergency department visits, 82–83
    outpatient visits, 83
    overnight stays, 83
households, 84
housing, 22, 84–86
housing units, estimates, 86
Housing Vacancy Survey, 82, 85
hunting, 86

Idaho, 87
illegal immigrants, 87
Illinois, 87
immigration, 87
immunization, 88
income, 88
income inequality, 88–89
independent contractors, 89
Indiana, 89
industry employment, 89–90
infertility, 90
inflation
    calculator, 90
    how to adjust for, 33
insurance, health, 90–91
international demographics, 14, 63, 91, 136
Internet, 92
interracial marriage, 92
Investment Company Institute, 118, 166
Iowa, 92

job benefits, 93
Job Openings and Labor Turnover Survey, 176
job tenure, 93
job training, 93–94
jobs, 94–95
Joint Center for Housing Studies, 85
journey to work, 95

Kaiser Family Foundation, 73–74, 91, 110–111
Kansas, 97
Kentucky, 97

labor force, 99–100, 151
language spoken at home, 100
Latinos, 100–101
laundry, time spent doing, 172
learning disabilities, 101
leisure, 102
life expectancy, 102–103
living
    alone, 102
    arrangements, 24, 104
    standards, 104
long-term care, 104
Louisiana, 105

Maine, 107
mapping, 107
marital
    history, 107, 113
    status, 107
marriage, 108
Maryland, 109
Massachusetts, 109
maternity leave, 17
Maternity Leave and Employment Patterns, 17, 118, 121, 132, 138, 190, 193
Mean Body Weight, Height, and Body Mass Index, 20, 127, 129, 184
media demographics, 109
Medicaid, 109
Medical Expenditure Panel Survey
    attitudes toward health care, 111
    children's health, 24
    chronic conditions, 26, 43, 74
    dental care, 42
    doctor visits, 44, 134
    emergency department visits, 55, 83
    health care costs, 73, 110
    health insurance, 74, 91
    health of older Americans, 71
    health statistics, 77
    hospital outpatient department visits, 83
    hospital overnight stays, 83
    prescription drug use, 47, 139
    Medicaid coverage, 110
    Medicare coverage, 112

medical expenditures, 110
Medicare, 110–111
men, 112–113
mental health, 113
metropolitan area statistics, 114
Michigan, 114
migration, 114–115
military demographics, 115, 179, 181
Millennial generation, 7
minimum wage workers, 115
Minnesota, 116
Mississippi, 116
Missouri, 116
mobility
   economic, 116
   geographic, 116–117
Monitoring the Future Survey
   alcohol consumption, 8, 46
   drug use, 46, 167
   smoking, 27, 161, 171
   youth risk behavior, 15, 72, 169, 195
Montana, 117
mortality data, 117
mortgage
   debt, 41
   interest, 164
mothers, 117–118, 131–132
multiple job holders, 118
multiracial, 145
mutual fund shareholders, 119–120, 166–167

natality, 121
National Ambulatory Medical Care Survey
   doctor visits, 44, 134
      emergency department visits, 55, 82
      hospital outpatient department visits, 83
National Association of Realtors, 85
National Bureau of Economic Research, 50, 185
National Compensation Survey, 16, 56, 93, 159, 179
National Health and Nutrition Examination Survey, 19–20, 72, 127, 129, 184
National Health Interview Survey
   alcohol consumption 9
   cell-phone use, 21, 168–169
   physical activity, 59, 134
   smoking, 27, 161
   weight 20–21, 127, 130
National Home and Hospice Care Survey, 81
National Hospital Discharge Survey, 83
National Household Education Survey
   adult education, 3, 50
   after-school activities, 5, 23
   child care arrangements, 22, 39
   homeschooling, 51, 82
   job training, 93, 173
National Household Travel Survey, 174
National Immunization Survey, 88
National Nursing Home Survey, 125
national parks, 122
National Sleep Foundation, 159
National Sporting Goods Association, 148, 163
National Survey of Family Growth
   birth control, 16, 34
   divorce, 44–45
   family formation, 61
   family planning, 61
   fathers, 62, 112, 132
   fertility, 64, 90, 118, 121, 138
   homosexuality, 67–68, 82
   marriage, 108
   men, 112
   mothers, 118, 132
   sexual behavior, 15, 157–158
   women's reproductive behavior, 17
National Survey of Fishing, Hunting, and Wildlife-Associated Recreation, 64, 86
National Survey on Drug Use and Health, 15, 46, 72, 167
nativity, 122
Nebraska, 122
neighborhoods, 122
net worth, 122
Nevada, 123
New Hampshire, 123
New Jersey, 123
New Mexico, 123
New York, 124
newspapers, 12
non-Hispanic whites, 124
North Carolina, 125

North Dakota, 125
Number, Timing and Duration of Marriages and Divorces, 44, 107, 113, 188, 190
nursing homes, 125
nutrition and diet, 125

obesity, 19, 127
Occupational Employment Statistics Survey, 49, 183
Occupational Outlook Handbook, 94, 127, 173
occupations, 127
Ohio, 128
Oklahoma, 128
Older Americans 2008, 6, 55, 129
older population, 128
online activities, 129
Oral Health of Older Americans, 71
Oregon, 129
overweight, 19, 129–130

parents, 131–132
parks, national, 132
Pennsylvania, 133
Pension Rights Center, 133
pensions, 133
people living alone, 133
Pew Forum on Religion & Public Life, 14, 150
Pew Global Attitudes Project, 14
Pew Hispanic Center, 14, 80, 101, 163
Pew Internet & American Life Project, 14, 21, 31, 92, 129, 168–169
Pew Research Center, 137, 140
Pew Research Center for the People & the Press, 14, 109, 149
Phi Delta Kappa/Gallup Poll, 51–53, 155–156
physical activity, 134
physician visits, 134
places of birth, 135
play, 135
Population Association of America, 42
population
   density, 136
   estimates, 135–137
   projections, 137
Population Reference Bureau, 91, 136, 194

Population Trends Along the Coastal United States, 34
population, United States, 63, 135–137
poverty, 5, 13, 20, 24, 81, 101, 113, 124, 137, 147
pregnancy, 138
prescription drugs, 139
price index, 139
prison population, 139
Private School Survey, 52, 139, 155
private schools, 139
A Profile of the Working Poor, 193
Program on International Policy Attitudes, 14
Project for Excellence in Journalism, 12, 14, 109, 170
projections
   education, 139
   employment, 140, 151
   population, 140
public
   assistance, 140
   opinion, 13–14
   schools, 141
Public Transportation Fact Book, 173

quality of life, 143

race, 145–147
reading, 11–12
recreational activities, 147
regions, 148
religion, 148–150, 158
renters, 150
Residential Energy Consumption Survey, 58
retirement, 150–152
Retirement Confidence Survey, 16, 56, 152, 154, 162
Rhode Island, 152
Roper Center for Public Opinion Research, 14
rural population, 153

savings, 154
school
   districts, 54, 141, 156
   enrollment, 154–155
   general statistics, 156

    private, 155
    public, 155–156
School District Demographics System, 54, 141, 156
School Survey on Crime and Safety, 37
schools, satisfaction with, 155–156
self-employment, 157
sexual behavior, 157–158
Sexual Behavior and Selected Health Measures, 67–68, 82
shift work, 157
shopping, 157, 159–160
sick leave, 159
single-person households, 159
sleep, 159–160
Sleep in America Poll, 159
smoking, 26–27, 161
Social Security, 161–162, 164
South Carolina, 162
South Dakota, 162
Spanish, spoken at home, 162–163
spending, 163–165
sports, 163
Sourcebook of Criminal Justice Statistics, 37
standard of living, 163, 165
step-children, 3
State and Metropolitan Area Data Book, 114, 165–166
state data centers, 166
state demographics, 165–166
The State of 50+ America, 6, 55, 129
The State of the Nation's Housing, 85
Statistical Abstract of the United States, 40, 42, 81, 166
statistics, demographic, 166
stocks, 166–167
Student Financing of Undergraduate Education, 28, 176
students, attitudes of, 167
substance abuse, 167
Summary Health Statistics for U.S. Adults, 20, 26–27, 43, 46, 74, 113, 127, 130, 134, 161, 171, 186
Summary Health Statistics for U.S. Children, 24, 26, 43, 74

Survey of Business Owners
    American Indians, 9
    Asians, 11
    Blacks, 4, 18
    Hispanics, 80, 100
    Internet home page, 20, 145
    women, 188
Survey of Consumer Finances, 13, 32, 40–41, 119, 122–123, 152, 154, 167, 184
Survey of Income and Program Participation
    child care arrangements, 22, 39
    children's after-school activities, 5
    economic well-being, 143
    family life, 23–24, 62, 131
    field of training and economic status, 78
    learning disabilities, 101
    living standards, 104, 186
    public assistance, 140, 186
Swing generation, 7

taxes, 164, 168
technology, 168
teenagers, 169
telephones, 169–170
television
    audience, 12, 170
    time spent watching, 160
temporary workers, 170
Tennessee, 170
tenure, job, 170
Texas, 171
time use, 160, 171–172
To Read or Not to Read: A Question of National Consequence, 11
tobacco use, 26–27, 171, 173
tract data, 173
training, job, 173
transportation, 173
travel, 174
Travel Industry Association, 174
travel to work, 174
Trends in College Pricing, 28, 176
Trends in Educational Equity of Girls & Women, 188
tribes, American Indian, 174, 176

tuition, college, 176
turnover, labor, 176

unemployment, 177
Uniform Crime Reports, 36
union members, 177
United Health Foundation, 72
United States Life Tables, 102
unmarried partners, 178
urban, 178
Use of Contraception and Use of Family Planning Services in the United States, 16, 34, 61
Utah, 178

vacation
　days, 179
　homes, 175
vehicles, 164
Vermont, 179
veterans, 179, 181
Virginia, 181
vital statistics, 181
volunteering, 181
voting, 180–181

wages, 183
Washington, 184
We the People: American Indians and Alaskan Natives in the United States, 9, 174
We the People: Asians in the United States, 11
We the People: Blacks in the United States, 4, 18
We the People: Hispanics in the United States, 78, 100
wealth, 184
weekends, 184
weight, 19, 184–186
welfare, 186
well-being, 186
West Virginia, 187
What's It Worth: Field of Training and Economic Status, 78
whites, 187
Who's Minding the Kids, 22, 39
widows, 188

wildlife-associated recreation, 188
Wireless Substitution: Estimates from the National Health Interview Survey, 21, 168–169
Wisconsin, 188
women, 188–190
Women in the Labor Force: A Databook, 189, 193
work, 190–191
work arrangements, 191
work-at-home population, 191
work experience, 192
work schedules, 65, 192
work time, 160, 192
workers
　alternative, 9
　contingent, 34
　discouraged, 43
　full- and part-time, 182
　minimum wage, 115
　multiple job holders, 118
　on flexible schedules, 65, 157, 192
　self-employed, 157
　shift, 65, 157, 192
　temporary, 170
working mothers, 192–193
working poor, 193
working, reasons for not, 193
The World Factbook, 63, 91, 193
world population, 193–194
world public opinion, 14
World War II generation, 7
Wyoming, 194

The Yearbook of Immigration Statistics, 87
youth, 195
Youth Risk Behavior Surveillance System
　alcohol consumption, 9, 46
　drug use, 47, 167
　risk behavior, 16, 72, 169, 195
　smoking, 27, 161, 173

zip code demographics, 197